Animal Models of Human Psychology

Animal Models of Human Psychology

Critique of Science, Ethics, and Policy

by
Kenneth Joel Shapiro

With a foreword by
Jane Goodall

 Hogrefe & Huber Publishers
Seattle · Toronto · Gottingen · Bern

Library of Congress Cataloging-in-Publication Data

Shapiro, Kenneth Joel.
  Animal models of human psychology : critique of science, ethics, and policy /
by Kenneth Joel Shapiro.
  p. cm.
  Includes bibliographical references and index.
  ISBN 0-88937-189-X
  1. Psychology, Comparative. 2. Human behavior—Animal models. 3. Animal
experimentation—Moral and ethical aspects. 4. Animal psychology. I. Title.

BF671.S48   1998   156—dc21   97-26436 CIP

Canadian Cataloguing-in-Publication Data

Shapiro, Kenneth Joel
  Animal models of human psychology : critique of science, ethics, and policy

Includes index.
ISBN 0-88937-189-X

1. Psychology, Comparative. 2. Human behavior – Animal models. 3. Animal
experimentation – Moral and ethical aspects. 4. Animal psychology. I. Title

BF671.S48   1998   156   C98-9300330-6

Copyright © 1998 by Hogrefe & Huber Publishers

USA:	Suite 485, 218 Main Street, Kirkland, WA 98033
	Phone (425) 820-1500, Fax (425) 823-8324
CANADA:	Suite 514, 1543 Bayview Ave, Toronto, Ontario M4G 3B5
	Phone (416) 482-6339, Fax (416) 482-5127
GERMANY:	Rohnsweg 25, D-37085 Göttingen
	Phone +49 551 496090, Fax +49 551 4960988
SWITZERLAND:	Länggass-Strasse 76, CH-3000 Bern 9
	Phone +41 31 300-4500, Fax +41 31 300-4590

Printed in the United States of America

ISBN 0-88937-189-X
Hogrefe & Huber Publishers
Seattle • Toronto • Göttingen • Bern

Table of Contents

Chapter 3
Animals as Models 85

Chapter 4
Selected Animal Models 111

To Ann, Deb, Joel, Stormcloud, Black Arrow, and Atalanta

Foreword

This is a book for everyone who is concerned with the experimental use of the nonhuman animal as a tool in the struggle to better understand and treat physiological and psychological disorders in the human animal. It will be particularly helpful to those wrestling with the ethical problems generated by the use of animals in invasive, stressful, and painful experiments. The animals rights movement is increasingly forcing science to justify its use of laboratory animals. The standard justification maintains that animal experimentation contributes to the understanding and treatment of human physiological and/or psychological disease and is essential to progress in medical science.

Shapiro questions whether this is true, particularly with regard to the development of animal "models" of various psychological disorders. Of course, grant proposals address current human health and welfare issues (such as anorexia nervosa), because this kind of research is more likely to be funded, and funds are desperately needed to pay the salaries of researchers and staff. (Grants also serve to fuel the multi-billion dollar industry that is associated with the breeding, feeding and other maintenance requirements of laboratory animals.) The discovery of a new treatment for some major human disorder would bring credit and financial gain to the individual and/or to the institution. But research based on animal models of human psychological disorders has proved disappointing in this respect.

Some animal experiments, even though they have not led to any immediate benefit to humans, are defended by the researchers involved because they provide new information of academic interest. They provide information about the response of various laboratory animals to a variety of tests. Changes in response can be measured and correlated with an endless number of variables of a type that will depend on the interests of the individual experimenter. For example, increase or decrease in aggressive behavior can be correlated with varying amounts of food, water, space, presence or absence of companions, differences in rearing experience and other types of early experience, introduction of various drugs, hormones, chemical substances and so on—sometimes in a highly invasive way such as via needles and tubes into brain, stomach, or other organs. Each set of experiments will trigger hypotheses that will generate another set of experiments. Research of this sort can (and does) provide eager young students with material for their PhDs, and professors with material for the "publish or perish" games of modern academia.

Animal rights activists typically criticize animal experiments on moral and ethical grounds. If it can be established, on the basis of similarities of brain and central nervous system, that pain is likely to be experienced by the animal subject in the same sort of way as it is by us, then it can be argued that experiments involving procedures likely to cause pain are unethical. Unfortunately, the extent to which nonhuman animals actually feel pain is impossible to measure. Pain thresholds vary even among human subjects. Nevertheless, it is very widely accepted today that nonhuman animals do feel pain much as we do, so it is fair to assume that invasive research methods that appear to cause pain to the subjects are unethical. In addition, it can be shown that nonhuman animals with complex brains almost certainly experience emotions similar to human emotions. My own study of chimpanzees has, perhaps more than any other research, helped to bridge the divide between "man" and "beast." Of course we are different from nonhumans, but we are not as absolutely unique as we used to think. An understanding of chimpanzees nature proves convincingly (as I also learned from my dog, as a child) that we humans are not the only living beings with personalities, not the only beings capable of rational thought, above all, not the only beings who experience emotions like joy and sorrow, fear and despair, and mental as well as physical suffering. This knowledge leads to a new respect nor only for chimpanzees, but for other nonhuman beings with complex brains and behavior. And this, in turn, leads many of us to conclude that not only are the experiments resulting in physiological pain unethical, but so too are those that induce psychological stress.

In defence of their use of animals, researchers, even though they may admit that they are causing their subjects to suffer pain, are unashamedly anthropocentric, asserting the superiority of the human species. The fact that nonhuman animals may suffer, physically or mentally, is they agree unfortunate—and to be avoided, and certainly minimized, whenever possible. But, nevertheless, they assure us that, provided their experiments yield results that are beneficial, or *might be* beneficial at some future time, to human beings, the end justifies the means.

Shapiro's book examines the actual usefulness of animal experiments to the clinical psychologist. How helpful is an animal "model" of a human condition to those seeking to treat the problem in humans? How accurately does this model reflect the precise nature of the human disorder it attempts to reproduce in a nonhuman? Careful research shows that the animal model is typically neither helpful nor accurate.

For example, animal models designed to further understand bulimia (binge eating and vomiting) can only focus on the physiological characteristics. The sociopsychologi-

cal factors believed by most clinical psychologists to underlie this disorder in humans (issues of self-image, fear
of ridicule, and so on) can scarcely be replicated in rats,
dogs, or even monkeys.

To what extent do those working with human patients
in hospital, clinic, or consulting room make use of findings that emerged as a result of contemplating various
human conditions in specially created animal models of
those conditions? Shapiro investigates this question
through rigorous surveys handed to people working in
the field, and an equally rigorous analysis of citation lists
in papers published by investigators working with human subjects. When these methods were used to evaluate
the usefulness of a set of experiments (that involved animal models of various human eating disorders) to clinical
psychologists working with human patients, it was clear
that the experiments were contributing neither to further
understanding of the human conditions, nor to advances
in their treatment. It also became clear that most clinical
psychologists specializing in the treatment of eating disorders were unaware of the research that was being carried out on animal models of those disorders. And the
professional journals they read had almost no overlap
with the journals that reported the animal research. Yet
the animal research was extensive and costly—and it involved many procedures that caused a great deal of physical and psychological distress in the various animals
used.

Whilst we may disagree with an investigator who believes that nonhuman animals are in this world expressly
for the benefit of humans, to be used in many way we see
fit if this will improve the human condition, it is difficult
to disprove his point of view. But if he is using animals in
a way that is both cruel (because of inflicting pain and/or
psychological stress) and unhelpful in the search to cure
human disorders, his *research* can be strongly criticized.
Shapiro provides evidence showing that a great deal of

research using animal models (at least as it is supposed to relate to finding cures for humans) is, at the very least, wasteful of the taxpayers' money. He describes the world of the animal lab and the world of the practicing clinical psychologist as two separate world with few links. The investigator working with humans is gradually making progress in the understanding, diagnosis, intervention, and treatment of a whole variety of psychological disorders. The investigator working with animals, preoccupied with high-tech methods of creating ever more sophisticated nonhuman models of those disorders, and with testing the hypotheses that the animal research generates, accumulates vast amounts of information which, by and large, has very little relevance to curing human psychological disorders. Indeed, a recent study by Scott Plous concluded that mental health workers would not be seriously hampered by a total ban on animal research.

Shapiro predicts that the use of animal models of human psychological disorders will be phased out in the medium-range future. It is to be hoped that he is right.

Jane Goodall

Introduction

This book is about the use of nonhuman animals in science. Current debates over animals include numerous contexts of their use from laboratories to zoos to farms. But modern science itself, which constructed the laboratory and installed "laboratory animals" as its inhabitants, remains at the center of the controversy over the status of nonhuman animals.

Many believe that animal research is senseless and wrong for fundamental and personally compelling reasons. Their firm and deeply held beliefs are critically captured by other recent titles—*Victims of Science* (Ryder, 1975); *Slaughter of the Innocent* (Ruesch, 1978); *Arrogance of Humanism* (Ehrenfeld, 1978); *Three Blind Mice* (Giannelli, 1985); *Cruel Deception* (Sharpe, 1988); *The Unheeded Cry* (Rollin, 1989)—and shown positively in a philosophy that recognizes the interests and rights of individual nonhuman animals (Regan, 1983). To these readers, animal research is unacceptable at its core. There is no need for yet another treatise on the subject, certainly one that features, as this does, prolonged treatment of concepts, re-interpretation of the history of science, and extended analyses of contemporary examples of the practice of animal research.

However, others believe as strongly that animal research is a necessary basis of science and that, in most instances, the pursuit of understanding must take priority over concerns of the use of animals. Their beliefs are indicated in terms such as "scientific freedom," "the inviolateness of human life," and in the espousal of those humanistic or human-centered philosophies that have been the foundation of Western culture and have produced one of its crowning achievements—science.

The intent here is to address both points of view. Both sides of the issue are vulnerable to misconceptions about animal research. Furthermore, while accurately grasping each other's arguments, both sides maintain negative and extreme views of the other side (Paul, 1995). Many scientists, particularly those who are outspoken advocates of animal research (King, 1984a; Morrison, 1992), argue that if the public were simply more educated, particularly in the use of animals in science, they would be more accepting. Available data do not support this assertion (Furnham & Pinder, 1990; Pifer, Shimizu, & Pifer, 1994). In a study of the public's attitude toward animal research in 14 countries including the United States, these investigators found no consistent relationship between scientific knowledge, or lack thereof, and attitudes toward animal research (Pifer, Schimizu, & Pifer, 1994, pp. 101–103). And yet, here I undertake to educate the public, the animal rights community, and those in the academic community who both do and do not use animals in research. A full exposition of animal research practice will produce better understanding and openness to change.

Discussion and examples are largely restricted to my own field, psychology. To further indicate my point of view, my other field of work is animal advocacy. For over a decade, I have worked to promote a re-examination of psychology's practice of using animals in research laboratories and classrooms. In writing this monograph, it is not my intent to hurt but rather to help the profession of psychology. As a professional I believe it is in psychology's interest to reconsider the basic approach psychology employs in animal research; and I personally am indebted to psychology for the rich intellectual home it has provided for me since I first wandered into an "Intro Psych" class 35 years ago.

The focus of this monograph is the present-day use of animals in psychological research. After indicating the scope and character of the research and its strategy of developing animal models of human psychological disorders, an illustrative area is systematically examined, animal models of eating disorders, from both scientific and ethical points of view.

First, however, a description of how psychology developed its reliance on animal models of human psychology and how the present challenge to its use of animals arose is given and a historical sketch of psychology's life-span, highlighting the path that led it to put nonhuman animals in a laboratory and to form certain attitudes towards them. An analysis and critique of the concept of animal models, the major strategy in psychology's use of animals, follows. Finally, the recent rise of the animal rights movement is sketched, highlighting the several philosophies upon which it is based. These philosophies are analyzed in terms of their specific application to psychological research and to those policies currently governing it.

In effect, the weave consists of three threads: (1) the science, both its general approach and the tactics embodied in its everyday practice; (2) the animals, both the general attitudes toward them and, as it were, "a day in the life of" an animal in the laboratory; and (3) the cases for and against animal research, including those ethical, political, and empirical considerations necessary to the full presentation of this complex tapestry.

From the outset of the contemporary animal rights movement, psychological research was singled out for criticism. In what quickly became the "redbook" of that movement, *Animal Liberation: A New Ethic for our Treatment of Animals*, Peter Singer took psychology to task for the high level of suffering imposed on the animals and the "often trivial and obvious" results obtained (1975, p. 40). Following this opening salvo, it was generally thought, at least within the ranks of that movement, that psychological research would be an early casualty leading up to the more formidable target, biomedical research. And, indeed, psychological research did supply the *cause célèbre* of the movement when Edward Taub, a psychologist using primates as an animal model of stroke, was brought to court for his mistreatment of the animals involved. More than any other event, the lengthy unfolding of this case established public awareness that animal-based psychological and biomedical research exist and that the practices are problematic.

However, as the biomedical community developed defensive strategies in response to the animal rights movement, it became apparent that psychological animal research was not a pushover, in large part because the distinction between it and biomedical animal research is not clearcut. Psychologists often study physiological aspects of disorders, while biomedical investigations often include behavioral aspects. Hence, the boundaries between the two enterprises often overlap.

Two Stories: Transcendence and Reduction

Two contrasting and oversimplified accounts provide preliminary landmarks. In a sense, no one is *for* animal research just as no one is *for* war. Generally, people do not want to cause suffering to or to kill animals to help find cures for human illnesses. As waging war to gain peace is an undesirable last resort, so, surely, is using animal models of human disorders to enhance our species' health.

However, people tell two very different stories about this enterprise. In both, animals in the laboratory are not themselves. In the first account, their transformation is a transcendence of their mundane nature, while in the second it is a reduction.

In the story featuring transcendence, told by research proponents, animals transcend their own being by virtue of their laboratory existence to become models of some aspects of a human beings. The rat is not a rat, but rather he or she is more than a rat. Through modelling certain physiological or psychological processes, he or she is transformed into an analogue of us, transcending inter-species differences.

The more fundamental transformation is that the rat becomes a scientific object, an object of scientific investigation. Through this elevation, by becoming the repository of phenomena under rigorous investigation, the rat makes that investigatory enterprise possible. The rat is a transcendent object because the enterprise is dedicated to transcendent ends, those of enhancing understanding and human welfare. Whatever suffering and death is involved is justified, for the animal is a "sacrifice" (Lynch, 1988). Science is a set of transcending secular rituals through which a "naturalized" animal is lifted to a higher plain to become an "analytic animal, a bearer of generalized knowledge" (Lynch, 1988, pp. 266–269). Within this abstract and mathematized space, scientists are entitled and indeed obligated to pursue any phenomenon of interest in the name of academic freedom. They need only to induce and then to experimentally analyze it in their animal subjects—employing virtually any means to do so. This account often includes the assertions that the results of animal research have provided both the foundation or basic principles of the field and substantial benefits in applied clinical settings, and that those who oppose this form of science are sentimentalists and in some cases terrorists.

By contrast, in the second story, told by critics of animal research, the same rat is not more but less than a rat. By virtue of the laboratory existence, he or she is no longer either an autonomous and free individual, or a member of that at once marvelous and terrible species that so successfully occupied natural and human-made cultural niches around the globe. Rats and the many other species kept in the laboratory are "lab animals," a distinct category of being in which both individual and species identity are de-emphasized. Lab animals are reduced to models of those physiological and psychological processes under investigation. They are lab animals in the sense that they are part of the lab, extensions of the instruments comprising it. These intelligent, social, and sentient beings are reduced to "preparations," passive recorders of the results of the experimental manipulations to which they are subjected. Such artifacts are neither like themselves nor like us. This reductive enterprise is destructive of both their individual and species-specific nature and causes great suffering and harm; it is also ineffective and cumbersome for human purposes. This account often includes the assertions that animal-based scientists are sadists and some are frauds.

In researching and preparing the present monograph, both of these stories are taken seriously. Inevitably, the result of this effort is yet another story, although one clearly more sympathetic to the reductionist theme offered by the critics of animal research than to the transcendent theme of the proponents.

A Social Scientific Approach

As a social scientist, I am influenced by recent studies in the sociology of knowledge (Latour, 1987). This literature offers a correction to the traditional view that science is primarily shaped by and understandable in terms of the underlying philosophy of science, positivism. According to this philosophy, science is a rational and objective practice in which a detached investigator, by dispassionately forming and testing hypotheses, discovers hidden facts and relations. In the popularized version, a lone investigator in a single breakthrough study finds the cure for a major disease. Through this traditional philosophy-based view, science claims a special status for itself "founded on the superior rationality and objectivity of scientific knowledge, which are themselves due to the rules of scientific method" (Fuchs, 1993, pp. 1–2).

In contrast, in the sociology of knowledge critique, science is, "just another social practice" (p. 3). It is shaped by and understandable in terms of the social institutions in which it occurs—the subcultures of the laboratory, the university, and the profession. Moreover, "[b]uilding scientific knowledge is a *messy* business ..." (p. 5, quoted from Collins, emphasis added). Doing the work of science involves "tinkering and groping" (p. 10), and "false leads, lucky breaks, accidents, idiosyncratic circumstances, and personal biases" (p. 14). Part of this messiness is perhaps inherent in the practice, given the complexity of the phenomena under investigation. Ironically, part of it is a result of the rationalistic and precise positivist philosophy governing it. This traditional philosophy ultimately introduces obscurity by distancing the investigator from and limiting the permissible approaches to the object of study. Beyond this, and here is the thrust of the critique of the sociology of knowledge, the practice of science occurs in a social institution complex in itself and complexly situated among other social institutions and forces. As a result, personal biases, competitiveness, interpersonal dynamics, politics, and economics—both inside and outside the laboratory—all play significant roles in determining the way the work is done.

Building on this account, I add that complex social relations across species also are part of the institution of science and greatly influence scientific work. Notwithstanding the distinct claims of the first two stories that the animals are absent, having been either transcended to abstraction or reduced to instrumentation, there they are. Scientists, technicians, and their animal subjects form complex relations consisting of "bonds," expectations, and implicit contracts which cross species lines. The presence of this network of cross-species relations confounds and undercuts the traditional account of science as being based on dispassionate, neutral observation and rational inference. Science is one of the crowning achievements of human culture, but it is not what it seems nor is it what it should be. While neither a romance featuring the heroic efforts of an isolated individual nor a horror story starring a Frankenstein-like doctor playing malevolent god, there are serious scientific and ethical problems raised by the use of nonhuman animals to construct animal models of human disorders.

My story and the intent of this monograph is the disclosure of these problems. It is effected through a mixed (and, yes, messy) methodology consisting of historical interpretation, conceptual analysis and original data, the latter gathered by employing survey, citation analysis and other empirical methods.

Organization of the Book

For many readers, even the existence of animal-based psychological research is news. Chapter 1 introduces these relatively uninformed readers to psychology and its use of nonhuman animals. Approximately 10% of psychological research involves nonhuman animals. While there is some evidence of a reduction in these numbers over the last two decades, levels of suffering and harm do not show a similar trend and remain substantial. An instrument originally developed by the author provides an empirical tool for the measurement of these levels.

The most common use of animals in psychological research is as a model of a human disorder. Models of virtually every known problem in the human condition with a psychological component have been developed through experimental manipulation of animals in every possible way—genetically, surgically, pharmacologically, socially and environmentally.

A history of psychology that highlights its reaction to the contemporary animal rights movement reveals that the field was caught unprepared, as a disproportionate number compared to the total animal research enterprise of psychologists became campaign targets—despite the fact that the field had developed some modest institutional mechanisms in response to the animal protection movement at the turn of the century. The introductory chapter ends with a sampling of the broad spectrum of attitudes toward the practice of animal research within the field, demonstrating that it is currently divided over the issue.

Chapter 2 provides a social constructionist account of the "laboratory animal" in psychology. Modern psychology chose the laboratory, rather than, say, the consulting room or some more "naturalistic" setting, as the "locus classicus for scientific psychology" (Capshew, 1992, p. 132). Through selective breeding and environmental shaping, psychology fit nonhuman animals to the lab and the lab to them. This reciprocal retrofitting, carried out in housing conditions, instrumentation, and other technological innovations, transformed the "wild" rat and animals of numerous other species into "lab animals" who function as preparations, repositories of data, or "highly specialized scientific instruments" (Phillips, 1994, p. 136).

Chapter 3 provides a conceptual analysis of the strategy of constructing animal models of human disorders. The important distinction is made that a model is an analogy to a disorder and not the disorder itself. As such, at best it is a hypothesis that ultimately must be validated in its human setting. Despite this fact, much literature in biomedicine and psychology, both scientific and frankly promotional, has oversold animal models as identical with,

and literally as re-presenting, a given disorder. More critically, I argue that psychology's use of animal models has
not even fulfilled the modest function of providing a heuristic, of generating hypotheses that are then tested in a
clinical population. Rather, these models serve to generate
additional models within the laboratory and are never
properly validated. To the degree that they do have an
impact in clinical settings, they merely provide rhetoric,
images and metaphors of the disorder, rather than genuine insights into it or interventions for its effective treatment or prevention.

Chapter 4 examines this animal model strategy through
an extensive and intensive study of a related set of models: those employed in research on eating disorders. As the
incidence of bulimia and anorexia nervosa has dramatically increased in recent years and their effective treatment remains elusive, it is one of the most pressing areas
of investigation. Examples of such animal models include
surgically producing a hole in a rat's stomach (fistula) to
mimic the binge-purge behavior found among bulimics
(both are "eating without nutrition"); and placing a rat in
an exercise wheel cage, where he or she grossly reduces
the amount of food eaten, as does an anorexic.

A close reading of this literature reveals that the ideology of the laboratory, with its heavy emphasis on technology, quantification, and explanation at a micro-process
level, constrains and shapes the original conception and
development of these models more than does direct clinical knowledge of the disorders. The result is that these
research efforts have very little influence on the relevant
treatment settings. I present original empirical survey and
citation analysis data showing that these models have not
resulted in effective treatment innovations, are not cited
in relevant applied literatures, and are not even known to
specialists in the treatment of eating disorders.

The final two chapters discuss, respectively, ethical and
policy considerations. Several contemporary moral phi-

losophies are reviewed to extract their specific applications to the policies governing the practice of animal-based psychological research. While there are several distinct and evolving ethical systems that address the status of nonhuman animals in innovative ways, my general finding is that current policy and practice in psychology have either avoided these or adapted their language in ways that preclude any progressive movement. Thus, while adopting its language, utilitarian theory specifically developed to deal with the ethics of nonhuman animals is given only lip-service (Singer, 1975). Requisite cost-benefits analyses are not undertaken. Despite the availability of instruments to measure the costs to animals, no rigorous assessment of costs is performed. Benefits are globally asserted rather than assessed on a case by case basis.

A second theoretical discourse evident in policy statements and guidelines, the humane ethic, similarly has been assimilated in a form that simply justifies current practices. In effect, all suffering is necessary, and therefore, humane if it has been customary practice.

Other progressive ethics, rights (Regan, 1983), and feminist issues (Donovan, 1990) have not been addressed or incorporated into current legislation and guidelines.

The conclusion includes recommendations that would substantially curtail the use of animal models in the study of human psychological disorders.

There are two omissions from the present work that may strike the informed reader as odd. I do not discuss alternatives to animal model research. I believe the present analysis cuts deeper than the critique implied in the argument that such research is unnecessary because alternatives not involving nonhuman animals exist. If animal model research is found to be ineffective, we are not required to have an alternative strategy in place before we can justify abandoning it. In any case, most research in psychology is and historically has been human-based, including research on topics for which animal models have been sought. While I will show that the animal model strategy has unduly and in negative and unproductive ways influenced the approach of human-based research, the latter enterprise is an approach that antedated that for which it presumably must provide an alternative.

I also do not review and evaluate human-based research in psychology. Rather, I rely on a more direct and internal examination of the animal model research itself. I do include an evaluation of it based on its relation to relevant treatment interventions.

Language and Style

Finally, a note about language and style: both my own style and, more importantly, features of language that I believe are an important facet of the current debate over our uses of nonhuman animals.

In the tradition of scholarly writing I have attempted to keep to dispassionate discourse. This involves careful documentation, wherever possible, of the origin of ideas and facts and, at the risk of disrupting the flow, the provision of ample sources in the text. I also identify and distinguish historical interpretation, conceptual and logical analysis, and empirical findings, for each has its own rules of evidence and persuasion. However, as I am also an advocate, I do occasionally depart from this academic prose with attempts at more evocative language (e. g., the tapestry and salvo metaphors).

Just as the women's movement deconstructed the generic "he," so must any responsible speaker or writer come to terms with those linguistic conventions bearing on the animal issue. When referring to nonhuman animals, where appropriate and possible I use "he" or "she" for "it," and "who" for "which," for these beings have some personal attributes. I also prefer "animals in the laboratory" to "laboratory animals" as a reminder that they are first animals and only recently and unwillingly part of the inventory of the laboratory. Further, I do not hesitate to attribute autonomous action and experience to nonhuman animals when I am reasonably certain it is descriptive. Any reluctance to do so reveals the Cartesian legacy, outmoded since Darwin, in which any attribution of mental state commits the error of anthropomorphism. In the present work I restrict that error to the attribution of exclusively human capabilities to nonhuman animals (Noske, 1989, p. 88). Clearly, nonhuman animals are experiencing beings who act on the world that they experience.

In addition, there is the sticky problem of the use of the generic term "animal" to refer to all animals other than humans. "Nonhuman animal" is an inadequate corrective as it retains and indeed reinforces the importance of the categorical cleavage between human and all other animals. Ideally, one should use this term only in the specific contexts that demand that distinction, reserving "animal" for contexts in which a reference inclusive of human and nonhuman animals is intended. Of course, the problem is that "animal" is typically taken as "nonhuman animal" where that being is devalued relative to human being. In the present work, I cannot resolve this issue and use "animal" to refer to nonhuman animals.

Social scientists perpetually argue whether to adopt a neutral, unambiguous, and universal language, a discourse peculiar to science; or whether to employ language rich enough to fully evoke the phenomenon under study with its many meanings and connotations. There is also a tension over language used outside the laboratory in common discourse. While some people are concerned about language that is disrespectful and discriminatory, others disapprove of language that is empty—talk that, while superficially nodding to respect, substitutes etiquette, just talk, for genuine caring and committed action.

More than just talk and beyond the effort to educate and analyze, I intend the present work as a polite and respectful but strong and objectively founded call to action.

Chapter 1
Psychology's Use of Animals
Current Practices and Attitudes

Introduction

Modern psychology first became well-known to the public during World War II as an applied rather than as a research enterprise. For this reason, the person on the street is often surprised when informed that not all psychologists are therapists and that many are engaged in animal-based laboratory research. Yet it is estimated that 8–10% of research psychologists study nonhuman animals (American Psychological Association [APA], 1984). Furthermore, their research often involves considerable suffering and impairment to the animals involved. Because psychology is a popular course of study in undergraduate and, increasingly, secondary curricula, and since its texts often graphically feature animal-based research, the field is highly influential in forming and maintaining attitudes toward animals in contemporary society and especially among those considered well-educated.

The Field of Psychology

Psychologists research and practice in a wide variety of settings: the laboratory, school, clinic, hospital, industry, advertising agency and courtroom. The breadth of the field is also indicated by the variety of "units" that different psychologists take as the object of their research or practice. In addition to feelings, thoughts, motivation, attitudes and behavior, some psychologists focus their attention on a physiological system or even on a single type of neuron in the brain. Still others take as the organizing unit of their work a human relationship, a family, or a formal institution such as a corporation.

A listing of the subfields of psychology provides an additional view of the scope of the field. The *Directory of the American Psychological Association* (1989, p. xlviii) divides the field into 58 "major fields" including, but not exhaustive, biological, clinical child, consumer, ecological, engineering, exercise and sports, forensic, pharmacological, philosophical, psychoanalytic, rehabilitation, and transpersonal psychology. "Specialties" within these major fields number several hundred.

Finally, there have been several different dominant theoretical frameworks or, loosely, paradigms in the brief history of modern psychology. At first, introspectionism, structuralism, functionalism, gestalt theory, and psychoanalysis all vied for dominance, then behaviorism largely replaced them, while cognitive psychology currently prevails, perhaps soon to give way to or amalgamate with neuropsychology.

In approximate numbers (see Rosenzweig [1992] for actual estimates), there are 500,000 psychologists in the world. The number has doubled in the past decade (1982–1992). Of the current total, approximately 80,000 (16%) do research as part of their work. Research psychologists include those using both human and nonhuman animal subjects. The United States has roughly half the world's psychologists (250,000) and half the number of research psychologists (40,000).

It is generally agreed that since the early 1950s, when applied psychology came into its own, there has been a decrease in traditional academic and research areas relative to the number of psychologists in applied or "health-service-provider" areas. Evidence of this is the proliferation of professional schools of psychology that produce psychologists whose exclusive interest is clinical practice. An older model of the psychologist as scientist-practitioner, a person who combined the pursuit of scientific research with its direct application in the clinic, is no longer dominant. The shift is also evidenced in the relative numbers of students earning doctorates in research as distinct from applied subfields. While in the 1950s and 1960s, the ratio of PhDs in health service subfields versus research and academic subfields was 1 to 3, this ratio was reversed by the 1970s and 1980s (Boneau, 1992, p. 1588). Despite an absolute increase in the numbers of researchers, this relative decline is a matter of considerable concern to some within the field.

One concern is that the decline exacerbates the perennial tension between researchers and practitioners in the field. There is a common perception that this tension is resulting in a growing rift between these two groups. A survey of the views of "senior" psychologists toward "psychology's past and future" (Boneau, 1992) is illustrative: "... [S]cientists and practitioners seem further apart than they were then [comparing 1962 to 1987]" (p. 1589); "There will be a continuing and growing split between the academic/scientific group and the practice group" (p. 1592).

The growing rift between "psychology's two cultures" (Kimble, 1984) is seen in professional organizational political tensions. These tensions culminated in 1988 when a group of predominantly academic and research psychologists broke away from the American Psychological Association (APA) to form their own organization, the American Psychological Society (APS). The rift is also evident in the relative lack of communication between researchers and practitioners. There is "... a major flaw in the bridging function of research; very little research is done that is helpful to the practitioner and very little in the world of practice has influenced research" (Schneider, 1990, p. 523). Researchers and practitioners read and publish in different journals and relatively rarely cite each others' work—in effect, they live in different worlds. The significance of this separation as it exists between animal researchers and practitioners is examined in Chapter 4.

The relative decline in the research arm of modern psychology is a threat to the field's view and presentation of itself as a science-based enterprise. "... [T]he dramatic shifts of recent years [from psychology as a scientific discipline to one dominated by practice] have the potential for drastically altering the discipline" (Rosenzweig, 1992, p. 721). The concern is that the field "would be a psychology without a science" (p. 721).

One "solution" is that the field will succumb to "centrifugal" forces (Spence, 1987), which will push some of the research subfields into existing fields or new amalgamations no longer recognizable as psychological science. For example, physiological psychology will become part of biology or neuroscience; while cognitive psychology and psycholinguistics will become part of the new field of "cognitive science" (see Stillings et al., 1989). Spence, a former president of APA, states: "In my worst nightmares I foresee a decimation of institutional psychology as we know it" (p. 1053).

There is, then, a certain vulnerability in the academic/research side of psychology. This is not to say that practitioners do not have their problems. Changes and upheavals in health care systems may be a threat to the traditional private practice approach of many practitioners (Schneider, 1990, p. 521). However, despite all these developments, we should not lose sight of the fact that psychology as a field is presently very robust and continuing to grow. If the numbers of undergraduates enrolling in a particular field is any measure of its future, the well-being of psychology is assured.

Animal-Based Research in Psychology

Psychology's reliance on animals has varied in the different paradigms, both now and in the past. Research in introspectionist and Gestalt psychology was laboratory and human-based, while psychoanalytic research was and is clinical- and human-based. In its heyday, behaviorist research was, and to a somewhat lesser extent still is heavily reliant on lab animal studies. Cognitive psychology is largely a human-based research enterprise, physiological psychology heavily uses animal subjects in the laboratory, and comparative psychology and ethology use animals in both laboratory and natural settings.

Numbers: Of Animals Used and of Users

The absolute number of animals used by psychologists in research is not readily available. Several countries provide data on the number of animals used in research, but these data are not broken down to indicate specific use of animals in psychological research. Furthermore, U.S. data typically do not include rats, mice, and birds, those animal groups most commonly used in largest numbers in psychological research.

In a 1985 publication produced by its public information office, the APA stated that "252,000 animals [were] used in psychological research in university psychology laboratories in the U.S. in 1983 ... " (APA, 1985a, p. 2). This number is a gross underestimate of the number of animals that psychologists use annually in research in the U.S. It is based on a survey of only universities and does not include the various other settings in which psychologists conduct psychological research: notably, undergraduate psychology departments (of which there are several thousand), medical centers (particularly departments of psychiatry), industry (e.g., Bell Laboratories), and governmental agencies (e.g., National Institutes of Health [NIH]). In addition, the item in the survey that asked for the "number of animals used" did not stipulate annual use. It is more likely read as requesting the number of animals in the lab at the time the survey is being completed. Given the resulting underestimate from this critical survey item and considering the actual number of institutions in which psychologists conduct psychological research, the actual number of animals used annually in psychological research in the U.S. is probably 5–10 times greater (1.25 to 2.5 million) than reported.

In addition to this admittedly rough estimate of the absolute numbers, there are some data available on the percent of psychological research involving nonhuman rather than human subjects. Gallup and Suarez (1980) state that approximately 7.5% of psychological research is animal-based. They derive this estimate from a survey of the articles in *Psychological Abstracts* in 1979. This publication presents abstracts of published studies in psychology. The abstracts are not exhaustive since only selected studies from selected journals are included.

Finally, there are some data on the percent of research psychologists using animal rather than human subjects. An APA brochure offered that roughly 5% of its then 60,000 members (or 3,000 individuals) "are involved directly in research with animals, either as scientific researchers or educators" (APA, 1985a, p. 2). Assuming that 16% of psychologists do research (Rosenzweig, 1992, p. 718), this would mean that roughly 30% of research psychologists use animals. This is discrepant from the 7.5% estimate derived from *Psychological Abstracts* of published animal-based research since there is no reason to suppose that researchers using animal subjects publish less than do those using human subjects. Other possibilities are that they publish their research less, or are less frequently cited in *Psychological Abstracts*. (The implications of high rejection rates, unpublished and uncited animal-based research is discussed in Chapter 4). Another interpretation is that Gallup and Suarez's estimate of 7.5% animal-based psychological research is an underestimate. Perhaps there is a bias in Gallup and Suarez' method—the figure was offered in the heat of a rebuttal to Bowd (1980) who had tendered some "ethical reservations about psychological research with animals." Or, there could be a bias against animal-based research operating in the selection process in *Psychological Abstracts*.

Several studies offer data pertaining to the trends in the numbers of animals used. Gallup and Suarez (1980) found that the proportion of animal-based research articles in *Psychological Abstracts* fell from 10% in 1939 to 7.5% in 1979, a result they offer in support of their claim that the field's reliance on animal research has "[not] changed appreciably." Benedict and Stoloff (1991) reported no decline in the number of animal facilities for psychology, at least at "America's Best" colleges. Domjan (Thomas & Blackman, 1991, p. 208) reported a reduction in the number of animal-based research articles by American psychologists in four relevant journals during the preceding 10 years. Schneider cites a study showing that all research fields in psychology, with the exception of developmental psychology, a largely human-based research enterprise, have "suffered major losses" in the number of doctoral degrees awarded since the mid-70s (1990, p. 522). Finally, Thomas and Blackman (1991) offer, to them, "disconcerting" data all of which point to a considerable decline in animal-based research in the United Kingdom. Comparing data from surveys in 1977 and 1989, they found the following significant reductions: numbers of psychology departments with animal facilities (25%), animals used (69%), staff conducting animal-based research (35%), and graduate students engaged in animal studies (62%). They bemoan what they take to be "a fundamental change [that] may be taking place in psychology's scientific base"

Table 1. Numbers of Animals Used in All Research Settings, by Country

Netherlands	40% decline from 1978 to 1990 (The Alternatives Report, 1992, 4, 5, p. 1) 5.9% decline from 1989 to 1990 (SCAW Newsletter, 1993, 15, 1, p. 11)
Switzerland	declined 8 consecutive years (1984–1991 inclusive) (SCAW Newsletter, 1993, 15, 2, p. 5)
West Germany	declined about 50% from 1981 to 1991 (The Alternatives Report, 5, 2, p. 1)
Italy	55% decline 1978 to 1989 (The Alternatives Report, 1992, 4, 4, p. 4)
United Kingdom	declined every year but one (1991) from 1979 to 1993 for a total reduction of 58% (The Animal Policy Report, 1995, 9, 1, 1–3)
Canada	38% decline from 1977 to 1989 (Resource Newsletter, 1992) and 3% decline from 1986 to 1989 (Science and Animal Care, 2, 2, p. 2).

(p. 208), issue a "call for action," and suggest "mount[ing] a defence" to stop the decline.

Taken together, these data suggest a decline over the past 15–20 years in numbers of animals used in animal-based psychological research. It remains to be seen if this relatively recent trend is a portent of a long-term decline or a short-lived fluke.

Trends from the use of animals in all research settings (experimentation, toxicity testing, education) also point to a reduction in the total number of animals used worldwide in the past 15–20 years. Table 1 presents a sampling, beginning with selected European countries and working back to the U. S. by way of Canada.

Turning to the U. S., data on both trends and absolute numbers is limited and equivocal, and what data is available is controversial. In her recent review of current data, Orlans concludes that "with the current information available in the United States, it is impossible to tell whether use is increasing, declining, or holding steady" (1994, p. 223). A Congressionally mandated report (U. S. Congress, Office of Technology Assessment [OTA], 1986) states:

Upon reviewing all the data sources available for predicting the laboratory-animal use in the United States, it is clear that no source accurately portrays the number of animals being used. Each has methodological problems that prevented it from accurately counting all users of animals (p. 53).

The difficulties stem from inadequate governmental record-keeping and from the failure to count rodents and birds as animals under the Animal Welfare Act. These problems have forced reliance on production and sales information from the laboratory animal breeding industry, estimates which have their own problems. Despite its disclaimer about the inaccuracy of any estimate, in its 1986 report the OTA offered the figure of 17–22 million animals used annually. The lower end of this range, 17 million, has been enshrined as the definitive number by pro-animal research groups such as the Biomedical Research Foundation while being disputed by animal rights groups (McArdle, 1988).

Arguing from Charles River sales records, the largest breeder of laboratory animals, and from Jackson Laboratory, another major breeder, Rowan concluded that the lower end of an accurate estimate for all types of research is 70 million animals (1984a). According to the OTA report, Rowan later adjusted his estimate to 25–35 million (U. S. Congress, OTA, 1986, p. 56). McArdle (a member of the OTA advisory panel of experts on laboratory animal production) stated that "the best current estimate of overall animal consumption is between 60 and 70 million" (1988, p. 15). We are left unclear whether the absolute number of animals used in the U. S. in the mid-80s was 17 or 70 million! (It is interesting that a recent controversy over the number of cats and dogs killed in shelters annually in the U. S. provides estimates that also differ by a factor of 2 or 3 to 1 [5–12 million], and that some of the same people are arguing the numbers [Clifton, 1993]).

Without valid data on the absolute number of animals used in a given year, tracking trends is obviously problematic. The OTA report concludes that data on trends in animal use should be "assigned a confidence rating of 'poor'" (1986, p. 57). This notwithstanding, the report offers several data sources indicating declines comparable to European and Canadian trends (p. 57). In his most recently published observation on the issue, Rowan (1994) gathers evidence from individual pharmaceutical facilities and from the Department of Defense laboratories that indicate that trends in the U. S. are comparable to those found elsewhere and that the current trend is still downward. However, he also notes that "official data" (United States Department of Agriculture [USDA] and the Institute for Laboratory Animal Resources) are "limited and flawed" (p. 3).

Clearly, the claim that there is a downward trend in the number of animals used in the U. S. is in contention. Orlans notes that the number of research sites has almost doubled (from 1932 to 3495) in the period between 1975 and 1991 (1994, p. 221). Consistent with this and accepting its limitations, her presentation of USDA data from 1973 to 1994 shows "no marked decline in animal use in the U. S." (Orlans, 1996, p. 154).

As for explanations of a decline (if, indeed, one has occurred), there are several offered. The cost of animal care has risen; animal care regulations have partly contributed to this cost; technical advances in the use of alternatives have greatly reduced use of animals, particularly in toxicology and product testing; and animal rights activism has provided political pressure for increased regulation and also encouraged investment in the development of alternatives.

In psychology specifically, Viney speculates that animal care costs, animal rights activism, and changes in research interests have all contributed to declines in the numbers of animals used (1990, p. 324). While Gallup and Eddy (1990) argue that animal rights activism has not been an important influence, Thomas and Blackman hold that "decline in work with animals stems largely from changing student attitudes" and that these attitudes "are in tune with current widely shared concerns for the natural environment and animal welfare" (1992, p. 1679). In citing changes in research interests, Viney is referencing the shift from behavioristic to cognitive psychology. He quotes a "definitive text" on cognitive psychology: "Information-processing [cognitive] psychologists, in contrast to the neobehaviorists, largely ignore the literature on animals; the only animal data cited in this book are some interesting recent studies of language-like behavior in primates" (1990, p. 325).

For all their vagaries, the U. S. figures allow us to return in a roundabout way to the primary issue of the extent of animal-based research in psychology. Citing a 1979 report of the British Psychological Society, Rowan states that "psychological research accounted for approximately 8% of the annual British use of laboratory animals" (1984a, p. 138). If this percent is applied to absolute numbers of animals for all uses in the U. S., the number of animals used for psychological research in the U. S. can be estimated. This assumes that animal-based psychology research represents the same percent of all uses in the U. S. and U. K. However, because the U. S. has half the world's research psychologists (recalling Rosenzweig's finding cited earlier), psychology in general and presumably animal-based research in psychology may be more than 8% of the total animal usage in the U. S. This would make the following an underestimate. If the moderately low estimate of 20 million for the total annual U. S. animals is used, psychological animal-based research accounts for 1.6 million animals annually; while if the moderately high estimate of 60 million is used, the number of animals used in psychological research is 4.8 million. The 1.6 million estimate is within the range of the earlier estimate (1.25–2.5 million) based on upwardly adjusting the figure from the APA survey. This adds some confidence that this number has some validity.

Species Used

What species of animals do psychologists use in their research and what are the trends in relative usage by species? Again, data from the UK are helpful. In their study comparing usage in 1977 to 1989, Thomas and Blackman found that psychologists in the UK most commonly use rats, pigeons, and mice, in that order; that those three animal groups comprise 95% of the animals used; and that this same order of animals frequently used is true in both years studied (1991, p. 209). In 1989, other animals used in the order of frequency of use are: invertebrates, monkeys, other mammals, other birds, and fish (p. 208).

Relying primarily on *Psychological Abstracts*, Viney, King, and Berndt (1990) calculated animal use in each year from 1967 to 1988 for 17 species. In 1988, the number of articles reporting use of a particular species is, in order of frequency beginning with the most frequent: rats, mice, pigeons, cats, rabbits, hamsters, dogs, chimpanzees, gerbils, baboons, snakes, bats and guinea pigs (tied), dolphins, gorillas, and lemurs and seals (tied). Comparable to the UK study, the first three animal groups comprise 94% of the studies published. In terms of trends, the authors note that in the years surveyed the "absolute number of studies on standard laboratory animals such as rats, pigeons, and guinea pigs remained relatively stable, whereas the absolute numbers for larger, more specialized animals, such as cats, dogs, and rabbits, have been declining" (p. 324). The number of articles describing use of chimpanzees, bats, hamsters, mice, and snakes are stable.

Nature and Scope of Use

Different paradigms or subfields of psychology differ in the degree of their reliance on animal research—for example, cognitive psychology uses fewer animals than behavioristic psychology. The use of animals in psychology also has different purposes that are more or less distinct. Some psychologists study animals to understand just those animals or to understand the differences among them and other nonhuman species. These "comparative psychologists" are interested in understanding animals as an end in itself. However, other psychologists study animals to discover processes that they believe to be universal, that is, that they believe will help understand the behavior of all human and nonhuman animals. Typified by the behaviorists, they hope to illuminate the general processes of learning, motivation, memory, and perception.

A third group studies nonhuman animals to understand particular conditions in humans. Sometimes such conditions, or at least arguably similar conditions, occur naturally in nonhuman animals. These, then, can be induced in laboratory animals. However, more often, comparable conditions do not naturally occur in nonhuman animals and investigators must attempt to devise situations that induce what are at least analogous versions of the human condition under study. In either case, this purpose and strategy is called "animal model" research. A fourth use of animals, and one of more recent vintage than the other three, is in applied human clinical and institutional settings where they are utilized as an adjunct to therapy. This "pet-facilitated therapy" will not be dealt with here.

The focus in this monograph will be on animal model research. It should be noted, however, that the "universal processes" style of research is closely related to the animal model strategy. For these researchers, in effect, any animal is a model for all other animals, including humans, based on the working assumption that behavioral processes exist that apply virtually independent of species. In addition, some comparative psychologists do extrapolate results of their studies to further understand human behavior and some even characterize their efforts as the search for animal models (Rajecki, 1983). Typically, their emphasis remains the understanding of an animal for its own sake. DeWaal states this emphasis explicitly, "although I draw parallels between animal and human behavior, even at the level of international politics, I am not in search of an animal model of our species. Each organism deserves attention for its own sake, not as a model for another" (1989, p. 3).

Animal model research proper has a typical distinguishing style. In it, there is little direct interest in understanding animals or animal behavior in itself. Further, it is directed less at the study of universal processes than at particular undesirable human conditions—disorders, pathology, and dysfunctions. One hallmark of animal model research is the attempt to induce just these negative conditions in laboratory animals.

To illustrate this feature and, as well, the scope of the contemporary animal model enterprise, selected examples of typical conditions for which animal models have been sought are listed in Table 2. They are taken from the subject index of a recent APA publication, *Animal Models of Human Pathology: A Bibliography of a Quarter Century of Behavioral Research, 1967–1992* (Overmier & Burke, 1992).

It should be clarified that typically there are many specific models within each of these general categories. For example, according to Willner, "the list of animal models of depression has grown to include more than 20 experimental procedures" (1991, p. 131). He organizes these into several families of models: (a) stress models (such as learned helplessness, behavioral despair, and chronic unpredictable stress) induce depression through stressing the animals in different situations; (b) separation models induce depression through maternal separation and social isolation; and (c) pharmacological models induce depression through the use of drugs, the use of one drug to block the effects of another, or withdrawing the use of a drug following an addiction (p. 132).

Table 2. Typical Conditions for Which Animal Models Have Been Sought

affective disorder	Huntington's Chorea
aging	hyperactivity
alcoholism	insomnia
Alzheimer's	lead poisoning
amenorrhea	learning disorders
amnesia	liver disorders
anorexia nervosa	malnutrition
anxiety	maternal deprivation
asthma	memory disorders
attachment disorder	mental retardation
attention deficit disorder	motion sickness
autoimmune disorders	movement disorders
brain disorder	multiple sclerosis
bulimia	muscular disorders
cerebral vascular disorder	neonatal disorders
child abuse	neuromuscular disorders
cigarette smoking	neuroticism
cold exposure	noise effects
colon disorders	obesity
concussion	obsessive compulsive disorder
coronary disorders	pain
coronary prone personality	panic disorder
crowding effects	phantom limbs
depression	phobias
dermatitis	posttraumatic stress disorder
deviant behavior	premature birth
diabetes	prenatal exposure
drug addiction	reading disabilities
drug side effects	rheumatism
drug withdrawal	schizophrenia
emotional trauma	self-mutilation
endocrine disorder	sensory deprivation
environmental stress	separation anxiety
epilepsy	sexual function disturbance
failure to thrive	sleep deprivation
gender disorders	social isolation
genetic disorders	stress disorders
hallucination	ulcers
headache	visual disorders
hearing disorders	vitamin deficiency disorders
helplessness	

As another example, Reines describes three families of models of schizophrenia: (a) conditioned avoidance response models, in which animals are trained to press a lever to avoid a shock and then different potential anti-schizophrenia drugs are tested for their effects on behavior; drugs that reduce the avoidance response are said to be effective potential treatments of schizophrenia; (b) hallucinogenic drug models, in which drugs are injected to see if they produce schizophrenic-like behaviors; and (c) reward-appreciation deficit, in which the reward or pleasure appreciation center of the brain is destroyed by injection of a toxin, to test the hypothesis that schizophrenia is a loss of ability to appreciate reward or pleasure (1982, pp. 19–28).

From this partial listing, it is evident that psychologists have attempted to develop an animal model for virtually every known problem in the human condition that has even a remotely psychological cast. Indeed, one would be hard pressed to think of a problem to which their considerable ingenuity has not been applied. Although analysis of the motivations of investigators will not be attempted here, particularly the economic and political motivations that attracts them to this strategy of using nonhuman animals to understand human animals, one investigator offers the following conjecture:

> Surely *model* has become the most overworked word in animal research. I attribute this to the exigency of obtaining grant support: The research must be interesting, it must be relevant, and thus, it seems to have been concluded, it must be a model of a human disease condition if it is to be funded (Silverman, 1994, p. 659; emphasis in original).

The scope of the procedures devised to create the models are as broad as the conditions to be modeled. In general, the procedures extend from (a) genetic manipulation—animals are bred for certain dispositions, such as susceptibility to seizures from auditory stimulation, or, more recently, genetic engineering techniques manipulate certain susceptibilities or deficits; to (b) manipulations of the nervous system—different parts of the brain are implanted with electrodes, electrically stimulated, lesioned or cut, surgically ablated or removed, or destroyed through toxic injection; to (c) invasive manipulation of other parts of the body—different systems and organs of the body are monitored through fistulas (surgically created holes), stimulated through substances introduced into cannulae (surgically implanted tubes) or destroyed; to (d) behavioral and environmental manipulations—food or drink are made conditional on the performance of certain tasks; avoidance of painful conditions such as shock, heat, or cold are made conditional on the performance of certain tasks (or abruptly applied independent of any performance, or made conditional on another animal's performance); all manner of basic, even life-sustaining social supports and environmental stimulation and enrichments are withdrawn or otherwise manipulated; and all manner of painful, distressing or harmful social and environmental stimuli are presented.

Suffering Involved

The nature of the conditions for which models have been sought (and, as will be discussed, the goal in this research strategy of duplicating those conditions experienced by humans in every respect possible) raise the question of the amount of suffering that animal model research involves. Surprisingly, there is disagreement in the field about whether there is substantial suffering, and a fuller discussion of that controversy and of other issues associated with the question of suffering are deferred to Chapter 6.

Because part of the disagreement stems from determining what constitutes suffering, a working definition suggested by DeGrazia and Rowan is "suffering is 'the unpleasant emotional response to more than minimal pain and distress'" (1991, p. 199, emphasis deleted). Note that suffering is not the pain or distress itself, but the emotional response to it, and that such an emotional response is not limited to pain. Most people involved in both animal research and animal protection agree that the concept of suffering should be broadened from a narrow notion of pain to the inclusion of experiences such as distressful situations. In fact, as will be seen, such broadening is often incorporated in recent animal welfare policy and guidelines. However, there is disagreement as to whether harm and injury should be included as forms of suffering. While typically harm and injury are accompanied by pain or distress or both, in some instances harm can involve the loss of capabilities that are not so experienced. For example, in the case of the deprivation of a capacity from birth, an individual could be harmed without experiencing that deprivation as a loss. Under this working definition such harm would not be accompanied by suffering. More importantly, the definitional constraints of the term "suffering" aside, should we include such losses in our concerns about animal welfare? The same arguments are raised about death. When there is no pain involved or little anticipatory distress, as in nonsurvival surgical procedures, the death of an animal does not necessarily involve suffering. However, animal protectionists, most philosophers, and many animal researchers now do count death as an animal welfare issue, conceiving of it as the ultimate harm.

One other point of clarification to be made regarding suffering in psychological research is a general contrast between it and biomedical research. On the one hand, as the list of animal models above suggests, psychologists do study many conditions usually considered biomedical or medical in nature, and psychological research does include the study of physiological processes. On the other hand, it should be clear that most psychologists are primarily interested in behavior and experience, and only secondarily interested in physiology. This interest has important implications for the degree of suffering involved in psychological research. Although, to some extent, physiology, such as the physiology of a particular disease process, can be studied in an unconscious animal, the study of behavior and experience usually requires the animal subject to be conscious.

When psychologists study the behavioral correlates of depression, the structure of environment and behavior that maintains an eating disorder, the social effects of maternal deprivation, the mood correlates of chronic pain, the cognitive deficits associated with schizophrenia, or the lifestyle features correlated with the incidence or consequence of cardiac disease, they typically study the fully conscious "intact organism." While physiologically as well as environmentally invasive procedures are often part of animal model psychological research, investigators typically require the animal subjects to survive and recover from the invasive procedures so that behavioral and experiential effects, the primary phenomena of interest, can be studied. In much of the biomedical research, by contrast, animal subjects are not allowed to recover and do not experience any pain or subjective distress from the procedure. They cannot, then, be said to have suffered.

While on the surface, to a layperson it is apparent that animal model research in psychology involves considerable suffering, research psychologists are distrustful of such face validity and require more exacting evidence. They limit their inferences to conclusions drawn from the application of instruments that measure the phenomenon of interest. Fortunately, several rating scales have been developed that measure invasiveness. The term "invasive" is used for any procedure, whether genetic, physiological, psychological, or environmental, that causes suffering (Field & Shapiro, 1988). One of these instruments

specifically measures the invasiveness of typical psychological experimental manipulations (Field & Shapiro,
1988). In this chapter, the Scale of Invasiveness is employed simply to further describe and illustrate the nature
and scope of animal model research in psychology by
highlighting the varying degrees of suffering associated
with such studies.

The Scale of Invasiveness rates psychological experiments on a 6 point scale, ranging from 0 (little or no invasiveness) to 5 (highest level) (Field & Shapiro, 1988, p. 43).
(See Table 3 for abbreviated definitions and examples of
the scale points.) The actual scale provides more detailed
specification and definition than given in Table 3, amount-
ing, in effect, to a scoring manual that "reliably" (independent scorers agree on assigned ratings) allows the as-
signment of a scale point to virtually any experimental
procedure in the psychological literature.

To ensure that the examples offered are representative
of mainstream research accepted or highly valued within
the field, several studies have been selected that were
published by investigators who have served as chair of an
APA committee that promotes and oversees animal research in psychology, the Committee on Animal Research
and Ethics (CARE) (Field, Shapiro, & Carr, 1990). Most of
these experiments offer further advantages in that two
independent raters assigned the scale points, and data are
available that establishes its reliability (p. 3) (see Table 4).

The study "A Model of Early Social Deprivation and its
Treatment" scored a 5 and is part of an extensive literature
describing the development of models of maternal and
other social deprivation, using nonhuman primates. (See
Stephens [1986] for a critical review of over 350 studies
conducted between 1950 and 1984; see Sackett [1988] for
a critique of Stephens' critique). Some of the research in
this literature claims to provide models for early attachment and its dysfunctions, for the "nature of love" (Harlow, 1958), for depression, and for a so-called total isola-

Table 3. Abbreviated Definitions and Examples of Scale Points from Scale of Invasiveness

0.	Field studies involving virtually no pain/distress or harm. This includes observational studies or the capturing of an animal followed by its immediate release.
1.	Field studies involving little or no pain/distress or harm. This involves monitoring of physiological variables, simple behavioral tests such as perceptual discrimination and preference testing, with no reduction in weight below free-fed levels.
2.	Laboratory experiments and certain field studies involving mild pain/distress and no long-term harm. Examples include mild pain or distress such as frequent blood sampling; brief visual deprivation; mild electric shock; procedures involving anesthetized animals with mild postoperative pain/distress and no long-term harm.
3.	Laboratory experiments involving moderate pain/distress and little or no long-term harm. This includes surgery for electrode placement, negative reinforcement, or inescapable noxious stimuli involving moderate pain/distress, food deprivation (in rats resulting in 80–90% of ad lib body weight) and limited sleep deprivation.
4.	Laboratory experiments involving an extended period of pain/distress or moderate long-term harm. This includes surgery or inescapable noxious stimuli producing an extended period of pain/distress or moderate long-term harm; food deprivation greatly exceeding the species' requirement (e. g., in rats 70–80% of ad lib weight); drugs or toxic agents causing an extended period of pain/distress or moderate long-term harm (e. g., in rats, use of anxiogenic drugs).
5.	Laboratory experiments involving an extended period of extreme pain/distress or severe long-term harm. This would include prolonged physical immobilization (weeks); use of curariform agents on unanesthetized animals; use of inescapable noxious stimuli causing an extended period of extreme pain/distress or severe long-term harm.

tion syndrome. In some of the studies, the deprivation is total rather than partial, involving "chambering" animals in settings in which they have no social contact, by even the most narrow definitions. In more recent studies there is a trend toward employing shorter periods of deprivation, isolation, or separation.

Table 4. Selected Studies of Chairs of the APA's CARE Committee by Level of Invasiveness and Disorder Modeled

5. Laboratory experiments involving an extended period of extreme pain/distress or severe long-term harm.

A MODEL OF EARLY SOCIAL DEPRIVATION AND ITS TREATMENT

"Therapeutic effects of an imposed foraging task in disturbed monkeys" (Rosenblum & Smiley, 1984).

Twelve bonnet macaques were raised in "partial social isolation" for the first several years of their lives. In this arrangement their "socialization" occurs in the absence of any physical contact with another animal, although they can see and hear other monkeys. We score the study "5" because the social isolation is for "extended periods of time relative to species' needs."

Following the period of isolation, the investigators house the animals in social groups and test a wide range of behaviors under two conditions: a pre-forage condition in which food is immediately available and a forage condition in which food is only available in a feeder box which has access holes in the mesh sides. Behaviors observed include abnormal self-directed behavior such as unusual clasping behavior ("left arm fully extended upward while grasping repeatedly at the air and simultaneously pulling the skin on his belly," p. 488); floating limbs ("limb ... rise slowly in the air without the apparent awareness of the subject," p. 488), stereotyped pacing and various self-injurious behaviors ("one male ... was seen to chase his own tail, do repeated somersaults, bite his inner thighs ... and leap into the air and attack his feet before landing, p. 488)." Investigators also observed various abnormal sexual behaviors. The results of the study suggest that an imposed foraging task has therapeutic effects only on partially social-isolate monkeys who rank high or low in social dominance. Mid-ranking individuals, however, show a dramatic increase in abnormal behavior, following the foraging feeding arrangement.

4. Laboratory experiments involving an extended period of pain/distress or moderate long-term harm.

A MODEL OF STRESS-INDUCED GASTRIC ULCERATION

"The ulcerogenic effects of a rest period after exposure to water-restraint stress in rats" (Overmier, Murison, & Ursin; 1986).

Rats are restrained in plastic tubes that are suspended vertically in tanks of 19°C (66°F) water, with 15 cm of the 21 cm long tube under

Table 4 continued

water. "... [T]he animal's head was always safely well above the surface. The animals did have the possibility of small movements within the tubes and also of biting the securing bolts" (p. 374). The partial immersion extended over a 2 hour period at which point some animals were killed while others returned to their home cage for a period of 2 hours and then were killed. Their stomachs were then removed to measure the extent of ulceration. We score the study "4" because the noxious stimulus of restraint and immersion in cold water causes "an extended period of pain/distress and moderate long-term harm"ù in this case both.

3. Laboratory experiments involving moderate pain/distress and little or no long-term harm.

A MODEL OF MARIJUANA USAGE

"Chronic marijuana usage and sleep-wakefulness cycles in cats" (Barratt & Adams, 1972).

The investigators implanted electrodes in the brains of six anesthetized cats. Following recovery from this surgical procedure, they administered marijuana to the cats orally in the form of a capsule, daily for 180 days. While in a semi-sound proof cubicle for eleven hours each day, physiological measures of various stages of sleep and wakefulness were occasionally recorded, utilizing the electrodes. We score the study "3" because of the surgical procedure done under anesthesia and involving little long-term harm. The changes in the sleep-wakefulness cycles are not judged to be distressful or more than mildly harmful.

2. Laboratory experiments and certain field studies involving mild pain/distress and no long-term harm.

A MODEL OF A TASTE MODIFYING SUBSTANCE

"Reduction of sucrose preference in the hamster by gymnemic acid" (Faull & Halpern, 1972).

Male hamsters were tested to determine their preference for sucrose solutions, at several different concentrations, compared to distilled water. The experimental condition involved squirting different concentrations of gymnemic acid into their mouths prior to the taste preference taste. We score the study "2" because the animals are deprived of water for a number of hours prior to the test.

Table 4 continued

1. Field studies involving little or no pain/distress or harm.

A MODEL OF EARLY INFANT STIMULATION

"Nongenetic transmission of information" (Denenberg & Rosenberg, 1967).

Female rat pups were handled once daily for the first 20 days of their lives. "Handling" involves being placed in a tin can partially filled with shavings for 3 minutes and then returned to their home cage. When themselves pregnant, female offspring of these rats were placed either in stainless steel maternity cages or free environment boxes, compartments with food, water and toys available. Their female offspring were tested for activity level at age 21 days and then weighed. The measure of activity was number of squares touched in open field divided into 64 squares. We score the study "1" for "procedures involving simple behavioral tests such as perceptual discrimination, preference testing, handling or petting.

0. Field studies involving virtually no pain/distress or harm.

The experiment "A Model of Stress-Induced Gastric Ulceration" scored a 4 and confirms the investigators' hypothesis that a rest period immediately following a period of stress increases the degree of ulceration, that is that the effects of stress continue after termination of the stressful condition. This is one of numerous different animal models of stress-induced ulcers (Overmier, Murison, & Ursin, 1986, p. 372). Within this model featuring restraint and cold water immersion, these investigators have explored many variations. For example, Overmier and Murison (1989) founded increased degree of ulceration when rats were subjected to a post-stressor rest period in which they were exposed to cues previously associated with "80 five-second uncontrollable electric shocks distributed over four sessions" (1989, p. 1296). These investigators (Overmier & Murison, 1991) also found that rats subjected to footshocks prior to the restraint and partial immersion had more ulceration, whether or not the footshocks were predictable, i.e., signalled prior to onset.

The experiment "A Model of Marijuana Usage" scored a 3 and is "part of a larger research project ... aimed at studying the effects of chronic marijuana usage on brain function and behavior" (Barratt & Adams, 1972, p. 207, emphasis deleted). The results indicate that chronic use of this drug does change sleep and awake patterns and that these changes persist for at least 40 days after the termination of the drug. The investigators also found that a decrease in a stage of sleep (slow-wave) had been reported elsewhere to result in a decrease in aggression.

The results of the study "A Model of a Taste Modifying Substance," scoring a 2, confirms the investigators' hypothesis that gymnemic acid reduces sucrose preference. The investigators state as a goal of the study "the search for a nonhuman model of the effects of [gymnemic acid] in humans" (Faull & Halpern, 1972, p. 903). The investigators present no discussion of a broader context of interest in the model. Related studies refer to the physiology of taste in humans and to "suppression of sweet sensitivity." Presumably, one area of application of the model is to dieting and possibly to eating disorders. Several other studies using this paradigm are more invasive than the present one because they involve physiological measures of gustatory nerve activity.

Scoring a 1, the study "A Model of Early Infancy Stimulation" showed that the handling of female rats in infancy affects the activity level and weaning weight of their grandchildren. It is part of an extensive literature on the effects of early infant environment on subsequent development, in this case on the development of a later generation. It should be noted that while this study is relatively noninvasive, some experiments in the infant enrichment/deprivation literature can be highly invasive. For example, the same senior investigator (Denenberg et al., 1978) incorporated surgical removal of one hemisphere of the neocortex with subsequent handling.

No example for the "0" point on the scale is offered because animal model research almost by definition is not done in the field (as opposed to the lab) and, in any case, rarely involves no pain or harm. There was not one instance of a 0 score in the sample of 135 experiments in the study of research conducted by CARE chairs from which these other examples were drawn. In fact, only 12 of the 135 scored a 1, while 46 of the 135 scored a 4 or a 5 (Field, Shapiro, & Carr, 1990, pp. 4–6). It is also interesting to note that of those 46 highly invasive studies, 22 (48%) involved monkeys, cats, and dogs, while 24 (52%) involved mice and rats. The relatively high percent of the former species contrasts dramatically with the data reported earlier on the 90–95% of rats, mice, and pigeon typically used in psychological research. Clearly, a disproportionate amount of highly invasive research involves nonhuman primates, dogs, and cats. It is not clear why this is the case. One speculation is that investigators perceive these species as providing "higher fidelity" (more similar) models and assume that only such models can justify highly invasive procedures.

The five examples presented here suggest that developing or finding animal models of human psychology is a complex enterprise. The extent of "variations on a theme" is almost inexhaustible. In addition, it should be clear that most models are of pathological conditions, although occasionally normal or even optimal conditions are modeled. The predominant use of models which attempt to faithfully create pathological conditions assures that this kind of research is typically quite invasive.

Trends in Invasiveness

While the results are mixed, the several available studies of invasiveness trends in psychological research, all employing the Scale of Invasiveness, indicate that the level has not changed and remains moderately high. Examining research published in both physiological and comparative psychology journals, Field (1988) found an increase from 2.60 in 1947 to 3.12 in 1967 and then a decline to 2.34 in 1987. However, both Lindquist (1990) and Schmorrow (1993) found no decline during a comparably recent period. Lindquist rated five journals, featuring behavioristic, physiological, and comparative psychological research, for invasiveness. The comparison of studies in 1975 and 1989 revealed no statistically significant difference, and the average score was around "3." There was a statistically insignificant trend toward less invasiveness and a trend toward fewer studies scored as "4" or "5," while more were scored as "3." Schmorrow rated studies in a behaviorist journal from 1958 to 1992 and found no change in level of invasiveness, which remained between "3" and "4" (except for 2 years in the 1960s when mean invasiveness levels were over "4").

Psychologists' Attitudes Toward Laboratory Animals

While not of direct interest, the literature on public attitudes toward laboratory animals and research is extensive and provides some general findings that are consistent with and features that characterize psychologists' attitudes.

From her own study and from her review of the literature, Driscoll (1992) concludes that such attitudes are "unitary," "consistent," or "hard." This means that individuals have consistent attitudes toward animals in general, and that these attitudes likely form at an early age and endure over time.

This is not to say that attitudes toward animal use are simple or logically coherent on the surface. A number of investigators have found that attitudes vary according to the species involved (Driscoll, 1992). Herzog notes that "human likes and dislikes about an animal species are often based on emotional criteria such as how cute they are and how we define their social role" (1991, p. 246). The culture distinguishes many categories of animals including "pets," "exotics," "pests," "endangered species," "farm animals," "sea food," and "feeder animals" (those fed to pets and exotics). It also does not imply that attitudes do not change, since with the advent of the animal rights movement, many people have become more sensitive to issues of animal suffering and exploitation.

The morally acceptable practices that are built up around this panoply are necessarily complex and inevitably involve many conflicts of interest. As an example of "treading these murky [moral] waters," Herzog (1988) describes the different "moral status" accorded to different categories of animals of the same species within a research laboratory—mice that are objects of study (laboratory animals), those that live outside the cages within the laboratory walls and corridors (pests), and those that are raised to feed other laboratory animals (feeders).

However, attitudes toward animal use are strong and enduringly held despite the complexities of the philosophical issues and of the many distinct cultural "niches" that we have constructed for (or actually from) animals. Perhaps because they occupy a peculiar moral space between people and things, nonhuman animals are important to us, and our attitudes toward specific uses of them reflect this: Gluck and Kubacki report informal evidence "that Congress has received more mail on this issue [specifically, the use of animals in research] than any other topic in the history of the country (1991, p. 157). Jamison and Lunch (1992, p. 439) cite an article in the *Congressional Quarterly* which asserts that letters on the treatment of animals make up the third largest volume of mail to Congress.

Many studies find a strong gender-based bias in attitudes toward the use of animals. Fulero (1992) found females to be less accepting of animal research than males. Gallup and Beckstead found that females appeared "more concerned for pain and suffering in animals than did males" (1988, p. 475). In their cross-cultural analysis of attitudes, Pifer, Shimizu, and Pifer (1994) found that women opposed animal research significantly more than men, in 10 of 15 countries studied, with a trend in the same direction in the remaining five countries. Consistent with this, according to Plous (1991, p. 194) women comprise 80% of the animal rights movement. In addition, Jamison and Lunch (1992, p. 445) found that 68% of people, selected through a randomizing procedure for interviews at the March for the Animals rally in Washington in the summer of 1990, were women.

Kellert and Berry (Driscoll, 1992) found a complex but negative relation between age and concern for animals in that younger people are more concerned with animal welfare. A possible implication of this is that somehow we (de)educate children from being animal welfarists to becoming animal exploiters (Shapiro, 1990b).

Turning to a more directly ideological demographic variable, liberals more than conservatives are animal welfarists. This finding encompasses both religious affiliation and political persuasion. Bowd and Bowd (1989) found this relation between individuals affiliated with liberal as compared to conservative Christian denominations in Australia, while Kimball found that U.S. Congressional "Representatives who exhibited a strong interest in the welfare of creatures that *can't* vote ... also exhibit a strong interest in legislation that *directly* supports the liberties and freedom of expression of individuals who can vote (1989, p. 7, emphasis in original). In their study of activists attending the 1990 March for the Animals, Jamison and Lunch (1992, pp. 450–1) found that they are "moderately liberal or liberal."

Nibert's study (1994) of the relationship between a belief in animal rights and opinions on various other social issues broadens these findings of religious and political ideology and affiliation. "The way people regard animals is related to the way they regard people" (p. 122). Nibert found that support for animal rights is associated with more tolerance of human diversity, specifically, acceptance of rights for women, homosexuals, and persons of color. In the context of the frequent assertion by their opponents that proponents of animal rights devalue humans, Nibert offers that the two concerns, the welfare of human and nonhuman animals, are typically held by the same individual.

Hills (1993) also provides evidence that attitudes toward animals are more often associated with, rather than divergent from, attitudes toward humans. Using a scale that distinguishes between people who are more oriented toward or interested in things and those who are more oriented toward other people, Hills found that "interest in animals is more strongly associated with interest in people than interest in things" (pp. 106–7). One possible implication of this finding is that those people who have "emotional concerns" for animals also have such concern for other people (pp. 108–9).

Consistent with this positive correlation of attitudes toward humans and nonhuman animals, a recent poll reported that nearly one-half (47%) of Americans believe that animals "are just like humans in all important ways" (Balzar, 1993). Sixty-one percent of people 18–29 years old and 52% of women espouse this view.

In terms of individual psychology, Broida, et al. (1993) found that certain personality types are more likely to oppose animal experimentation: intuitive and feeling types more than sensate and thinking types. The former are more focused on relationships, while the latter emphasize process. In the context of animal research, intuitive and feeling type individuals attend more to the effects and ethical implications, while sensate and thinking types key on the process of scientific investigation.

Evidence regarding the general level of opposition to the use of animals in research is mixed. While a number of studies converge on the finding that, on the average, individuals espouse a middle position when asked about their attitude toward the use of animals in research, a recently published large-scale study surveying individuals in 15 different countries finds a high level of opposition (Pifer, Shimuzu, & Pifer, 1994).

In his review of five studies, Plous reported two general themes: while concerned about the well-being of animals, most survey respondents do support the selective use of animals, including their use in research (1993, p. 14). Driscoll concludes from her finding of a grand mean "right on the neutral point" that "there is little evidence of strong public opposition to the use of animals" (1992, p. 36). While his findings are consistent with these other studies, Takooshian interprets the middle position as an indication of "mixed feelings" with regard to this issue (1988, p. 8). This is based in part on his observation that respondents "explicitly note their discomfort over this issue [animal research] when returning their surveys" and are suspicious of the motives and bias of the investigator (1993). It is worth noting that it is difficult to distinguish between neutrality and strong but mixed feelings on an issue in survey research. It also should be clarified that an *average* middle position does not imply that many individuals do not take extreme positions. For example, Gallup and Beckstead found that 14.5% of a student population agreed that "most psychological research done on animals is unnecessary and invalid" (1988, p. 474).

Using a survey item that asked over 11,000 respondents from 15 different nations to weigh the benefits to human health against harm to "popular" animals, Pifer, Shimizu, and Pifer (1994) found high levels of opposition (over 50% disagreed or strongly disagreed with a statement permitting painful/injurious research) in most of the European Community nations, with only Greece and Portugal having less than a majority opposition. The authors suggest that the higher level of opposition found in their study is a function of what species of animals are referred to in the item—here dogs and chimpanzees, rather than rats as in some of the studies reviewed above.

Turning from the general public to scientists' views, Takooshian included groups of scientists, not necessarily psychologists, in his general surveys of the public (1988). He found that, like the general public, scientists have mixed feelings about the use of animals in invasive research ("vivisection") (1988, p. 8). He also found that for both the public and scientists an individual's attitude toward vivisection is more related to his or her views toward animals than it is to views about science. "Pro-animal" people, including scientists, are also "anti-vivisection," while a high faith in science does not predict any particular attitude toward the use of animals in research (1988, p. 8).

Scientific literacy does not predict attitude toward animal research any better than does faith in science. Of 14 nations surveyed, Pifer, Shimizu, and Pifer (1994) found that for the general public scientific knowledge is not consistently related to attitude toward animal research. In some nations there is a positive relation with individuals with higher levels of knowledge supporting animal research, while in others the relation is negative. In the U.S. sample, no significant relation was found.

Paul (1995) studied the views of scientists involved in a British organization dedicated to the defense of animal research. Both these scientists and a group of animal rights activists were asked to generate arguments that support their own position and that of their respective opponents. While both groups tended to have a negative and somewhat extreme view of the other, each also had a "... clear knowledge of the arguments and ideas on both sides of the animal experimentation debate" (p. 17). Both groups presented their own views as moderate, relative to the perceived extremism of their opponents. At least half of the participants of each group made concessions to their respective opposition: the scientists allowed that some animal experimentation is inadmissible; the animal rights activists allowed that some is admissible. While both groups agreed that animals have the capacity to suffer, scientists focused their attention and concern for such suffering higher up the phylogenetic scale than did animal rights campaigners. Also, scientists, contrary to the activists, took the potential benefits of experimentation as their starting point when making judgments about admissibility, with suffering being given only secondary consideration.

Finally, Plous has conducted a major attitude survey of psychologists in practice (1996a) and undergraduate psychology majors. The results are largely consistent with findings in the general public. Based on a sample of 3982 psychologists and 1188 psychology students, he found a high level of support for research involving observation and confinement (1996a, p. 1171). However, when asked about research involving pain or death, a large percentage of both groups replied that it is not justified. Even when the research is described as "institutionally approved and deemed of scientific merit," 62.1% and 44.4% of psychologists indicate that research involving pain or death to primates and rats, respectively, is unjustified (1996a, p. 1171). Consistent with this are the results of a survey of psychologists selected from members of APA and APS, in which O'Sullivan found that "psychologists believed psychological research with animals to be important, however, the more invasive a research activity is, the less it was found to be acceptable" (in submission). O'Sullivan measured degree of acceptability of experimental procedures varying in invasiveness through sub-items derived from the Scale of Invasiveness, discussed earlier.

On various measures, psychology majors are even less supportive of animal research than are psychologists. For

example, the percentage of students who are strong supporters of animal research is less than half that of psychologists (14% vs. 31%). Further, psychologists who received
their doctoral degree during the 1990s are much less likely
to support animal research than those earning it before
1970. Also, as reported in other studies, women are less
supportive of animal research than men. The number of
women enrolling in graduate programs in psychology is
escalating dramatically, as is true in several other profes-
sions. These findings and developments, taken together
with the documented decline in the numbers of animal
facilities, animal-based articles published, and doctoral
degrees in animal-related subfields, all suggest that support for invasive animal research in psychology is corrod-
ing and will continue to corrode.

I conclude with one additional study that bears on psychologists' attitudes, as it provides data on students'
views of their psychology teachers' behavior with respect
to laboratory animals. Keith-Spiegel, Tabachnick, and Allen (1993) studied students views of the ethics of certain
actions taken by their professors. While also dealing with
student rights, two of the items bear on the ethics of psychologists' use of animals. Specifically, 62.1% of students
view a professor's requirement that students use electric
shock on rats as unethical under many or all circumstances. Similarly, 48% of students consider a professor's requirement that students watch a film on how to do surgical brain implants in monkeys as unethical under many
or all circumstances.

Psychology and the Animal Rights Movement

In Chapter 2, I shall present an historical account of the
introduction of laboratory animals into the emerging field
of modern psychology in the late 19th century. Here I sup-
plement the relatively impoverished literature of formal

studies of psychologists' attitudes toward animal use reviewed above with a brief sketch of the relation between psychology and the animal rights movement.

Most psychologists, indeed the profession as a whole, were caught short by the prominence given to psychological research involving animals by the contemporary animal rights movement. Three early events early established that prominence: (1) the publication of Singer's *Animal Liberation* in 1975, (2) the protest of the work of Lester Aronson in 1977, and (3) the exposure of the research of and subsequent trial of Edward Taub in 1981.

In a chapter entitled, "Tools for Research," Singer clearly singled out psychological research with the statement, "Many of the most painful experiments are performed in the field of psychology" (p. 34). He then provided a dozen pages of graphic examples of psychological research which he found particularly unacceptable.

Just one year after the publication of Singer's book, animal rights activists, headed by Henry Spira, organized a protest at the American Museum of Natural History where Aronson was studying the sexual behavior of cats. The research involved blinding, deafening, and castrating cats, and surgically removing parts of their brains (Garfield, 1980, p. 104). The protest and attendant media attention prompted the museum to terminate the research (Jasper & Nelkin, 1992, p. 28). Ironically, whether or not Aronson was a psychologist depends on one's definition. He did not earn his doctorate in psychology. However, he was chairperson of the Department of Animal Behavior at the Museum of Natural History and the APA's own newspaper, the *APA Monitor* ("Animals in research," 1982), referred to him to as a psychologist.

Taub's research involved cutting the sensory nerves of monkeys' arms to see if they could learn to use the affected limbs. This highly invasive procedure, deafferentation, was an attempt to provide a model for stroke and was funded by the National Institute for Neurological and

Communicative Disorders and Stroke, a branch of NIH. Following the first of its kind arrest of a researcher and the seizure of laboratory animals, NIH first temporarily and then permanently suspended Taub's grant. The NIH review committee found inadequate veterinary care, housing, and review committee expertise (Shapiro, 1989, pp. 4–5) and "grossly unsanitary" conditions (Rowan, 1984b, p. 175) in Taub's lab. In addition to the inquiry by NIH, Taub was tried and convicted of animal cruelty in a state court. However, the conviction was later overturned when the appeal's court ruled that his federal funding exempted him from the provisions of the state's animal cruelty statute. As the publication of *Animal Liberation* launched the contemporary animal rights movement, the trial of Taub provided it with its *cause célèbre*, kicking off an uproar that continued for a decade.

While the vigor and strength of the contemporary movement caught most psychologists by surprise, there had been an earlier movement. In fact, Dewsbury concludes his history of its impact on the field of psychology at that time with the assertion that, "the resemblances between the antivivisectionist movement at the turn of the century and the current agitation far exceed the differences" (1990, p. 325). If that were the case, if the earlier movement was truly a rehearsal for the present one, one would have expected psychology as an institution to have been more prepared than it was to deal with contemporary criticisms of invasive animal-based psychological research.

In any case, as Dewsbury notes, animal-based psychology developed at the end of the 19th century just as the Victorian antivivisection movement "was in full swing" (p. 316). Some psychologists became targets of the antivivisectionists, with the latter often receiving the support of press media. A notable example is James Watson, known in psychology as the father of behaviorism. In its original form behaviorism was an animal-based research enterprise which urged that observable behavior rather than "mental life" is the proper focus of study of science of psychology. Watson responded to criticism of his research on sensation and learning in rats with a justification of his research:

> Much has been written about the artificiality, the abnormality—yes, even the brutality of the present "laboratory" method in animal psychology. However well founded they may be in certain cases, these criticisms cannot with justice be urged against the present set of tests (quoted in Dewsbury, 1990, p. 322).

In our terms, his research was highly invasive, involving "removal of the eyes, destruction of the tympanic membrane, removal of the olfactory bulbs, cutting of the vibrissae, and anesthetization of the soles of the rats' feet" (p. 320). By systematically destroying in turn every sensory capability of the rat and then testing their learning in mazes, Watson intended to explain the sensory basis of learning in rats.

Other conflicts were played out more quietly within the field. William James, an early giant in psychology and philosophy, took a "moderate position" (Dewsbury's term) against his former student, Walter Cannon. James opposed the use of animals in classroom demonstrations and criticized his colleagues for opposing all regulation of animal research. However, James also stated:

> Man [sic] lives for sciences as well as bread ... To taboo vivisection is then the same thing as to give up seeking after a knowledge of physiology; in other words, it is sacrificing a human intellectual good, and all that flows from it, to a brute and corporeal good (quoted in Dewsbury, p. 318).

Here is a statement of Cannon's more extreme pro-vivisectionist view, in which he rails against

> the propaganda and ill-advised restrictive proposals of that small minority of our fellow citizens who make a fetish or a religion of "antivivisection" and who sometimes act as though other organisms are more worthy of considerate treatment and preservation

from accident or disease than is man (quoted in Dewsbury, 1990, p. 319)

In the context of media attacks on psychologists, conflict within the field, and the more threatening antivivisectionist attempts to pass state legislation against animal research, the APA, at Cannon's instigation, formed a Committee on Precautions in Animal Experimentation in 1925 (Dewsbury, p. 324). The charge of CPAE was to

> cooperate with other organizations interested in safeguarding animal experimentation, and which shall endeavor with them to disseminate accurate information about animal experimentation and to combat attempts to prevent or restrict it ... (Young, 1928).

Both the occasioning contexts and the formal charge of the committee indicate that its primary purpose was to protect animal research by "combat[ting]" attempts to limit or reform it. The charges do not refer to protecting animals or to animal welfare more generally. Further, from the outset CPAE took a "low-profile" on the issues and was a relatively inactive committee (Dewsbury, 1990, p. 324).

Not until the emergence of the contemporary animal rights movement and the three events described above that thrust psychology again and more prominently into the limelight did the committee add, in the early 1980s, the protection and welfare of animals to its official charge (Field, Shapiro, & Carr, 1990, p. 2). While retaining the earlier charges about safeguarding animal research and combatting attempts to restrict it, the Committee proposed and the Council of Representatives approved language requiring it to "... review the ethics of animal experimentation" and "... to disseminate ... guidelines protecting the welfare of animals used in research, teaching, and practical applications ..." (Dewsbury, 1993, p. 11).

Psychology and the Animal Rights Movement

Relative to their share of the total output of animal-based research in science, the number of psychologists targeted by the contemporary animal rights movement has been disproportionately high. Speculatively, the reasons for this come from within as well as from outside the field. From within, I have described the divided camps separating research from applied psychology. Through sheer numbers, applied psychologists have had political control of the APA. Professionally, they have little or no vested interest in protecting laboratory animal research. Personally, they tend to be caring people who are relatively uncomfortable with the notion that some individuals, whether human or nonhuman, would have to suffer for the sake of the presumed benefit of others. As mentioned, in 1988, the tensions between researchers and practitioners culminated in the formation of a split-off organization primarily backed by researchers and academicians, the American Psychological Society.

The general public is less aware of animal-based psychological research than of biomedical research. When informed of the former their response often is that psychological or behavioral research is less important than its counterpart in biomedicine, for it is not perceived to directly contribute to their own health. As I have described, animal-based psychological research is often highly invasive.

Through a survey of selected animal rights organizations who undertake campaigns on the laboratory animal issue, I have identified 15 psychology research laboratories that have been the target of a major protest, published critique, or exposé following infiltration (see Table 5).

Research selected for criticism and campaigns involves relatively highly invasive research. These targets are strikingly nonrepresentative of animal-based research with respect to the species used: only two of the 15 campaigns

Table 5. Campaigns Launched by Animal Rights Organizations Against Psychological Research in the US by Area of Research and Species

- Sexual behavior in cats
- Drug addiction and aggression in monkeys
- Physiology of color vision in cats
- Physiology of taste in rats
- Visual deprivation and physiology of vision in cats and monkeys
- Maternal and environmental deprivation in monkeys
- Maternal deprivation in monkeys
- Social deprivation in monkeys
- Sleep deprivation in cats
- Drug addiction in rats
- Maternal deprivation in monkeys
- Visual deprivation in cats
- Depression in dogs

noted are directed at research utilizing rats, mice and pigeons, animals selected for over 90% of psychological research. As noted earlier, however, psychologists disproportionately select primates, dogs, and cats for highly invasive research. Research on cats and primates predominates in the targeted research. Campaigns are predominantly launched against major university facilities. Areas of research coalesce around topics that are clearly high on the contemporary health or social problem agenda: addiction, aggression, depression, sexual behavior, and heart disease.

It is interesting to note that a number of psychologists who have borne the brunt of criticism have responded by becoming spokespersons for animal research. Of course, another scenario is that these self-appointed pro-research spokespersons, through that exposure, have become campaign targets.

On the other hand, a number of psychologists who were trained to conduct and conducted laboratory-based animal research, often quite invasive research, have gone through a kind of conversion experience in which they quite dramatically renounce that enterprise. Some of these, together with a few individuals from areas of psychology not involving nonhuman animals, now devote their full professional effort to animal protection issues. Adding to the many different areas in which psychologists work, there now are psychologists who are career animal protectionists.

Psychologists' Sound-bytes and Sound Advice

It is no surprise, then, that within the field of psychology, as in the general public, there is a broad spectrum of views about animal research. I close this chapter with a brief discussion that displays the scope and diversity of positions taken by the many psychologists who have chosen to publish their views on this issue, leaving an analysis of the complexities and nuances of arguments as the burden of the remainder of the monograph. The discussion is organized into several selected points of contention.

Regarding the philosophical question of whether rights should be attributed to nonhuman animals, Fox argues in the affirmative based on their "intrinsic natures and interests" (1988, p. 6). King states that "[M]an [sic] is justified and moral in his denial of rights to animals and his use of them in his own self-interest" (1986, p. 406). Without depending on rights talk, Ryder provides the term "speciesism" to "describe the widespread discrimination that is practiced by man [sic] against other species" (1975, p. 5). Also, independent of reliance on animals' rights, Segal refers to "ethical obligations" as "(o)ver historical time, the perception of who constitutes 'family' ... has gradually expanded" to include nonhuman animals (1989, p. xii). Seligman clings to the traditional ground that scientists' "basic commitment is to the alleviation of human misery," so that not to do animal research "would be un-justifiable" (1975, p. xi).

Baldwin asserts that "(t)he most persuasive argument for using animals in behavioral research ... is the untold benefit" gained from that use (1993, p. 123) and Gallistel offers that "science cannot progress without [experiments on animals]" (1981, p. 360). Yet Ulrich abandons his career as animal researcher because, he comes to believe, that research is artifactual and does not contribute to the un-derstanding of human phenomena (1992, pp. 384–385).

Gallup asserts that "there are simply no viable alterna-tives to the use of live organisms in behavioral research" (1985, p. 110), while Heim urges the direct study of human subjects "wherever this is practicable" instead of inducing disorders in animals and drawing an analogy between that condition and the allegedly comparable human dis-order (1978, p. 17).

Miller refuses to set "a limit on the degree of suffering that may be produced in an animal experiment," lest that reduce our understanding of the human conditions that produce the most suffering (1984, p. 8). Other psycholo-gists are concerned with the effect that such inductions may have on themselves and the general public. Bernstein writes of the costs of learning "detachment" (1987, p. 156); Bowd describes a moral callousness that results from treating animals as "simply complex research tools" (1980, p. 203). Finally, Gluck and Kubacki argue that a "state of siege exists" on the issue of animal research, and chide animal research scientists for adopting a "strategic defensive posture" (1991, p. 158). In their survey of the treatment of animal welfare issues in scientific literature, Phillips and Sechzer (1989) found a marked increase in defensiveness between the 1960s and the 1980s. Hopeful-ly, by clarifying some of these divisive points through con-ceptual analysis and empirical data, the following chap-ters will contribute to increased openness.

Chapter 2
Construction of a Science

Viewed from the outside, most scientific fields appear unified, as if they consisted of one discrete subject matter and/or one general way of studying it. However, the view from within typically reveals a disparate array of subject matters and varied and often competing ways of investigating them. This is certainly true of the field of psychology both at its inception near the end of the 19th century and as it is today. In fact, ever since the publication of his monumental six volume work *Psychology: A Study of a Science* (1959–1963), one respected critic of psychology, Sigmund Koch, has denied the possibility of there being a single, unified field called psychology:

> My argument has been that psychology is misconceived when seen as a coherent science or as any kind of coherent discipline devoted to the empirical study of human beings. Psychology, in my view, is not a single discipline but a collection of studies of varied case, some few of which may qualify as science, whereas most do not. (1993, p.902).

Efforts at identity formation were and continue to be necessary because all fields are constructed rather than discovered (Foucault, 1970). A field of study is a human invention. Things and phenomena in the world only suggest what needs to be studied and how it should be studied, and define where one field of study might begin and a second might end. Most fields, like psychology, were carved out of pre-existing fields which already laid claim to the area of knowledge which the new field sought to appropriate. Traditionally, philosophy included many areas of study that we now include in the domain of modern psychology.

Merely naming a field only begins to answer the questions of what will be studied and how. Was this modern "psychology" to study behavior, what we do and why we do it; or was it to study what we experience, the meanings we find in and give to the world? Is behavior describable as the movement of a muscle, as the execution of an individual's intention or as a family's communication style? Should we look inside the individual at the organization of his or her nervous system or outside at the organization of the family and his or her role in it? Should we infer mental operations from behavior, look at the immediate environment that may control behavior, or perhaps look at past environment? At the history of the individual or of the culture? These questions still are alive in psychology and the field is robust and vitally pluralistic according to some observers, and still immaturely struggling to define itself according to others.

By most accounts and certainly in the predominant view, the original impulse for this emerging field in the late 19th century was to separate itself from the arm-chair speculations of philosophy by constructing a field that would be closer to the natural sciences than to the humanities. However, from the beginning of this effort, there was another identity for psychology vying with this intention to achieve the legitimacy and status accorded a natural science. There were and are at least "two psychologies" (Cahan & White, 1992): one "based on the methods of the natural sciences, and a second, subjective psychology based on the human sciences" (p. 224). This "second psychology" or human science approach developed its own methods distinct from those of the experimental method of the natural sciences. These involve introspection and reflection, interview and attitude survey, individual case study and observation in real life settings. Generally, these are methods that focus on the task of clarifying and understanding the *meaning* of experiences, on questions of what people experience and how an individual's purposes and intentions form experience and behavior.

By contrast, the construction of psychology as a natural science largely restricted itself to the study of directly observable events. Instead of a focus on the meaning of behavior, there was an emphasis on predicting its occurrence, frequency and intensity—all of which endeavors lent themselves to quantitative description. With this more external ("objective") focus, the investigator applies his or her ingenuity to the development of apparati that induce behavior in such a way that it can be directly recorded and expressed in mathematical or statistical forms. The investigator then makes predictions about these quantitative results, using strict rules of logical inference. These "hard" methods, as distinguished from the "soft" approaches of human science psychology, require that the investigator be impartial and detached from what he or she observes, as a physicist records measurements on a gauge.

This natural scientific method was in accord both with the practice and the philosophy of science of the time. The "positivist" philosophy of science held that science is founded on impartial observations which can be quantified and from which inferences can be drawn governed by strict rules of logic. Only by using such a method could one be positive or certain of one's findings. Any other approach reverts to the uncertainty and speculation of the earlier efforts of psychology in philosophy.

Another tenet of positivism is that it is partial to reductionistic explanations (Bannister, 1981, p. 308). Rather than describing complexity as it appears (called phenomenology, this philosophy underlies the human science approach to psychology), employing terms borrowed from common sense (Rollin, 1989, pp. 1–23), or searching for principles of organization that only arise with increased complexity (emergentism), complex phenomena are understood by breaking them down into simpler components. As physics had its micro-particles, chemistry its basic periodic chart of basic elements, and biology its genes and later its DNA sequences, the new natural science of psychology would understand complex human experience and behavior in terms of building blocks of simple linked stimuli and responses.

Interestingly, this natural scientific approach mixes a very strict or restrictive method of observation and verification with an ideal of open and unfettered freedom of inquiry. The ideal of free inquiry was reactive to the dogmatism and limitations on inquiry that were often part of Medieval religious thought. It substituted a faith in reason and "man" for faith in God. Following this ideal, the scientist was invited and propelled to inquire into the nature of anything and everything. Like a child, he or she insatiably asked questions. Nothing was to be taken for granted, everything was fair game. This openness and freedom were among the most precious developments of Western culture.

While we still hold to this ideal, we have come to recognize and accept competing interests that constrain the scientific enterprise, as they do any other human enterprise. For example, we give priority to individual human rights and require the scientist to obtain informed consent before conducting a study involving people. And we now are debating to what extent nonhuman animal rights should limit scientific inquiry.

While we have legislated and institutionalized these further restraints on science, certain other restraints have been lifted, primarily through a critique of the positivist philosophy of science. For example, recent philosophers of science have shown that the scientist is not impartial or detached: the questions asked, the observations made, the inferences drawn and the descriptive language chosen are all at least partly dependent on the culture and historical period in which the scientist lives and on the theory that he or she presently entertains (Shapiro, 1986a; Wertz, 1986b; Polkinghorne, 1992). Once the impossibility of detachment is admitted, the investigatory enterprise becomes more open regarding the research questions posed, methods employed, and the form of presentation of the results.

Some sociologists studying scientific knowledge have provided a stronger critique. For example, Fuchs (1993) sees the positivist claim to a "privileged system of knowledge" (p. 1) founded on the superior rationality and objectivity of scientific knowledge as false. Such rationality is limited to the "positivistic rhetoric" presented in scientific publications and in public pronouncements. In practice, science proceeds more through "tinkering and groping" (p. 10) and through personal investment and persuasion than through strict rules of evidence of a pure rational empiricism. "... [S]cience is just another social practice or form of life and does not provide the rest of our culture with safe and rational foundations" (p. 3).

These critiques of positivism have had the liberating effect of allowing more participatory methods in mainstream science, such as those developed in the human science approach. It also has underscored the point that not only is a particular scientific field a human construct, so is the more general approach we call the scientific method itself a construct—one in which the rules often dramatically change over time.

Experimentalism

The field of modern psychology emerged at a time when the pulls of both the ideal of relatively unfettered inquiry and the restrictions on method espoused by positivism were strong. While several prominent early thinkers

(James, Baldwin, Wundt, Dewey) subscribed to the idea of there being two psychologies, and held that at least part of modern psychology should be a human science distinct from the reigning positivistic natural science, most investigators insisted that a scientific psychology must strictly emulate the physics and biology of the time (Boring, 1963). It must be an *experimental* science.

Experimentalism quickly became the established view of this modern psychology. An experimental approach builds on the positivistic ideas of inquiry: The investigator restricts study to a directly observable object, observes that object from a detached or impersonal point of view, measures it in quantitative terms, and explains it by reducing it to simple component parts. To this ideal, experimentalism adds the notion that the thing observed, and particularly the conditions under which it is observed, must be varied systematically.

To effect this experimental variation, it is necessary for the investigator to have control over the object of study. Only in that way can the scientist be sure of the actual causes of something. In nature (and in culture) too much is going on at once. To effect this control, the object of study must be taken out of its (or his or her) natural setting and placed in a more controllable and simplified setting. Experimental science gives rise to the idea of a laboratory.

Construction of the Laboratory

The enduring motif in the story of modern psychology is neither a person nor an event but a place—"the experimental laboratory" (Capshew, 1992, p. 132). Psychologists realized that the achievement of the primary features of experimentalism could be assured most fully in the laboratory. Physically, the laboratory allowed detachment of the investigator, unimpaired observation, and relative control of the object of study. It also provided a site in which to develop technology to enhance and extend the limits of observation, and instrumentation to quantify and record results of observation. The lab was a place away from the buzzing confusion, the uncontrollable flow of events of the ordinary world. It was, as it were, outside of history and culture. Events observed and measured there could gain a claim to universal generality. In the simplified and controlled setting of the lab, psychology could become an exact or "hard" or "pure" science.

Beyond these physical fits with the parameters of an experimental science, the laboratory had strong symbolic value for the emerging field:

> In symbolic terms, the laboratory provided a focus for the disciplinary aspirations of psychologists, functioning as an icon of the transcendent power of scientific knowledge. In the process, it became as much a spiritual home as an experimental workplace (Capshew, 1992, p. 132).

In his review of the history of the laboratory and of the accounts of it that exist in psychological literature, Capshew establishes that it had a "central role in the construction and maintenance of psychology's scientific identity," that it became a "metaphor for scientific psychology itself." Clearly, the establishment of laboratories was seized upon as the way toward the establishment of psychology as a science.

Construction of the Laboratory Animal

All that was needed to complete the laboratory as the *"locus classicus for scientific psychology"* (Capshew, 1992, p. 132) was an object of study compatible with its physical and symbolic parameters. As none was available, one was constructed. It is important to understand that neither "wild" nor even domesticated animals were immediately at hand for this role. As the field of modern psychology and the site of its operations had to be constructed, so did what we now call "laboratory animals."

"[S]cientists are continually engaged in ... an activity of social construction. Far from existing as a given in nature, the laboratory animal is the product of this constructive activity" (Phillips, 1994, p. 120). This class of objects is "a distinct category, which is painstakingly differentiated from other culturally available animal categories such as pets, wildlife, or vermin" (p. 120). "Social construction" refers to the explicit or implicit consensus formed by a group of people regarding the meaning held for them by an object or class of objects.

The term "construction" emphasizes the active role that people and institutions play in conferring that meaning. It also underscores the power of such conferral in actually producing an entity. "Construction" is not limited to attitudes—it is not simply "in the eye of the beholder." The way people think and talk about, and look at things affects those very things. It plays a formative role in making them what they are (Gergen & Davis, 1985).

As I shall show, the lab animal is a product of the variety of ways that scientists and other workers in the lab procure, breed, house, care for, experiment on, and dispose of them. More subtly, that class of objects is also constructed through the philosophy of science underlying lab animal science, through the language scientists use formally in publications studies, textbooks, and research proposals, and informally in the lab to refer to lab animals, and through the ethics and policies they develop regulating their treatment of them. "Lab animal" is an actual construction achieved through the complex interplay of attitudes, language, philosophy, purpose, and practice that constitute laboratory animal science.

In this section, I describe the role that the philosophy of science adopted by experimental psychologists had on that construction. In the next chapter, still on an abstract level, I describe a primary purpose of their use, that is to be models of human pathology. Obviously, this overriding purpose strongly shaped the social construction. To anticipate, if the purpose of the lab animal is to provide an analogy to understand human animals, it must be constructed as being a stand-in for humans, not as being worthy of study in her or his own right. In Chapter 4, I show the actual practice toward animals involved in developing specific animal models and, in the final two chapters, the role ethics and policies relating to the use of animals in psychology play in that construction.

To begin the story, enter the "albino rat" (Lockard, 1968). Both the black rat *(Rattus rattus)* and the brown rat *(Rattus norvegicus,* the Norway rat) had a long history of involvement in human affairs before their selection for the psychology lab. In the 14th century, following the introduction of a bacterium hosted by black rats who were in turn escorted by the Crusaders returning from the Holy Land, the Bubonic Plague decimated Europe several times over.

On the one hand, rats were among the most adaptive and successful animals. A social history dedicated to them documents their marvelous capacities for proliferation and survival (Hendrickson, 1983). On the other hand, they have long been considered a scourge and pest, and provide an apt symbol of our own villainous and scurrilous potential ("take that, you dirty rat"). There is considerable irony, then, in the selection of this unruly, nocturnal, and destructive species (Wertz, 1986a, pp. 144–5) as the primary inhabitant of this highly controlled, rule-bound, broad-daylight laboratory of exact, objective science.

Only a few decades after the first recorded use of them in modern science, rats were used for the first time (in 1898) in psychological research (Lockard, 1968, p. 735). This was made possible by a process of selective breeding albino forms of the Norway rat. Birke notes that the expertise developed in the controlled livestock breeding in the 18th century and, later, in the selective breeding of "fancy" cats and dogs "[were] taken into the laboratory by the early 20th century" (1993, p. 195). Quinn (1993) offers an intriguing account of how paintings of cattle provided an ideal image toward which breeders of so-called "fat cattle" could strive. This process of domestication in the lab or, using the more appropriate term suggested by Lockard, this process of "laboratorization" accelerated when Meyer and Donaldson selected albinos from a population of Norway rats (Wertz, 1986a, p. 151). This became the now commonly used Wistar breed of laboratory rats. In 1903, Watson wrote a doctoral dissertation entitled "Animal education: The psychic development of the white rat" and Donaldson published *The Rat* (1915). Through generations of selective inbreeding, strains such as the Wistar and Long-Evans hooded rat were established that had virtually identical genetic characteristics. This was in the service of the experimentalist ideal of eliminating as many "extraneous variables" as possible (Phillips, 1994, p. 130).

The differences between these constructed breeds and the Norway rat from which they were developed are striking, and clearly show how psychologists intentionally created breeds that would fit the requirements of their emerging experimental laboratory-based science. As Hediger states:

> In the case of the white rat ..., a domesticated animal may be fundamentally different from its ancestral wild stock. Since the wild rat was much more difficult to handle, it was replaced in 1895 by the far more docile standardized white rat in laboratory experiments in animal psychology. Thus instead of making the experimental method fit the animal, the sort of abstract animal form, nicely adapted to the experimental apparatus, was made (quoted in Griffin, 1984, p. 13).

As compared to a wild or even a first generation captive Norway rat, an albino rat is less vicious, less fearful of people, and less excitable and intent on escape (Lockard,

1968, pp. 735–6). He or she also has lost the "threat posture," and fighting is reduced to playful behavior; mice killing is much reduced as is cautiousness in response to novelty and vocal communication. In general, the albino is more quiet and tractable and, from the experimenter's point of view, easier to manage, handle, and control.

By the mid-1920s a survey indicated that roughly 25% of psychology labs in the United States included animal facilities (Capshew, 1992, p. 136). The white rat had become a common fixture of experimental psychology, both actually and symbolically. The animal laboratory was the place where psychologists did their work and the laboratory animal was the object of study. The construction through selective breeding of the laboratory rat and other species such as the mouse and guinea pig have recently been supplemented by more sophisticated means of transformation. Through biogenetic engineering, transgenic animals have been developed that more efficiently and comfortably meet the needs of scientific investigators. On the level of cultural symbols, will "oncomouse" (cancer-prone) soon be as significant as Mighty Mouse and Mickey Mouse? The central aspiration and commitment of the new field of experimental laboratory psychology was that the study of rats, mice, and pigeons in the controlled setting of the lab would reveal the nature of learning, motivation, and perception at the most basic and universal level.

The new science's preoccupation with instrumentation and technology was built around rats and pigeons. The tiers of animal cages, the mazes, the automated food dispensers, the Skinner box, the controlled environment (lighting, temperature, noise, bacteria), the restraining devices, the electronic recorders—all were designed to snugly fit the laboratory animal. As I have described, psychologists achieved this fit through change in the other direction as well, as they transformed "wild" rats to rats "adjusted" to life in the laboratory. Restraining devices, such as stereotaxic equipment and specially designed plastic restraining tubes with openings to withdraw needed blood and other fluid samples completed the fit.

Critique of Experimentalism

As I have described, modern psychology from its beginning consisted of a critical tension between two psychologies, an experimental science modeled after the natural sciences and a qualitative human science more akin to the interpretative methods of literature and history. The former approach reached its predominance in the 1940s and 1950s with the heyday of behaviorism. While there has generally been a healthy critique of experimentalism and positivism among qualitative scientific and philosophically inclined psychologists, beginning in the 1960s this critique became more robust and influential.

McCullough critically identifies the exaggerated value given to the experimental approach and labels it the "experimenting bias" (1979, p. 410). To exemplify the "unconscious" operation of this bias, he observes that theories that generate the most experiments are for that reason alone valued most highly. The degree of understanding and significance of discovery are simply equated with a greater number of published studies.

With this bias, forms of investigation conducted outside the experimentalist's lab are relatively devalued. Studies conducted in the "field" (meaning, precisely, outside the lab), in the clinic, classroom, or street; nonexperimental methods of data collection, such as demographic, correlational, clinical case, and historical studies are all relegated to the limited role of generating suggestive leads which then must be tested in the experimental lab.

At the extreme, this over-valuation of the experiment and devaluation of other forms of investigation becomes a refusal to consider the results of the latter as scientific.

The experimental lab is a closed shop. By definition, all facts are those observed, and all relations among facts are those demonstrated in an experiment. The experimentalist is a Sergeant Friday whose retort, "Just the facts, ma'am," provides the exclusive "dragnet" in the development of evidence. No one outside the experimentalist's lab knows anything for sure, as certitude (positivism) has its exclusive residence there. Nothing is already known. Both the common sense of the layperson and the understanding and judgments reached by practitioners of applied psychology, are degraded and considered to be inferior forms of understanding. All are eclipsed by the "common sense of science" (Rollin, 1989, p. 8).

This common attitude in the field of psychology is aptly referred to as an "ideology" (Capshew, 1992, p. 132) for it is a set of beliefs resting on certain assumptions themselves not subject to question. The bedrock assumption is that understanding is developed if and only if certain investigatory procedures dictated by the rules of experimentalism are followed.

Given the importance of observability and the quantification and control of the observable, certain features of the experimental lab situation become preoccupying. The experimentalist does not remain a passive observer of naturally occurring behavior; rather he or she attempts to produce observable effects. Following Francis Bacon, one of the architects of the natural scientific approach, the laboratory is precisely the place where understanding is best pursued through "the production and reproduction of effects," not through naturalistic observation (Smith, 1992, p. 218).

To produce effects, nature must be "squeezed and molded" (Bacon in Smith, p. 218). Experimental psychologists turned to technology to develop this manipulative power over nature. Psychology adopted a "technological ideal" (Smith, p. 216). The predominant focus became the development of apparati and instrumentation through which effects could actively be produced. In effect, psychologists were engineers constructing a highly mechanized and automated laboratory. One occupational hazard of this preoccupation is the loss of the original impulse in psychology to directly observe and understand the subtleties of naturally occurring behavior.

An equally dominant focus is in part a consequence of this technologizing of the laboratory. While apparatus and instrumentation allow the control and production of behavior, the resultant effects are recorded rather than directly observed. Observations are expressed mathematically. What is seen is, in effect, only "visible" as a statistical effect. This is true in two senses: we see numbers rather than behaviors and even the numbers do not directly show the effects we are seeking to produce. For those numerical effects are typically so small that in order for differences to be revealed, complex and sophisticated statistical manipulations must first be performed. The development of these statistics became another preoccupying interest of psychologists.

The "persistent 'technophilia'" of psychology and its "fascination with the technology of experimentation" (Capshew, 1992, p. 132) leaves psychology vulnerable to the critique of technology, to what Smith refers to as the "general decline of the technological ideal in recent decades" (p. 216). Smith's critique of behaviorism, the paradigmatic example of the attempt to control behavior through technology, applies more generally to experimental laboratory psychology: "Can a movement that has so wholeheartedly embraced the technological ideal, and that has drawn on the general prestige accorded technology in our culture, escape the devastating critiques of technology that have arisen in the last half of this century ...?" (p. 216).

The self-imposed insularity and artificially constructed technopolis of the laboratory have led to the criticism that its findings are not extrapolable ("generalizable") or relevant to the real world of everyday experience and behavior. It is important to note that this critique of laboratory psychology as irrelevant and inapplicable is brought against research involving human as well as nonhuman laboratory subjects.

Experimental lab psychology is also vulnerable to a feminist critique. One of the characteristics of this social construction of modern psychology as an experimental science is that it is male-centered, that it perpetuates a masculine style and male dominance in our society (Riger, 1992, p. 737). This is evidenced in the emphasis on the "distance of the researcher from the subjects, manipulation of the subjects and the environment, and the use of quantitative data" (Carlson in Riger, p. 733). This distance is a "refusal of a social relation with them [the animals]" (Weston, 1994, p. 157). Weston calls for a "transhuman etiquette" that through "(n)aming, meeting the look, touching and being touched" researchers would establish and maintain "social relations" with members of other species (p. 153). Similarly, Riger calls for a "... communal style of research that emphasizes cooperation of the researcher and subjects, an appreciation of natural contexts, and the use of qualitative data" (Riger, p. 733).

Critique of the Laboratory Animal

Psychologists constructed both laboratories and "lab animals" under the rubric of positivism and the ideal of experimentalism. What kind of being emerged from this project? Here I describe the peculiar kind of being that was the unwitting byproduct of the experimentalist program with its attempt to gain experimental control, investigator detachment, objective observability, measurability, and the reduction to simple components. The end result is a version of Shelley's story of Frankenstein. In showing here how the lab animal so constructed is a "monster," my intention is to highlight rather than to detract from the real suffering of an individual animal in his or her cage.

Construction or Deconstruction: Positivism or Mystification?

Every animal is an individual and a member of a particular species. His or her identity consists both of those aspects uniquely individual and those shared within a species. Animals of a particular species vary in the degree of individual and species-specific behaviors that constitute their identity.

While you probably nodded to these generalizations, the predominant Western modernist philosophy, humanism, is built on their denial. It is a basic tenet of humanism that individuality requires rationality and that only human beings are rational (Shapiro, 1990a). In the humanist tradition, nonhuman animals are instinct- and need-dominated; they are not autonomous, self-determining beings; they are not individuals.

Modern science is also known as scientific humanism since it developed directly from the humanistic philosophy spawned during the Enlightenment. It is no surprise, then, that the social construction of lab animals features the "loss" of their individuality. Some of the features identified that effect this deindividuation include: the large numbers of animals used, the brief time many of them live, the focus on parts of animals rather than on whole animals, the press for genetically identical animals, the need to kill the animals, and the production of animals bred solely for research (Phillips, 1994, pp. 135–6). Experimental manipulations both promote and assume that there are no individual differences. Observed differences are primarily understood as results of the experimental manipulation, while any residual differences are attributed to errors in measurement, age or species.

Phillips describes a more subtle way in which "individual identities are consciously and systematically obliterated" (1994, p. 130). Her ethnographic study of 23 contemporary biomedical and behavioral research laboratories and Arluke's study of 20 labs show that "animals were almost never named" (Phillips, p. 126). Fouts observes the same reluctance to give animals names among research scientists in zoos and also attributes it to "an attempt to deindividualize the animal" (in press). In the few instances where they were named, the names "functioned more as jokes than as true proper names" (Phillips, p. 127). Names were selected that had personal relevance to the namer and they were not used to address the animal. Even this limited use of names was "generally confined to undergraduate and nonprofessional staff" (Phillips, p. 129). In their more proper use, "proper names are linked to the social emergence of personality, which engenders a matrix of ideas and behaviors peculiar to one individual" (p. 123). Through naming, we construct an individual. Phillips goes on to suggest that without a name a narrative account of that life is precluded; that life is not a biography.

Phillips cites an account by Konigel (1987) of a rat referred to as number 1913 which begins:

> Down the metal chute he slid. He had no name, not even, as yet, a number. He was only a weight—part of an order for thirty male laboratory rats, weighing between two hundred and seventy-five and three hundred grams, destined for the psychology department at John Hopkins University, in Baltimore (p. 136).

While presenting the scientific context of the rat's life, Konigel through intended irony provides a biography of number 1913 and allows us to get to know him as an individual. This narrative account of an individual demonstrates by counterpoint what is absent in the standard scientific account in which laboratory animals figure. Failure to name an animal is a part of the process of deindividuation in the social construction of laboratory animals.

In a similar vein but in an intentionally anthropomor-
phic account of laboratory animals, Kotzwinkle's novel
Doctor Rat (1971) begins:

> In the colony I'm known as Doctor Rat. Having been part of this
> laboratory so long and having been studied so carefully, it's only
> right I be given some mark of distinction other than the tattoo on
> the inside of my ear, a mark that all the other rats have too. Some
> of them have tatoos and V-shaped wedges cut out of their ears.
> Some even have three or four wedges cut out of their ears, but that
> doesn't mean they are as learned as I. It simply means that they
> have had the liver removed (one wedge), the liver and pituitary
> gland removed (two wedges) ... (p. 1).

As does the account of Number 1913, Kotzwinkle's popular fiction shows by contrast that, as scientists have constructed them, laboratory animals are not considered individuals with a biography, fictional or real.

The rhetoric utilized in scientific reports further supports this deindividuation. Investigators describe what
was done to the animals rather than what the animal was
doing. Subsequent "action" by the animals is reduced to
an effect of the investigator's action in manipulating the
environment and the animal. The lab animal is not an
agent or autonomous being but a product of the experimental manipulation. Even the description of the animal
as passive respondent focuses more on the "technical procedures" than on the behavior of the animal (Birke and
Smith, 1995): "... [W]hat is actually happening to the *animal* is subordinated to the descriptions of what was done
in order to make measurements" (p. 31; emphasis in original).
When behavior of the animal is described, it is couched in
terms that make the animal as individual "disappear"
(Scholtmeijer, 1993, p. 72). An act by the rat, say to avoid
something (an aversive stimulus), becomes an "avoidance
reaction." The rat does not act; rather, under certain stimulus conditions, the avoidance reaction is effected. The rat
as individual, in the sense of autonomous agent, has dis-
appeared.

Another view of laboratory animals which sustains this deindividuation is that any particular animal is replaceable. When animals die, there are no individuals lost for lab animals are members of a "population," not unique individuals. Certainly, there is no loss in the more laden sense of aggrieved "loss," for there is no individual relation or bond between animal and investigator. What is lost is a replaceable member of a species. (Phillips notes in her study of research scientists that in one of the few instances in which an animal was named, "Sylvia" was still Sylvia even when the original Sylvia had been replaced by a second monkey [p. 129]). But is there even this more limited "loss"?

If there are no genuine individuals in the lab, surely there are different species and there are then differences among animals based on species-specific behavior. But to assume that is to underestimate the power of the social construction of lab animals. Psychologists and other scientists using lab animals commonly refer to them as "animals" (Phillips, p. 138). They are not "the rat (pigeon, dog)" but "the animal." The irrelevance and denial of species differences to psychologists is revealed by Beach's alarm at his observation that, by 1950, psychologists were "dedicating over 50% of their research to an animal that represented only .001% of the types of living creatures that might be studied" (Wertz, 1986a, p. 151).

In more formal settings such as scientific publications, another term that is used is "organism." This expresses a prevalent attitude that an animal under study is an organic process, a physiological and behavioral system. Rather than being an individual or even possessed of a species-specific physiology or behavior, the lab animal is reduced to a general process. The animal is "prepared" so as to eliminate any individual or species identity and to disclose for study a biological organism, a generic animal, a "preparation" (Devereux, 1967). This process of preparation culminates in the use of apparatus such as stereotaxic fixation, anesthetization, the Pavlovian sling, or other forms of restraint in the experimental procedure.

However, the construction of lab animal as a generic animal is a more extensive program that is not limited to the experimental procedure. It begins with selective breeding and, now, genetic engineering and continues with the provision of certain housing conditions, both of which further effect the stripping away of species-specific behavior. I earlier described this process in the case of the selective breeding that led to the production of the white rat, the standard bearer of the new lab-based science of psychology.

In terms of housing, the cage plays a major role, actual and symbolic, in the construction of generic animals. Caging an animal for much of his or her life without the company of other animals has a profound effect on most animals. Wemelsfelder (1993) describes the subsequent condition as "boredom." This boredom is more than an occasional passing mood which the animal can readily shake off. The behavior of a chronically caged animal is largely limited to bored behavior. At the extreme, the behavior of a chronically caged animal consists of repeated stereotypical movements and postures. It is important to note that these are similar for animals across species. A bored animal no longer demonstrates much of his or her species-specific behavior.

In an animal that has been caged for his or her entire life or even chronically caged for much of his or her development, this absence signals more than the immediate absence of an environment that would stimulate species-specific behavior. The animal has literally lost interest in his or her surroundings. The species-specific identity is lost. A lion that has no lion country is no longer a lion (Shapiro, 1989b). The scientist has succeeded in constructing a generic animal, an organism bereft of species-specific identity.

This is itself a form of harm, the loss of a capacity. Beyond the temporary deprivation of objects of interest, the chronically bored animal has lost the capacity to be interested in the environment as a source of stimulation. The bored animal no longer reaches out toward the world as a source of interest for he or she is no longer really living or engaging in that world. To the degree that an animal experiences the loss of that capacity and the loss of that engagement as distressing, boredom is accompanied by suffering.

A particular phase in the recent history of psychology provides a variant that illustrates this *despeciation* of the lab animal. In behaviorism, which was the dominant approach to psychology in the 1940s and 1950s, animals (and humans) were completely understandable in terms of observed behavior. Mind, subjective experience and consciousness, did not count in this attempt at a scientific psychology (Rollin, 1989, pp. 206–225).

An investigator fully adopting this approach assumed that animals *consist of* observable behaviors. Further, these behaviors are more or less exclusively a product of the animals' immediate environment. Behavior is "shaped" and maintained through aspects of the environment that "reinforce" particular behaviors. The identity of a given animal is predominantly a function of this shaping rather than of any membership in a particular species. All animals are either organisms or generic animals in that their learning and their behavior is governed by the same rules of environmental contingency.

It is precisely this environment which the investigator can, at least in theory, completely control. The investigator can shape the animal to perform any behavior, limited only grossly by species-specific capabilities. In this behaviorist psychology, the social construction of lab animals as the generic animal includes the "discovery" of the law governing organisms—they are eminently shapable by external forces, particularly the kind the investigator can readily control and manipulate. How convenient for a laboratory-based experimental science of psychology.

From individual to species to organism to preparation, there is yet one more turn of the screw in the social construction of the lab animal. I have described how the initial impulse to construct a scientific psychology involved a dedication to direct observation and how psychologists attempted to utilize technology and instrumentation to enhance and extend the range and depth of what they could observe. In a subtle way, this effort in practice eventually blurred the boundary between the instrument and the object of measurement.

Consider a rat that is chronically implanted with an electrode in his or her brain and is connected by a tether to machinery that sends stimuli and receives and records responses. As I shall illustrate in more detail in Chapter 4, the rat is more a part of the instrumentation than a discrete object of study. The animal is merely a conduit for certain energies, fluids, and electrical impulses. Certain relations between brain function, external stimuli, and movement are the object of study. The animal has lost his or her integrity in that only certain parts of the animal are the focus of interest (Phillips, 1994, p. 131). While psychologists often argue, as we will see, that there is no alternative to the study of the whole intact organism, they do not see him or her as a whole creature let alone as an individual.

The chronically implanted animal is not so much put "under the microscope" as made part of it. This exceeds fitting the technology to the animal. The integrity of the animal, of his or her individual and species-specific behavior, is dissolved; even the integrity of the generic organism presents no boundaries and is regularly violated. The rats are "*laboratory* animals" in the sense that they are *part* of the laboratory; they are part of this complex of sophisticated apparatus, instrumentation, and recording device that constitutes the site and object of study. They are "highly specialized scientific instruments" (Phillips, 1994, p. 136). They are *deanimalized*.

The attempt to enhance observation through instrumentation, to record results in strictly quantitative terms and to remove the person and bias of the investigator, all in the service of achieving objective and positive (certain) results, has the unintended result of confounding or *mystifying* the whole enterprise. When we selectively breed, genetically engineer, deindividuate, despecify, and deanimalize an animal, can we really pretend that we know what we have left? How can we have any idea what we are studying once we have reduced, trivialized, and bypassed these animals in this way? Can we have any idea of the relation between what we are observing and the particular human behavior that is typically the actual intended object of study? Ironically, the ideal of objectivity pursued in this manner results in mystification rather than positive understanding.

Again, behaviorism's effort to identify universal principles of learning offers an illustration of these points. The assumption that there are such universal principles across species justified the predominant use of one species, the rat. As Beach observed during the period when behaviorism was still the dominant paradigm in psychology, that assumption was wrong-headed and led to a narrow view of learning, a psychology of "rat learning" (1950). Beyond this restriction of study to one species, there is also the problem, discussed earlier, of the "laboratorization" of the albino rat through selective breeding. The many differences between the resulting laboratory animal and his/her wild counterpart "should convince any investigator that *albinus* is not the place to start looking for mechanisms nature has produced. It is at least a waste of time, if not outright folly, to experiment upon the *degenerate* remains of what is available intact in other animals" (Lockard, 1968, p. 739, emphasis added). These are the "risks inherent in developing a natural science around an unnatural animal" (p. 740): "One can imagine a sort of 'Schmoo' in a germ-free environment, surrounded by life-support systems and fitted with prosthetic devices, attended by technicians and still studied by scientists; its riddles of 'the learning process' still unsolved" (p. 740).

Clearly, when we study the laboratory animal or Schmoo we are so many times removed from the natural animal in his/her natural setting that we cannot claim to understand the counterpart in nature, any natural process or ourselves. Yet it is to increase understanding of human behavior to which much of this enterprise is dedicated.

This construction of the lab animal effected by the positivist ideal of experimentalism may be contrasted to that of the "pet" (Serpell, 1986; Tuan, 1984). As we have selected and constructed certain species of animals for study, so have we constructed others for emotional support—to be ancillary members of our family and to provide us with companionship in an increasingly urbanized and impersonal world.

On the face of it, the inflation of the being of the pet is in sharp contrast to the reduced being of the lab animal. However, in both contexts, the intent is to construct an animal as a human—in one case, to provide models or analogies to better understand ourselves, in the other to provide emotionally suitable playmates. The construction of pets is not without its costs (pet overpopulation and uncountable deaths, selective genetic breeding for human use that produces animals prone to various diseases and deformities, feral animals, and displacement of "wild" animals).

It is the burden of the remaining parts of this essay to show the "costs and benefits" of the construction of the lab animal. Here, I have described how, despite the intent to construct an animal that would accurately model the human animal, the construction ironically features a peculiar deindividualized, depersonalized, and deanimalized entity—Frankenstein's monster. The project to construct "animal" as human animal issues in animal as instrument or machine. While the original intent is predicated on the existence of a basic similarity or continuity between human and nonhuman animals, the outcome clearly underscores differences or discontinuity.

My account to this point must be qualified in two ways. I have been emphasizing the philosophical assumptions underlying the emergence of modern experimental psychology as they have effected the construction of the lab animal. As mentioned, other forces also play a role in that construction. Positivism and the language usage that embody it feature the animal as an object—more a thing or process than a subject with his or her own consciousness and autonomy. However, studies of the subculture of present-day animal laboratories show that the construction is often ambivalent in this regard. While supporting Phillips' finding of the prevalence of the view of lab animals as objects, Arluke (1988) finds considerable support that lab personnel perceive animals as subjects as well. In particular, lab technicians, those workers who deal with the animals on a daily basis (as distinguished from the principal investigator who designs and oversees the experiment), relate to animals as both objects and subjects. As subjects, lab technicians often form attachments to selected animals that are comparable to that seen in a typical human-companion animal relation.

Arluke indicates that the lab animal becomes a companion animal when the "process that transforms the animal into object is not fully effective" (p. 99). This suggests that the construction of the objectified animal has priority while that of the animal as pet is reactive and complementary. In his discussion of the occasional practice of adopting, that is actually taking, a lab animal as a pet involves "subverting the protocol." Elsewhere he speaks of "objectifications that may ... be defied." It is clear that the animal as subject, and specifically as companion animal, is largely a development of a subordinate class (the lab tech) within the laboratory culture. It is what sociologists call an "underlife" (Goffman, 1961) a part of a subculture that does not fully accept the official culture. Apparently, lab technicians and student research assistants often balk at attempts to socialize them into the regnant construction in which the lab animal is object—instrument, supply, and/ or scientific datum.

Turning to a second qualifier, Fox argues that laboratory (and domesticated) animals are not "degenerate forms" (1986, p. 101). Although constructed as instruments through selective breeding and the design of the laboratory, they still retain "complex behavioral systems such as territoriality, sexuality and aggression," though with altered thresholds and intensities (p. 101). For examples, they have a need for exploration and will cross an electrified grid for the opportunity to explore a maze (p. 102); and Brain (1993) reports that laboratory mice still respond with distress (as measured by changes in opioid levels) to the recorded call of a hawk. Wyers describes a study in which laboratory rats placed in outdoor enclosures with nest boxes familiar to them from the laboratory, quickly left the boxes to dig burrows "after the manner of wild rats" (1994, p. 31). He concludes that "for the white rat ... laboratorization produced effects that quickly rubbed off in the wild" (p. 31). Obviously, although formidable, the power of social construction is limited as many capabilities unexpressed in the confines of life in the laboratory remain latent but intact. Even when utilized as instruments, these animals are complex, sentient beings with rich behavioral repertoires which leave them vulnerable to our manipulations of them.

Further, the ideal of the detached investigator/unaffected object of study notwithstanding, the animals are affected by social interaction with their human experimenters. Dewsbury reviews findings that rats are motivated to learn when their only reward is handling by the investigator (in Davis and Balfour, 1992, p. 34); that human stimulation can accelerate their development and increase the effectiveness of their reactions to stress (p. 37); and that they are capable of differentiating among human handlers (p. 34).

As Scholtmeijer (1993) eloquently argues in her study of the victimization of animals in "modern" fiction (since Darwin), apparently animals resist our attempts to construct or deconstruct them. This resistance is largely a function of "the recognition that animals, in themselves and as they stand, possess by nature their own power to argue against the conventions in thought which license human aggression" (p. 6). The recognition of animals' resistance to victimization is partly a byproduct of science's construction of them. Through its insistence on rational understanding, devoid of personal interest, science itself has helped debunk the traditional projections onto animals—the animal as "beast" or "animal," as unrestrained emotion and as irrational or instinct-dominated—from the animal in itself—as a subject of his or her own world and as worthy objects of our sensibilities and moral regard.

In the case of the construction of the lab animal this force and counterforce is most apparent. The use of the lab animal as a means or instrument of understanding ourselves is in continual tension with the results of that research. The more investigators reduce the animal to instrument, the more it becomes clear that he or she is a sentient being. The lab rat is both a part of the lab, a *lab* animal, *and* an irreducible end in itself. He or she has intentions and subjectivity, and is a participant in his or her own society as well as that of the investigator, the complex social institution of the lab. The subtitle of a recently edited volume by Davis and Balfour (1992), *The Inevitable Bond*, refers to the fact that for all their efforts to reduce them to instruments and to data points, investigators or, at least, lab technicians, inevitably form subject-to-subject relations with them.

Conclusion

The application of experimentalism to animal research in the development of a modern psychology is, at best, a mixed achievement. To this day, psychology perennially struggles with tensions between the ideal of a psychology modeled after the natural sciences and one peculiarly adapted to the study of human beings, a human science. This split is most clearly apparent in the relative distance between clinical practitioners and laboratory research scientists within the field. The effectiveness of the natural scientific approach to the study of human psychology continues to be at issue.

The natural scientific ideal of detached rather than participatory observation, and the emphasis on measurement and quantification over meaning and interpretation led to the construction of laboratories as the preferred sites of investigation and to lab animals as the preferred objects of study. This ideologically driven choice resulted in a new category of animal and an additional enterprise of animal exploitation. The field was largely successful in creating the deindividuated, despecified and deanimalized entity that embodies and complements that ideal of objective investigator detachment—although, some evidence, both on biological and subcultural grounds, suggests that the construction was faulty.

The further evaluation of the enterprise of psychology's use of animals in research must await exposition of its primary strategy—the effort to construct animal models of human pathology, to which I now turn. In Chapter 3, I critique this strategy as a concept, while in Chapter 4, I present and evaluate a concrete example of an animal model in depth.

Chapter 3
Animals as Models

To complete the story of the creation of a laboratory animal-based natural science for psychology we must understand the strategy of developing animal models to represent human phenomena, for it is a dominant way in which psychologists doing animal research justify their work. In his introduction to a bibliography of references to research in "animal models of human pathology," Overmier states, "... animal models have been and continue to be a ubiquitous component of psychological research into human dysfunction" (Overmier & Burke, 1992, p. xi).

Properly understood, the strategy of studying human psychology by developing animal models to represent it is yet another problem for the ideal of direct observation. On the face of it, constructing a model and then investigating that instead of the thing itself is an indirect approach. It involves observing a stand-in and is yet another level of removal, another form of indirect observation for the investigatory enterprise. Given the ideal of direct observation, and the appeal of the common sense view that if we want to understand something the most effective way to proceed would be to study the thing itself, why did and does psychology bother with inventing, constructing, developing, and "validating" animal models?

The argument is involved but important to explicate if we are to understand the claims of animal-based research in psychology. I begin with a definition of models in science and two very different concepts of models. Historical examples from biomedicine indicate how, while one of these concepts was adopted as the official position justifying the use of animals, in practice the second concept is more descriptive of the use of animal models. I then turn to psychological research and discuss both scientific and ethical problems in psychology's use and misuse of animal models.

It will be helpful to offer an informal definition of a model. We are all familiar with models in the sense of a "model" airplane or the "scale-model" of a building. A model airplane can look strikingly like a real airplane and in some instances can be used to study some of the performance features of one. But, obviously, even a high-tech model airplane is not just an airplane that is smaller than the original. We may be able to fly it but not while we are in it. A model does not differ from the original only quantitatively, like Alice in Wonderland or the children in the recent movie *Honey, I Shrunk the Kids*.

Models are analogies. A model is analogous to but not identical to the original. Models have to do with similarity but they do not imply sameness, oneness or identity. The statement, "a rat is a model of a human being," makes the limited although undeniable claim that there are some ways in which the two are similar. However, it does not imply or really allow that they are identical (except that one is smaller). For, in the other direction, if a rat is merely a model of and not identical to a human being, it necessarily follows that there are some qualitative differences between the two. Interestingly, this quite straightforward distinction between the model and the modelled is a point of confusion in both animal researcher claims and animal rights critiques of animal models—but I am getting ahead of the story.

More formally, as defined by a contemporary philosopher of science, a model in science "allows us to analyze analogy relationships ... carefully and finely" (Harré, 1972, p. 173). The key term is "analogy" which is in turn defined as "a relationship between two entities, processes, or what you will, which allows inferences to be made about one of the things, usually that about which we know least, on the basis of what we know about the other" (p. 172). The potential usefulness of a model lies in the assumption that, "(i)f two things are alike in some respects we can reasonably expect them to be alike in other respects, though there may still be others in which they are unlike" (p. 172). "In general between any two things there will be some likenesses and some unlikenesses" (p. 172). Formally, any one thing that is not identical to a second is a potential model of that thing for there are at least some similarities between the two—a human being is like a banana for they both have skins which change in appearance with age . . . If A is analogous to B, this implies that (1) there is a set of similarities between them, (2) there is a set of differences between them, and (3) that A does not equal B, i. e., they are not identical. By this definition any thing that is not identical to a second thing is a potential model of it, and the whole problem of using or developing models is in the selection of a thing that will be helpful in understanding the original.

We now can clarify why scientists bother with constructing and studying analogies of the object of study instead of studying the thing itself. Of course, one reason is ethical. Particularly if the object of study involves human beings, ethical limits on the ways they can study humans encourage them to turn to models. As I will discuss more fully later, the current debate about animals revolves around the recent widespread recognition that using animals as models also has ethical limits.

Scientists also use models when the object of study is relatively inaccessible (stars) or very complex (the human brain). Finally, related to the demands of experimentalism, models are used because they are often more readily controllable and allow the investigator to vary one or two features of the model at a time.

Concepts of Models

Scientists forego direct observation of the actual object of study for the sake of accessibility, simplicity and control. They do so reluctantly and we will see that one of two major concepts of animal models actually allows them to think, or at least claim, that they still are making direct observations—to deny that they are looking at only an analogous stand-in for or model of the actual object of study. In their philosophical analysis of animal models in biomedical research, LaFollette and Shanks distinguish between two concepts of models, as "heuristic" and as "causal analogies" (1993a, p. 122). For reasons that will become apparent, here I adopt the terminology "weak analogy" and "strong analogy," respectively, in the following explication.

The use of weak analogy models is closer to our use of analogies in everyday experience, so let us start with it. To teach ourselves or someone else to understand something new, we often analogize to something more familiar. The unfamiliar computer is like a desk in which we organize things so that we can remember where they are and have easier access to them. This kind of model is based on a "heuristic analogy" (1993a, p. 13). A heuristic is a device that helps us think, learn or discover. By thinking about the computer as a desk, we are able to better understand concretely some of its abstract features and even to learn more about them by generating questions from what we know of desks—can we move information from one drawer to another; can we put only so much stuff in each compartment ... ? In this first concept, an animal model is a heuristic or generative device that helps us to conceptualize and guides our inquiry about the original.

It is important to understand that in this concept, the model can be helpful even if the actual suggested similarities do not obtain. For example, from the model desk, we generate the hypothesis that when we move information from one compartment to a second it is no longer in the first. Information is transferable but not duplicative. This hypothesis is disconfirmed when we turn to the computer. But although the desk model was invalid in this regard, the hypothesis has helped us discover something about computers, that information stored in them is both transferable and duplicative. Clearly, in judging the power of a model, validity is an inadequate criterion. In the final analysis, validity is less critical than productive generativity, that is, whether the hypotheses generated by it are productive of new information about the actual object of investigation. Such productive generativity is not a simple function of similarity as differences between the model and the modelled can also lead to further understanding of the original.

The second concept of animal models makes a stronger claim about the relation between the model and original. There is the additional requirement that a model go beyond the function of generative device to actually provide a strict analogue of the causal mechanisms in the actual object of study. Model and modelled must be causally, not merely heuristically, analogous. Causal analogy means that a causal relation in the model also operates in the thing modelled. In both model and original, there is an A that causes B. The power, then, of the model depends on its displaying common or, really, identical causal mechanisms ("isomorphisms"). This commonality is said to be a measure of the validity of the model. A model is a good one to the degree that the same causal mechanisms obtain in it as in the object of investigation. Generativity or usefulness is reduced to validity.

The requisite strength of the strong analogy concept of models is more apparent when we further note that biological and psychological processes are composed of many systems and subsystems all of which have some determining or causal power. This quickly leads to the desideratum, if not the requirement, that the "validity of any model depends on how closely it resembles the original *in every respect*" (AMA White Paper, 1988, p. 27, emphasis added).

It takes little sophistication about biomedicine to understand that by this criterion no animal model is fully valid. In the case of human disease, as Sharpe (1988), Bross (1987), and Kaufman and Hahner (1993) have shown for particular models and LaFollette and Shanks have argued on logical grounds for all models, no animal model can be similar to a human disease "in every respect." As I will show, this is even clearer in research on psychological phenomena. While a dog or rat can be depressed, neither the causes nor even the course and form of the depression resemble in every respect those of depression in a human being.

Yet the concept of animal model as causal analogy is the "official position" of the AMA, the primary professional organization of the biomedical community (LaFollette & Shanks, 1993a, p. 121). How and why does it take this position if it is virtually impossible to develop an animal model that would meet the strict test of providing the same causal mechanisms involved in a human pathological condition? While a full answer to this question would take us too far afield, some treatment of it is important since psychology, in its effort to emulate the natural sciences (here biology) borrows this strong analogy concept of animal model.

Historically, the animal model strategy in biomedicine was used early on in the study of infectious diseases such as tuberculosis. In the late 19th century, Koch helped develop the germ theory of disease. In this theory, diseases result from germs, usually bacterial, implanting themselves in and infecting a human body. The subsequent course of the infection is the disease process. Koch argued that an animal model of an infectious disease could be created by isolating the particular germ, infecting an animal with it, and then attempting to affect the course of the disease through drug or vaccine intervention.

Here "animal model" refers to the use of an animal as a host organism for another organism (the germ). The host's reaction to the germ provides the model of the object of study. It is easy to see how this situation readily leads to the strong analogy concept of animal model. After all, while the host organism (the model) and the original diseased individual (the modelled) are quite different, the germ implanted in the host animal is literally identical to the one that is also found in humans when they have contracted that particular disease, for the investigator may actually use that germ.

In this concept the animal is merely a receptacle for the original. The tubercular process, for example, is just that whether it occurs in a rat or human. For all intents and purposes, the rat is merely a small human and the process of interest is merely occurring on a smaller scale.

While this description is often adopted naively, it obviously is not an accurate description of the situation. Biological processes are composed of many systems and subsystems all of which have some determining power. The causal mechanisms, the course, and the form of expression of the disease are a product of these many interactive systems. Each system and its interactions are different in different species. In the terms of LaFollette and Shanks, "there is always room for systemic disanalogy" (1993a, p. 123). Even subtle systemic differences can result in "widely divergent responses to the same stimuli, be it bacteriological, virological or pharmacological" (1993a, p. 123).

For example, there is no tubercular process that is independent of its host. An animal model of tuberculosis does not resemble the original tuberculosis in humans in every respect. In fact, systemic disanalogy is also the rule in different strains of the same species and even in different individuals of the same strain (see Zbinden & Flury-Roversi, 1981, for discussion of differences in rodent strains). Recent theoretical advances in various sciences have revealed that extremely small differences in the initial conditions of any system, whether inorganic or organic, may produce very significant results (Gleick, 1987). In his discussion of "chaos theory," Gleick describes the butterfly effect. In attempting to predict the weather, meteorologists have to deal with the fact that "tiny deviations" say on one side of a continent eventually can have powerful effects on the weather thousands of miles away (illustrated only "half-jokingly" by the fluttering of the wings of a butterfly in Peking that produces a storm system in New York) (pp. 11–31).

Nonetheless, the relatively close match across species in the case of infectious diseases facilitated biomedicine's adoption of the causal analogy concept of the animal model. So we have the 19th century biomedical pioneer, Claude Bernard, claiming, "All animals may be used for physiological investigations, because with the same properties and lesions in life and disease, the same results everywhere recurs..." (1927). (This quote has received considerable recent discussion from academics apparently espousing both sides of the debate on the use of animals in biomedical research. LaFollette and Shanks [1993, pp. 8–9], who misquoted from the original Bernard text, were taken to task in a response also published in *Public Affairs Quarterly* [Willis and Hulsey, 1994, p. 215]). The AMA cites Bernard in its recent White Paper as a developer of "the principles of the scientific method" (1988, p. 6).

Bernard's use of the adjective "same" is telling. The "strong analogy" of this concept of animal model belies the fact that the model is only an analogy and uses instead the language of identity—of sameness not similarity. Tuberculosis is tuberculosis; a particular disease is that disease independent of host setting. This is the consequence of an early and naive grasp of the germ theory of disease: the disease consists of the germ and the inevitable and fixed consequences of its invasion of the host. In this view, a disease is such a robust entity that it is readily transportable, intact and without variation, across species lines.

A significance of espousing the strong analogy concept of an animal model is that scientists can then claim adherence to the important natural scientific ideal of directly observing of the object of study. Through this concept of the animal model, scientists can retain the notion that the lab is where the real action is. They thereby deny that the object of study is artificial, several times removed.

Infectious diseases and the germ theory lent themselves to the strong analogy concept and its attempt to develop models that involve the same causal mechanisms as the actual object of study. While in the case of infectious diseases that fit already involved considerable distortion, the advent of the current major diseases clearly demands a new concept of disease, and with it a new understanding of the actual function of models, whether animal or non-animal. Heart disease, stroke, and cancer—the contemporary major killers—are not discrete infectious diseases caused by a specific germ. They are more complicated and better thought of as families of diseases that implicate environment, life-style, attitude, stress tolerance, and several systems of the body in interaction (e. g., Castelli, 1984).

Despite this conceptual misfit, biomedicine has held onto the strong analogy concept in practice and as its official position. It also has inflated the results of medical treatments allegedly derived from animal research involving animal models of the infectious diseases (Sharpe, 1988; LaFollette & Shanks, 1993a). For example, while the AMA claims that the decline in death rates in the first half of this century from infectious diseases such as tuberculosis, pneumonia, influenza, and diphtheria are attributable to animal research leading to the development of vaccines and pharmacological treatments, medical historians trace most of the decreases to preventive measures in public health, such as improved nutrition, sanitation, hygiene, and water quality (McKeown, 1979). Even those residual gains resulting from biomedical research were often due more to clinical research than to animal experimentation (Reines, 1991; LaFollette & Shanks, 1993a).

Further, there are significant instances in which animal research delayed medical advance, misled research efforts, or even led to harmful and disastrous medical interventions. A recent debate suggests that animal models of polio may have delayed and misled research leading to the development of a vaccine. While accepting that animal research "may have facilitated some insights," Kaufman joins Sharpe (1993) in arguing that in the case of polio it was on balance responsible for significant delay and misdirection (1993). Sharpe (1988) puts forward the case that animal research involving the sedative thalidomide was largely responsible for the tragedy of thousands of children being born with gross birth defects in the 1960s. Others have rebutted this analysis, arguing that the historical data are much more complicated (Steinmetz & Tillery, 1994, p. 288–290).

As I have argued, the strong analogy concept of animal models is not supported in theory or practice. Rather than providing causal mechanisms of the original, both animal and nonanimal models operate in a more limited way. They are heuristic or generative devices which help scientists to think about the actual object of study.

Contemporary philosophers of science draw a distinction between two parts of the scientific enterprise, the contexts of discovery and justification (Hempel, 1966; Popper, 1968), where the latter refers to the problem of proof or validation. The use of models is largely limited to the discovery context. A model provides one of many possible generative or creative devices, ranging from the systematic study of a model to the openness to new ideas that comes while singing in the shower. Any leads suggested by a model must be validated in the original. Even when a hypothesis is validated in the object of study, it does not follow that the features of the model that suggested that hypothesis are the same as those in the original, nor need they

be. The model when applied to the modelled is either useful in furthering understanding or it is not. As I will discuss
later, any eventual scientific gain is an historical question:
Did a particular model help or hinder, hasten or delay
understanding; did it lead to beneficial applications?

Rhetorical claims notwithstanding, the proper and typical use of animal and nonanimal models is a limited one.
They do not directly provide understanding; they are
thinking aids that give leads about a line of questioning
or a way something might be understood. When the scientist constructs a model, he or she does not have the
original in hand. It is never simply a matter of extrapolating directly, as if a rat were simply a small human and one
could determine effects by multiplying by a factor representing that quantitative difference. The laboratory is not
a shrunken version of reality—it is not *Alice's Wonderland*.

Why this exaggeration of the benefits of animal research
and why the continuing claim that animal models give
actual access to the phenomenon of interest instead of
merely providing sometimes helpful heuristic aids? An answer would require an extended analysis of political and
strategic considerations. Suffice to note here that the enterprise of biomedical research has been a major target of the
contemporary animal rights movement. Sophisticated critiques of vivisection have been developed on both ethical
and scientific grounds. One thrust of that critique has been
the demand that the use of whole or "intact" animal-based
research be replaced by alternatives such as cell and tissue
culture, computer and math models, epidemiological studies (Stephens, 1989) and direct observation of human disease through access now dramatically provided by new
imaging techniques (Morris, 1989).

Although a significant part of the biomedical community has been instrumental in these developments, professional organizations such as the AMA have responded
with a defense of the status quo or, at least of the official
version of it. This has involved a reconstruction of history

which inflates the benefits of earlier animal research and distorts the actual function of animal models. It is claimed that, unlike computer simulations and other alternatives, only an animal model can "resemble the original in every respect." As LaFollette and Shanks (1993b) describe, a key plank of the "intact systems argument" is the notion that animal models and only animal models can provide causal analogies to human biomedical phenomena. We have seen that even for the infectious diseases there is no basis for this claim.

As a side note, the strong analogy concept of animal models can be expected to be revived by its proponents as recent advances in bioengineering begin to accelerate. As early researchers implanted a germ to create animal models of the infectious diseases, so may the technology of genetic engineering allow investigators to transplant human genes identified with a particular pathology into laboratory animals (Fox, 1992, p. 2).

Psychology's Use of Animal Models

In the next chapter I will examine in detail selected animal models in contemporary psychological research. Here I will characterize conceptually that use and certain misuses to which it is prone.

As discussed earlier, not all parts of the animal research effort in psychology rely on the animal model strategy. Comparative psychologists, who make up only a small proportion of the researchers using animals (Dewsbury, 1992), study animals as an end in themselves and to understand differences among species. The animals are not considered models of human behavior and any extrapolation to the human condition is considered incidental. Another group of psychology researchers studies animals to understand allegedly universal processes. For these researchers, any animal is a model for all other animals, including humans, since the working assumption is that the basic principles of learning, perception and other psychological phenomena apply equally to all animals. The group of researchers referred to here studies nonhuman animals primarily to understand particular conditions in human animals. Of course, these distinctions blur to some extent, but the three different groups are fairly distinguishable in terms of degree of selective breeding, species studied, reliance on the laboratory or field as site of study, degree of manipulation and invasiveness practiced on the animals, and journals utilized for publication.

Claims and Actualities

Given psychology's desire to emulate the natural sciences, it is no surprise that experimental psychologists, like biomedical researchers, invoke the same "strong analogy" function in their use of animal models, and inflate the benefits derived from them. Of course, early psychologists were aware of attempts in the biomedical science to study human diseases by creating animal models. By borrowing this strategy they hoped to understand the pathologies of the psyche or, to use more contemporary language, behavioral disorders.

As noted earlier, an additional significance of the espousal of the strong analogy concept is that psychologists, like biomedical researchers, can then claim adherence to the important positivistic ideal of direct observation of the object of study. With its emphasis on the provision of virtually identical causal mechanisms, adoption of the strong analogy concept allows investigators to claim that they still are making direct observations of the object of study.

In his discussion of the "elements of models" in psychology, Overmier states, "Now if a relation between the patient's physiology and behavior is hypothesized to parallel the empirical causal relation between the animal's physiology and behavior, a formal analogy can be drawn ... It is this formal analogy- the hypothesized parallelism of causal relations in the two domains [model and original]- that constitutes a functional model" (Overmier & Burke, 1992, p. ix). In a paper entitled, "The Value of Behavioral Research on Animals," Miller refers to "a point-to-point correspondence" between certain results of the learned helplessness animal model of depression and "the behaviors characteristic of human depression" (1985, pp. 432–3). Clearly, these psychologists' understanding of and claims regarding animal models are close to a strong analogy in which they provide causal, and not merely heuristic, analogies to human disorders. An APA Backgrounder (APA, 1984, pp. 3 and 14) and other official publications of APA also claim that animal models provide causal, not merely heuristic, analogies to human disorders. Gallup is an exception to this as he uses the phrase "heuristic value" and speaks of animal research as "an important source of hypotheses about human behavior" (1985, p. 1105).

We have described how the discovery in the late 19th century that many of the diseases then ravaging human populations were caused by specific bacteria led to the germ theory of disease; and how, in turn, an early form of that germ theory led to the idea that the causes and process of certain diseases could actually be duplicated in an animal models. If physical illnesses could be understood and studied in this way, psychologists reasoned, why not psychological or behavioral illnesses?

Experimental psychologists readily grafted the animal model strategy onto the construction of the laboratory animal. Psychologists selectively bred animals to model obesity (e. g., Greenberg & Ackerman, 1984), alcoholism (e. g., Li, Lumeng, McBride, & Murphy, 1987), high blood pressure (e. g., Elias & Schlager, 1974), depression (Willner, 1991. p. 133) or level of intelligence, and manipulated their environments to create models of depression, dependence, and various forms of social, perceptual, and intellectual deprivation.

However, many psychologists argue that behavioral disorders such as drug addiction, eating disorders, and child abuse are not illnesses in the biomedical sense, certainly not in the sense of infectious diseases caused by a discrete germ. We cannot understand or treat a person suffering from a behavioral disorder by thinking of him or her as a carrier or host of a germ. While there may be a genetic component in some mental illnesses and while there are physiological substrates of the condition which then can be a focus of drug intervention, more generally to understand and treat psychopathology we must more often deal with the structure of the family (Minuchin, 1974) and other socializing agencies, with analyses of interpersonal interactions (Carson, 1969), with stages of development, with attitudes (Ellis, 1973), and with language. These cannot be injected into the body like a germ that produces a particular disease entity, takes a certain course, and has a particular outcome.

Some psychologists and psychiatrists have argued further that the notion of behavioral disorders as mental illnesses is so wrongheaded that it is a myth perpetrated to justify social control or to assure that the treatment of these disorders would fall within the bailiwick of certain disciplines (Szasz, 1961). They offer as a more useful concept that behavioral disorders are "problems in living," complexly determined situations in which we find ourselves unable to live effectively or happily. Germs as cause and vaccine or pill as intervention are clearly inappropriate.

We need not fully subscribe to this "radical psychiatry" to realize that the likelihood of being able to develop an animal model that will "resemble the original in every respect" rapidly diminishes as we move along the following spectrum, roughly from infectious disease to problems in living: tuberculosis, heart disease, depression, eating disorder, addiction, and antisocial behavior. No reasonable person would wager that experimentally induced aggression in a rat can provide a causal analogue—a strong analogy model—to hostile aggression in a human context. Clearly, any usefulness of such an animal model is limited to providing a heuristic analogy. Again, when we examine more fully some selected animal models below, we can judge whether even by that more limited criterion, animal models of psychological phenomena are useful.

Degraded Heuristic

Putting aside the inaccurate claim that animal models in psychology provide strong or causal analogies to human disorders, is it not at least accurate to understand their use as heuristic or generative and are there not, then, benefits from this enterprise? In fact, there are several ways in which even the weak analogy concept of animal models is not descriptive of animal research in psychology.

If an animal model can lead to further understanding of the actual object of study through its use as a generative device, by the same token a given model can fail to so enlighten us. It can suggest ways of understanding that turn out to be dead ends. But at least if the models are truly functioning as heuristic devices, as leads that are then tested in the original, these false analogies can be caught. Unfortunately, animal models do not often operate this way in psychology.

As I have indicated, the model strategy is sometimes adopted precisely because the actual object of study is relatively inaccessible or because ethical constraints prevent its direct study. In practice, this means that the justification stage in which the ideas generated in the discovery stage are tested often never occurs. There are also sociological and professional reasons for this failure to validate the model in the original human context. In psychology those who experiment on animals typically are not the same people who treat or study people. Animal experimenters and clinicians are generally distinct groups who read and publish in different literatures and belong to different professional groups. Those who construct the models are relatively incommunicative with those who work directly with the object of study, and the models are never tested. They do not serve the heuristic function that is their proper use. Wade provides an even more narrowly constructed instance of this kind of sequestered turf behavior in psychology: "... the rat people are very parochial in that they only read the rat literature and only cite rat studies, so very frequently our [cat study] papers are not cited" (cited in Garfield [1980, p. 106]; attributed to Lester Aronson, a scientist whose invasive research at the American Museum of Natural History on the sex behavior of cats was the target of a campaign by Henry Spira in 1976). Neuringer (1984) provides another example of blinders between different parts of psychology and specifically between basic and applied areas. He is critical of the primary subfield of behavioristic psychology (operant conditioning, developed by B. F. Skinner), for what he terms its "oft-noted ingrown nature" (p. 399). He summarizes his concerns as follows: "Operant researchers rarely use the arena of applied psychology to motivate or to judge their research. Absence of tests by application weaken the field of basic operant research" (p. 397).

Models and research procedures become established as areas of research within animal behavior psychology. A literature gets built up in which a model, say for human depression, is established through many variations on the basic model. Instead of checking the model against the original behavior for which it is a model, the "validation" occurs within the paradigm of the model. Verification is limited to testing the degree of consistency of the new findings with other research within the literature on the same model. In this way, an entire research enterprise becomes "ingrown" and may be of little or no value in furthering understanding of the original object of study. An animal model so constructed can do serious harm not only by delaying understanding but by fostering a basic misunderstanding of the object of study. That the model is a model and must be empirically verified against the original is forgotten.

Rhetorical Device

As ineffectual and misleading as this is, another scenario is more insidious. Sometimes although no verification of it is obtained in the actual object of study, the model provides an image to describe the original. The model merely supplies a loose analogy for the object of study. For example, an animal in whom "depression" has been induced becomes a graphic image of depression. Our talk and imaginings about depression are influenced but it is not clear that any understanding has been gained for the model is never validated. The use of the model as a generative device degenerates into the model as a rhetorical device.

In her critique of Suomi and Harlow's model of human depression, Midgley notes that she was "dumbstruck" upon reading their account of the study "not to find better arguments. I had always assumed that a deeper structure of thought must be present ... " (1981, p. 332). To her surprise, she discovers that for these investigators to develop a model does not mean "to examine rigorously what the points of likeness and unlikeness are ... " (p. 332). Instead, she characterized what she found as "(c)rashing into this subtle and delicate structure [of depression] with a sledgehammer" (p. 333). The model of depression, separating infant monkeys from their mothers, and isolating and confining them in a vertical metal chamber for 45 days, merely provides a metaphor. Depression is like a "well of despair." Ironically, Suomi and Harlow's inspiration for the model that provided this metaphor itself was a metaphor already in the literature on human depression. As they note, depression has been characterized as similar to being in a "sunken well of despair." Their vertical chambering device was "designed to reproduce such a well both physically and psychologically for monkey subjects." (quoted by Midgley, p. 332). Rather than based on any original or thoughtful insight into human depression, the basis of their model was, in their own words, "intuitive" (p. 332).

Incidentally, psychology is not the only scientific enterprise prone to the loose use of analogic thinking. Sociobiology (Caplan, 1978) is in part an attempt to explain complex human social and cultural phenomena by finding evolutionary parallels in other species. Some critics find explanations provided by sociobiological models of, for example, altruism, scientifically inadequate, untestable, and implausible. They find accounts of the social organization of certain species of insects to be a kind of "just so" story clad in scientific garb.

In a different context, Haraway (1989) echoes Midgley's critique of Harlow and the enterprise of animal models of human psychopathology. "Harlow was a master narrator. He could design and build experimental apparatus and model the bodies and minds of monkeys to tell the major stories of his culture and his historical moment" (p. 231). The work issuing from the primate lab at the University of Wisconsin and much similarly highly invasive research subsequently produced by the 36 doctorates mentored by Harlow primarily serves a rhetorical function. Rather than scientific explanations that further understanding of human phenomena, depressed infant monkeys, surrogate cloth-covered or wire-meshed mothers, and rape racks provide images for and tell the story of aspects of the then current culture. As Haraway states, the "raped rhesus mothers ... were constructs for the literal translation of metaphors into hardware" (p. 238). Finally, in his comprehensive critique of Harlow's studies in maternal deprivation, Stephens (1986) also emphasized that the contribution of that work was largely rhetorical—"Many of these experiments were little more than *sensational illustrations* of what had already been established in humans" (p. 35, emphasis added).

Akin to this critique of models as metaphorical or rhetorical devices, Kotre (1992) offers that highly successful experiments, not just those employing the model strategy of experimentation, are more generally like stories. "What experiments do we care about? In one area of psychology [social psychology], at least, it's the ones that have potential as stories" (p. 673). Kotre analyzes the experiments in social psychology that have become "classics," and notes that they have the elements of good stories, in particular, they have the structure of parables: vivid imagery and conceptual simplicity (p. 673). Of course, unlike the studies under investigation here, experiments in social psychology tell a good story without expending animals.

A related way in which the animal model strategy fails to work even as a heuristic device involves a reversal in the relation between the lab animal model and target behavior. Instead of using the model to generate hypotheses which are then validated in the actual object of study, psychologists begin with some aspect of behavior already observed in humans and seek to demonstrate an analogous form of it in the animal lab. Rowan provides an example of this in the research of Edward Taub, whose research on deafferentation became the cause célèbre known as the case of the Silver Spring Monkeys. It was already well known that the extended period of disuse of limbs damaged by stroke in humans was frequently due to motivational and learning factors (Rowan, 1982, p. 226).

This tendency to develop a model to demonstrate what is already known is another example of the "experimenting bias." The assumption is that the controlled, objective, and instrumentalized setting of the lab is the only site where something can be confidently observed. The only "facts" of which we can be sure are those behaviors produced in the lab. The real world is in the lab, while the everyday world outside the lab is an "as if" world where what is observed can not be legitimately, in the scientific sense, believed. This is a sophistic turn which perverts the idea of an animal model. The model itself is taken as scientific fact rather than as generator of possible relations that must be verified in the original.

Harlow carries this experimentalist bias to the extreme by a twist of illogic one step beyond the above reversal where insight moves from the original to the model, thereby thoroughly corrupting the heuristic function of models. "Sometimes when monkey data fail to generalize to human data the answer lies in the superiority of the monkey data and the need to revise those data that are human ..." (quoted in Reines, p. 68). Here there is a denial of the need to test the model against the original. The data from the animal model are incontestable for it was generated in the lab.

Finally, another use of the model strategy further demonstrates how its proper function has been misunderstood. A kind of second order modeling occurs when investigators forget the original object of study and seek a model to understand what is itself only a model. For example, a computer model is constructed to help understand an aspect of animal behavior which was artificially induced in an attempt to model a certain human behavior. The presence of this peculiar thinking about animal models is often revealed when proponents of invasive laboratory animal research insist that there can be no nonanimal alternatives in psychology. They insist that a computer, for example, can never be a model of a whole, intact animal's behavior. Of course, a computer no doubt can provide weak analogies for animal behavior. However, the point is that those who deny that there are alternatives for animal research forget that the alternative need not be a model for *animal* research for that is only a generative device to help understand human behavior. They have invoked a generative device to aid another generative device while not moving toward the requisite testing of the model in the original.

A use of animals outside of psychology, in product testing, provides an interesting parallel to this peculiar illogic in the use of animal models. Toxicologists, producers, and animal protectionists currently are debating the problem of validation of alternatives to animal testing of ingredients used in cosmetics and other products. How is an alternative to an intact live animal model such as the Draize Test to be validated? The tendency is to utilize toxicity levels taken from the animal models themselves as the gold standard in evaluating alternatives. However, that data often is itself only a rough assay of the toxic effects of a particular substance on humans. In most instances, direct human data are not available, that is the animal model data remains an unvalidated hypothesis. To use such unverified data as the criterion against which to test an alternative is to rely on second order modeling and is to forget the hypothetical nature of the results of assays from animal model tests such as the Draize.

Complementing these degenerative uses of the animal model strategy is a logic that is overinclusive regarding what constitutes circumstances provides a prospect for a model in the first place. This "logical" turn includes virtually all possible species of animals as prospective models. To illustrate, in a research grant proposal involving bovine lactation, the investigator offers that "dairy cattle is [sic] also an excellent model for breast cancer studies. This is due to the fact that dairy cows rarely (almost never) develop cancer in the mammary gland." These animals, then, provide the opportunity to model the mechanism that protects the mammary gland from becoming cancerous. Of course, animals that do contract this cancer offer the opportunity to model the mechanism whereby the cancer arises. By this logic any mammal is a prospective model of human breast cancer as, presumably, absence or presence of such cancer of the mammary gland defines the entire class of mammals. I have seen similar logic used to justify selection of primate models of AIDS —both presence and absence of the syndrome.

Summing to this point, I have shown here how models should properly function; and, how, historically, this function has been misunderstood and the benefits of the use of animal models inflated. We have also described some misuses of those models. While the possible relations between the model and the modelled are complex and varied, animal models are limited to the generation of leads. They can not provide a description of causal relations that are duplicated in the original in all respects, because physiology and behavior are determined by many interactive systems that vary across species (and strains and individuals). Nor can an animal model provide verified facts or understanding; it can not by itself provide confirmation for such verification requires the original. Even within this limited proper function there are risks, for a model can be misleading. It also can be misused by forgetting its proper relation to the modelled, functioning as if it were the modelled itself. It then can become ingrown, merely "verifying" itself through achieving an internal consistency that provides no further understanding of the actual object of interest. Finally, any constructive generative use of the model can degenerate into a merely rhetorical or graphically demonstrative function that is uninformative, truncates genuine understanding, and suggests applications that have not been tested.

Ethical and Attitudinal Implications

Following a description and evaluation of specific selected animal models in the next chapter, I shall provide an extended discussion of ethical issues in psychology's use of animals in the concluding two chapters. However, certain ethical implications can be drawn even from this discussion of the concept and uses of animal models. As we will see, one of the major arguments of animal researchers is that their work is "necessary" (Giannelli, 1985) and that, therefore, any suffering associated with it is "necessary suffering." Once we understand that animal models do not live up to the traditionally touted claim of providing causal analogues, the argument that they are indispensable falls. LaFollette and Shanks conclude, "... if animal models are really heuristic analogies, then it is no longer clear that they are as *necessary* to advancement in the biomedical sciences as researchers allege" (1993a, p. 126; emphasis in original).

This is even clearer in the case of models of psychological phenomena. As we move along the spectrum from infectious diseases to disabilities that are more behavioral and sociocultural problems, the function of any animal model is more obviously limited to the provision of leads. But if animal models in psychology can at best only serve this heuristic function, then they are not indispensable. Rather, they may (or may not) be helpful in a given instance. Further nonanimal alternatives, epidemiological studies, and direct clinical investigations can serve the same heuristic function.

Models serve a discovery function; they are thinking aids. We can not know in advance whether any particular aid will generate ideas, let alone whether those ideas will then be verified in the original. A scientist can not claim in advance that a model is necessary to generate a verifiable insight into the original. It is not necessary to follow any particular "intuition" about a potentially helpful generative aid.

Human, animal, and economic resources available for research are limited. What is not limited is a scientist's ability to think and generate ideas about a problem. No one potential context of discovery is indispensable. The argument that developing animal models for this purpose is ethically justifiable because it is "necessary" is false.

Another ethical implication of this discussion of animal models is more psychological than logical. We have described how the social construction of the lab animal, including his or her construction as a model, results in animal subjects that are not themselves in several senses. They are, as it were, at several removes—from their naturally evolved genetic self, from their natural setting, from their species-specific behavior, from their individual behavior.

They are also not themselves in that, as models, they are treated as stand-ins for another species. From the psychology researcher's point of view, the animal subject is not him or her self but a model of something else. He or she is not a rat, even a laboratory-bred rat, but an aspect of some human disorder. One can look past the animal to the object of study, which is an aspect of human behavior. The actually present suffering rat is not there, for the focus of attention is an absent object of study. These several removals, this kind of absence of an animal that has any residual perceived integrity, promotes an atmosphere of indifference, callousness, and potential abuse.

Chapter 4
Selected Animal Models

1. PRESENTATION

In the last chapter I reviewed and critiqued the general concept of animal models, with special emphasis on how that concept is used in psychological research. Now I turn from those abstract considerations to a more concrete analysis of current animal models in psychology. The chapter is in two parts. In the first, I provide a closer look at how animals are used in psychology, referring both to the procedures involved and to their scientific rationale. I hope to do so in a way that is accessible to the reader with only a general background in science. At the same time I want to provide enough detail and depth so that a more informed judgment can be made about the animal model strategy in psychology.

In the second part, I provide a critique of the particular models presented. To do so, I utilize as critical frameworks the material in the previous chapters on the social construction of the "lab animal" and on the concept of models. However, I also will apply other more specific evaluative techniques, such as survey data describing the impact and use of the studies in relevant clinical settings, the frequency and context of the citation of studies presenting the research, and the level of invasiveness of the research. In turn, the application of these criteria will give an empirical basis for the subsequent discussion of ethical and policy considerations featured in the final two chapters.

Regarding the choice of models examined, that choice should be irrelevant given the degree to which the procedures and rationale involved are found throughout the field. Any model should do. On the other hand, I have tried to avoid certain obvious biases in the choices. For example, I decided not to select models involving researchers who have been the object of major campaigns by the animal rights movement, as this would be provocative and, in any case, that ground has been well-trod by both proponents and opponents of animal research. I avoided areas of animal research with which I was already relatively familiar and had already formed a clear judgment. I also did not select areas of research in which one would expect high invasiveness because of the nature of the phenomenon, such as pain or depression. This latter criterion was more difficult to adhere to than it might appear, as most of the animal models involve human psychological disorders that are painful and stressful, either intrinsically or as a secondary consequence of the disorder. Finally, I avoided areas that, although clearly psychological, are disorders predominantly held to be biologically caused. This arguably would introduce a bias toward more invasive research, as biological or physiological studies tend to involve more invasive procedures than environmentally caused disorders. Of course, for almost all disorders there is research being conducted to find both environmental and biological causes.

The area I chose to examine is *eating disorders*. In addition to the above considerations, the problem of eating disorders is of major current concern, both as a general social issue and in clinical settings. Certain forms of these disorders have reached epidemic proportions in some age groups and some subcultures. The *Diagnostic and Statistical Manual of Mental Disorders* (American Psychiatric Association, 1994) (DSM) indicates that among adolescent and young adult females the rate of occurrence of bulimia is 1%–3%. Among college women in the United States, the rate is even higher (Crandall, 1988). It is important to note that both bulimia and the other major eating disorder, anorexia, are largely restricted to females, with 90% of the occurrences in females. As will be reviewed, the literature implicates a growing interest in dieting as relevant to the dramatic increase in these disorders in recent times. It also shows that that increase is higher in urbanized and industrialized cultures. In the current crisis and debate involving health care in the United States, there is much discussion of the role of diet and nutrition. This area, then, combines social relevance and significant challenge for a psychological science.

My guiding question is: What contribution is the animal model strategy making generally to the understanding and solution of this social problem and to its more effective treatment specifically in applied psychological settings?

First, I will describe the phenomena of eating disorders as they are defined in the psychological literature, and discuss current forms of their treatment. Following an overview of the scope of animal models in this area, I will analyze several models more fully, indicating the procedures and species involved, the level of invasiveness, and the findings. Finally, I will provide data on the frequency of their citation in the animal, general psychological, and relevant clinical or applied literatures. Survey data on the level of impact of animal research on clinicians working with relevant populations will also be provided.

Eating Disorders

The two primary eating disorders are formally known as bulimia nervosa and anorexia nervosa. According to the DSM, which is the diagnostic system most employed by mental health providers and by the insurance industry, the essential features of bulimia are:

> ... recurrent episodes of binge eating (rapid consumption of a large amount of food in a discrete period of time); a feeling of lack of control over eating behavior during the eating binges; self-induced vomiting, use of laxatives or diuretics, strict dieting or fasting, or vigorous exercise in order to prevent weight gain; and persistent overconcern with body shape and weight (pp. 545–550).

The essential features of anorexia are:

> ... refusal to maintain body weight over a minimal normal weight for age and height; intense fear of gaining weight or becoming fat, even though underweight; a distorted body image; and amenorrhea (in females).... The disturbance in body image is manifested by the way in which the person's body weight, size, or shape is experienced. People with this disorder say they "feel fat," or that parts of their body are "fat," when they are obviously underweight or even emaciated (pp. 539–545).

While the two are listed separately in the DSM, they are clearly related disorders, possibly even variations on the same disorder. They both typically involve gross disturbances in eating behavior, such as binge eating and the use of laxatives; preoccupation and/or distortion of the individual's image of their own body (with near psychotic distortion in anorexia); and preoccupation with dieting and exercise as a means of weight control. While bulimia is more common, anorexia is more incapacitating, often necessitating hospitalization and sometimes resulting in death.

Both bulimia and anorexia are complex phenomena and cultural, familial, behavioral, and physiological components all are thought to be involved in their genesis. The question of their cause remains an unanswered one (Smith, 1989). However, most researchers and clinicians implicate the "slimming culture" (Booth, 1989, p. 123), i.e., the value placed on maintaining a certain body shape in our contemporary culture. Booth refers to the "religion of leanness" and to our "devotion to scrawniness." Echoing this, Seid notes, "We have elevated the pursuit of a lean, fat-free body into a religion" (1994, p. 4). In turn, these particular cultural factors point to the importance of issues of gender as a way of understanding the increasing and high incidence of these disorders among women in urbanized (and commercialized) cultures. A recent volume presents a feminist perspective on the eating disorders (Fallon, Katzman, & Wooley, 1994). However, in addition to these cultural factors, the role of family and individual dynamics may be necessary causes in the "selection" of the particular individuals afflicted. Some argue that, in turn, the underlying cause of differing individual vulnerability to the disorders may be physiological. It is clear that the course of both disorders have physiological consequences.

Identifying the etiology of these disorders, be they cultural or physiological, is an important task which guides the reliance on the animal model strategy. But cultural cause does not preclude attempts to develop animal models. Psychologists readily study "cultural factors" in the lab under the rubric of environmental variables and how they influence behavior and attitudes. For example, investigators study the effect on eating behavior of environmental features such as amount and type of available food. However, we will find that the search for animal models does bias research toward physiological causes, sustaining mechanisms, and secondary consequences of the disorders.

It is important to understand that, like their biomedical colleagues, psychologists conduct physiological research. While there is much psychological research that is purely psychological or behavioral, a significant percentage of it involves physiological variables. Just as medicine has a psychological specialty (psychiatry), psychology has a physiological specialty (physiological psychology), itself further specialized into neuropsychology and psychoneuroimmunology. Both fields use the same categories and definitions of disorders (the DSM); both fields draw from the same funding sources. This blurring of the fields also obtains in clinical settings as some psychological disorders have physiological causes and almost all have physiological consequences. Conversely, some physical disorders have psychological causes and almost all have psychological complications.

The relevance of these points is that it is often impossible to distinguish "psychological" from biomedical research. It is difficult and in fact arbitrary, to strictly limit this review of animal model research to psychology. Other supplemental definitions such as the academic degree of the investigator(s) and the name of the department or institute in which the research is conducted are helpful. But some psychologists have degrees in neuroscience and some work in medical school departments of psychiatry. In the following review, I have selected animal models in which psychologists, by at least one of these criteria, have been significantly involved.

One other definitional clarification: obesity is not considered a distinct psychological disorder or syndrome, strictly speaking. It is listed in the DSM as a physical condition that may be affected by psychological factors. We will deal with it only in passing while focusing on animal models of bulimia and, to a lesser extent, of anorexia. However, it should be noted that animal models of the three disorders overlap considerably. In fact, indicating why and how this is the case provides an organizing frame for the specific models to be considered below.

When I first began reading the research literature on eating disorders I was surprised at the density and difficulty of the material. Even with my background in academic and clinical psychology and a decade of critical reading of animal research in psychology, I found the literature confusing. The reason for this confusion soon became clear. It is true that bulimia and anorexia apparently are caused, occasioned, and sustained at many levels, including cultural symbols, family dynamics, individual disposition, central and peripheral physiology. And it is true that the array of variables being examined in the literature and the different technical languages employed are forbidding. However, these are no less the case for schizophrenia, depression, antisocial personality, and many other disorders. Rather, the confusion here stems from a simple set of inverse relations among the eating disorders (including here obesity).

In the logic of the positivistic philosophy of science underlying laboratory animal-based research, bulimia and obesity are reduced to (operationalized as) eating too much, while anorexia is taken as eating too little. While employing a simple conceptual rubric is often a powerful strategy in science, the result here is that any model of one eating disorder is a potential treatment of the other and, conversely, any treatment of one is a model of the other.

Any intervention at any level (cultural value, family or individual dynamic, immediate reinforcing environment, peripheral or central drug or other physiological intervention or manipulation) that *increases* food intake is a potential model of obesity and bulimia. But it is also a possible treatment of anorexia. Any intervention at any level that *decreases* food intake is a potential model of anorexia but also a treatment of obesity and bulimia. As we will see, the laboratory research enterprise is exhaustive (or opportunistic) in exploring all possible forms and levels of inquiry. The apparent confusion in reading the literature stems from the fact that a variable that plays the role of a potential model in one study is in another a potential treatment. Not only is there a cast of thousands, each actor plays several roles.

For example, various parts of the hypothalamus, an important portion of the brain, provide differential control over the amount of food to be eaten: there is a region that enhances eating (the so-called feeding center, the lateral hypothalamus [LH]), and a part that reduces eating, (the satiety center or ventromedial hypothalamus [VMH]). Any intervention, such as injecting into the LH a neuro-transmitter (a chemical that provides "communication" among cells) or an "agonist" drug (one that mimics a nat-urally occurring biochemical reaction) that further en-hances LH output is a model of obesity or bulimia and a treatment of anorexia; while one that enhances the output of the VMH is a model of anorexia and a treatment for obesity and bulimia. An intervention that impedes the functioning of the LH, through a lesion that destroys it or an "antagonist" drug that blocks communication to and from it, is a model of anorexia and a treatment of obesity and bulimia; while one that impedes the functioning of the VMH is a model of obesity and bulimia and a treat-ment of anorexia. These inverse or reciprocal relations also obtain at several levels, peripheral physiological (the gut), environmental (preferred foods, food with a certain history of association with certain critical nutrients, or stressful situations), and symbolic (subscription to *Elle* magazine). These levels function as remote-control cen-ters that enhance or reduce the amount of food eaten.

The confusion and complexity is only apparent. A sim-ple algorithm provides an organizing frame for this liter-ature: *any condition, mechanism or intervention that en-hances/reduces food intake is a model/treatment of obesity and bulimia, and inversely for anorexia.* Given this straightfor-ward rule of thumb and the numerous levels for possible investigation, each with numerous possible variables, the area of eating disorders is a field-day for investigators. Further, research in the three disorders intermingles since a variable for one is a potentially relevant variable for the other two. Two recent reviews of the literature combine consideration of animal models of the several eating dis-orders (Montgomery, 1991; Coscina & Garfinkel, 1991). The latter refers to the "vast number of models [of eating disorders] that have been generated" (p. 237).

In his review of animal models of obesity published over a decade ago, Scalafani provides in tabular form a "list of 50 or so," a number he finds "impressive" (1984, p. 491). Historically, the search for animal models of obesity antedates that for bulimia and anorexia. "Animal models [of obesity] have been investigated intensively since 1939" when the VMH syndrome was first described (Smith, 1989, p. 63). Anorexia did not receive intensive scrutiny until the 1970s and bulimia was not officially recognized as an entity distinguishable from anorexia until that time as well (Russell, 1979).

An examination of Scalafani's scheme of classifying animal models of obesity provides an overview of the range and type of models explored. As our discussion of the algorithm suggests, most of these models also appear in some form in the literature pertaining to the two major eating disorders. Scalafani organizes the models using an etiologic classification. These causal categories are neural, endocrine (the system that secretes hormones), pharmacological, nutritional, environmental, seasonal, genetic, viral, and combinations of these.

The neural models involve manipulating the brain through lesions (induced through surgery or applying electricity), injection (toxic, blocking, or stimulating), electrical stimulation, or ablation (excising a part of the brain). Some of these interventions can be done either unilaterally (one side of the brain) or bilaterally (both sides of the brain), and either acutely or chronically. Endocrine models can be effected by surgical damage or removal of glands or by the use of chemical hormones (insulin or glucocorticoids).

Virtually all the main classes of pharmacological agents have been explored, "... although as yet no pharmacological model of obesity has been fully developed" (Scalafani, 1984, p. 493). Various drugs do induce eating, including tranquilizers, antidepressants, antipsychotics, and serotonin, a neurotransmitter associated with the hypothalamus. Others reduce it ("anorectics") including the amphetamines, fenfluramine (affects serotonin), and naloxone (antagonizes the release of natural pain-killing chemicals in the body). These same drugs figure in the literature on bulimia and anorexia.

Some examples of animal models of nutritional states are force feeding excess calories through tube-feeding, meal feeding (for example, restricting eating to a certain number of large meals), diet restriction of nutrients and/or palatability (high fat or high sugar), "cafeteria" or "supermarket" dieting (designed to mimic human consumption of food types), postnatal overnutrition by "culling" to small litter size or by chronic tube feeding, and prenatal undernutrition by depriving the mother of food.

Environmental models involve involuntary or forced running and stress induction through tail-pinching, immobilization, or isolation. Physical restriction has not been systematically explored according to Scalafani, although caging itself limits physical activity.

Seasonal factors include the exploration of natural or spontaneously occurring changes in food intake, such as during hibernation, migration, or breeding.

The largest class of models is the induced genetic obesities, which include strains that are single recessive, dominant or polygenic, strains that produce severe and mild obesity, diabetes, varying types of adiposity (kinds of fat cells), and particular ages of onset of obesity.

A technique in the study of obesity not mentioned by Scalafani is parabiosis. This is a procedure in which two animals are joined surgically to produce a chronic blood exchange through which an obese rat can effect the amount of body fat in the parabiosed animal (Harris & Martin, 1986).

In these various models, in addition to effects on amount of food consumed, other behaviors are studied such as amount of work done to obtain food, food-hoarding, meal size, meal frequency, nutrient selection, palatability selection, finickiness, time eating, micro-gustatory behavior (bite size, or interval between bites), and level of activity.

As we will see, virtually all of these models (or some variation on them), as well as additional ones not classified here, appear in the literature on bulimia and anorexia.

In addition to there being an extensive range and variety of models, to grasp the scope of research in this area it is important to understand that it has a proliferating and recursive character. The logic of the scientific enterprise is such that investigators explore each new model and the variables associated with it in both in themselves and also as additional variables to be explored with respect to existing models. For example, an environmental model such as tail-pinching is typically further explored by looking at how it affects and is affected by endocrines, neurotransmitters, central neural activity, nutritional manipulations, other environmental manipulations, and pharmacological interventions. The enterprise grows by feeding on itself.

As we will see, there is a more serious irony in that the eating disorders, particularly the quasi-disorder obesity, remain recalcitrant to treatment:

> It is an unfortunate paradox that there are numerous experimental manipulations that reliably increase or reduce food intake and body weight in animals and yet the success rate for human conditions is disappointingly low (Montgomery, 1991, p. 177).

Even more discouraging, the National Center for Health Statistics reported in a recent study that the incidence of overweight adults jumped dramatically between 1980 and 1991, after remaining stable from 1960 through 1980. The investigator states, "(t)he problem with obesity is that once you have it, it is very difficult to treat. What you want to do is prevent it" (Burros, 1994).

If, according to the lights of experimental lab animal research, obesity and bulimia are reducible to peculiar forms of eating too much and anorexia eating too little, it would seem a simple matter to identify how a nonhuman animal "achieves" and maintains his or her eating disorder and then to transfer or teach that "ability" to a human animal suffering from an "opposite" disorder—from the obese and the bulimic rat to the anorectic human and from the anorectic rat to the obese human. Obviously, it is not that simple and we will revisit this irony following a closer examination of specific selected models in bulimia.

Bulimia Nervosa

As indicated, the criteria for the diagnosis of bulimia given in the DSM are recurrent episodes of binge eating accompanied by a feeling of lack of control of that behavior; the use of vomiting, laxatives, exercise and other means to prevent weight gain; and persistent over-concern with body shape and weight.

To portray this disorder more concretely, I present a composite sketch of an individual presenting bulimia in a typical college counseling center setting. The composite is based on discussions with counselors who specialize in the treatment of eating disorders, material from a casebook published in conjunction with the DSM (Spitzer, Skodol, Gibbon & Williams, 1981) and from my own clinical practice, which sometimes included college students with these complaints. The description is a mixture of the client's and the therapist's points of view. While much of it is a typical presentation by a client, more or less in her words, parts of it are typical therapist interpretations of or inferences from the material presented.

> This female sophomore is accompanied to the first session by her residence hall advisor who persuaded her to seek help. She is initially quite reluctant to talk about her eating habits. She is reticent, avoids eye contact, seems embarrassed, and speaks in vague and general terms. She states that she does not like the way she eats, that it is not healthy, that she eats too much. She says she is an

athlete and that her eating is affecting her ability to compete as a sprinter. She appears to be of average weight. She remains tense throughout the session and makes no commitment to counseling. She comes to the second session alone and proceeds to talk about her family. At first, she presents a conventional loving family scene. The family is Catholic, father is a professional, mother a homemaker. She has a younger sister. Gradually, she reveals that there is a long standing tension and conflict between herself and her sister. While the client is a serious student and athlete, sister has other interests and is more laid back in their pursuit. Her description of mother suggests that she is a very moralistic influence in the home, loving but judgmental. Father apparently wanted a son as his first-born and seems to live out that expectation through the client, grooming her for a brilliant professional career. He talks to her about how to get ahead. As early as her freshman year, he encourages her to begin to make contacts, to plan ahead. Home life is tense, with undercurrents of pressure and disapproval. Never a serious student, sister escapes and develops in other directions—a situation regarding which the client resents.

In high school, the client is slightly overweight and a boyfriend teases her about it. She is part of a social group that is very weight conscious. Also, mother perennially struggles with being over-weight and is quite concerned about it. The message from both school and home is that a woman is vulnerable to rapid weight gain and that its interpersonal and social impacts can be devastating.

Since beginning athletics in late high school, the client has been of average weight but feels concerned she is too heavy to compete as a runner. She is generally unhappy, feeling that she has not lived up to expectations of herself. The college track coach reinforces these concerns by commenting on athletes' weight and by encouraging weight loss.

Behind her composed but tense demeanor, the client is very insecure about some of her capabilities. This is typified by her concern about her body and weight. She has an exact ideal weight which she believes will guarantee her the self-satisfaction and social approval she feels she presently lacks.

It is not until the sixth session that she reveals that she regularly binges and throws up afterward. She indicates that this behavior began during a period of intense dieting. While typically she binges and purges two or three times weekly, she initially comes to the health center because she is beginning to do so daily, sometimes even more than once a day. She also has begun to drink alcohol in the evenings and purge following that. She indicates that during her freshman year she tried dexedrine (a stimulant and appetite suppressant) for weight control. There was also a period during which she would take a laxative before going to sleep. She indicates that many of these behaviors were common among her dormmates, particularly those also involved in athletics.

She is aware that the binge-purge behavior is more frequent when she is more stressed; but the cycle can be set off by a simple self-observation of the shape of her hips and buttocks in the mirror, or an off-handed remark by a member of the track team, or the coach criticizing a fat woman or one of the athletes. This prompts her to eat less. In hunger, she then finds herself eating foods she has labelled as unacceptable. Like her rigidity about an ideal weight, her perception of foods is organized into rigid categories of forbidden and acceptable foods. Highly preferred foods are forbidden, but when she eats them there is a sensual comfort and a general sense of filling a psychological emptiness in the act. It is just about the only time when she feels relief from her unhappiness. There is also a sense of being out of control, which is scary to her. Sometimes she plans binges, and the foods and way they are eaten, follow a certain ritual. Following the binge she feels grotesquely fat and delinquent and induces vomiting.

When about to purge she seeks out basement bathrooms where she is unlikely to be disturbed. While initially she has to use her fingers to induce vomiting, she now can do it without physical aid. The vomiting is accompanied by mixed feelings. There is some sense of peace or balance with the reassurance that she will not gain weight. But she also is disgusted with herself and her esteem is further undermined as she realizes that the cycle has been played out once again. In the vomiting, she is both back in control, of her weight, and out of control, under the tyranny of the cycle.

Her sense of emotional isolation is enhanced by the ritual and she more and more identifies herself as a grotesque and alien person. Although she knows otherwise, it is as if she feels she is the only one doing this. The behavioral cycle produces a psychological cycle where her awareness of weight gain is hypersensitized and her vulnerability to weight related remarks and stress increases.

With the increased frequency of the cycle, she experiences a chronic sore throat. She is aware of the possibilities of damaging her teeth and of esophageal tearing.

Animal Models of Bulimia: Sham Feeding

In common with people who struggle with obesity, a bulimic individual often has considerable experience with dieting and, indeed, often begins bingeing during a period of the disorganization of eating behavior that accompanies dieting (Polivy & Herman, 1985). However, the bulimic individual has arrived at a unique solution to the weight/food relation. He or she guards against the feared problem of being overweight through a behavioral sequence that incorporates a form of overeating—bingeing followed by purging. Depending on how soon after eating it is induced, vomiting reduces calorie intake by about 50 percent. However, some purging methods do not prevent food absorption (e. g., when a period of sleep occurs between the binge and the purge). Several animal models of bulimia key on this "strategy," whether or not it is effective, of "eating without calories" (Hoebel, Hernandez, Schwartz, Mark, & Hunter, 1989, p. 176). One model manipulates the external environment through periods of diet restricted to nonnutritional foods, such as saccharine. At the other extreme, through central brain stimulation, the neural effect of eating without calories is modelled. Finally, at a middle level, eating without calories is effected by "sham feeding." This model of bulimic behavior has been extensively utilized as a way of exploring bulimia.

Sham feeding adapts a procedure already available in animal research literature. The procedure involves surgically producing a fistula, a tube-like passage from a normal cavity to the surface of the body. In later developments, a cannula or catheter is fitted into the fistula with a screw or cap so that the tube may be opened or closed. Some fistulae are gastric (stomach), while others are esophageal (the canal into the stomach). Fistulae are utilized in sham feeding in such a way that the animal eats or drinks without receiving nutritional benefits. Sham feeding has been used on various species, notably dogs, monkeys, rabbits, and rats. According to Davis and Campbell, the gastric fistula is preferable with rats because the esophageal surgery is difficult, the survival rate is low, and the animal loses unknown amounts of body fluids and salts from an esophageal fistula (1973, p. 380). However, Mook (1989, p. 271) argues that the esophageal fistula is still preferable with rats. In their study using dogs, Lawson, Schiffman, and Pappas (1993), use both procedures on the same individual animals.

In a typical sham feeding experiment a stainless steel tube (cannula) is sutured into the stomach of an anesthetized rat (Davis & Campbell, 1973, p. 380). After coming out of the muscle wall of the stomach, the tube emerges on the back of the animal, under the shoulder. This tube is connected to a needle that is cemented to a fiberglass screen which provides anchoring under the skin. The needle tube is connected to a plastic tube extending up through a hole in the ceiling of the animal's testing cage. This tube can be connected to a syringe to draw out ingested (or, less commonly, to introduce) foodstuffs.

Since the etiology of bulimia is unknown (Smith, 1989, p. 69), sham feeding was adapted to create a condition that mimics a major feature of the bulimic behavior. It reproduces bingeing-purging in the very limited sense that, like these, it can allow the ingestion of large quantities of food without nutrient absorption. It is "operationally" similar to self-induced vomiting (Van Vort, 1988, p. 802). Of course, it is not claimed that sham feeding is a model of the cause of bulimia. It is an isomorphic rather than an etiologic model (Smith, 1989, p. 64). However, the implicit claim is that through this behavioral model, the conditions that give rise to and sustain bulimia can be discovered.

Van Vort (1988) argues that this artificially constructed situation was needed as natural occurring examples of binge-like behavior are rare in animals, except in the context of hibernation or during pregnancy or lactation. Purge-like behavior is also rare. While animals of some species regurgitate to feed their young, those of other species (such as the rat, the most commonly used animals in this research), are not capable of vomiting. However, in one of the relatively rare attempts in the animal literature to find a "naturally" occurring or spontaneous model of a human disorder, Gould and Bres (1986) explored regurgitation and reingestion, a common behavior in captive gorillas.

In any case, Van Vort asserts that sham feeding allows the "most *dramatic* example of hyperphagia [overeating] in animals" (1988, p. 798, emphasis added). With ingested food draining from an open esophageal or gastric fistula, "animals sham feeding for the first time increase meal size 3–6 times" (p. 798). By minimizing contact of the food with the stomach, the model interferes with absorption, stomach distention and other satiating effects of eating. At the same time, it enhances the oral pleasure of food by isolating these sensory and psychological aspects from the post-ingestive features of eating. By use of this arrangement which roughly and most "dramatically" mimics the eating-without-calories strategy of bulimia, a host of other variables including dieting, deprivation, administration of recreational and pharmacological drugs, central brain stimulation and lesioning, can be and have been explored in the exhaustive and recursive way that is characteristic of the research enterprise.

With the satiation signals blocked, sham feeding results in animals eating more with shorter intervals between meals. More significantly, they continue this behavior for several days after the fistula has been closed. It is hypothesized that the satiating mechanism has been weakened ("conditioned desatiation") (Van Vort, 1988, p. 800). Bruch (1973), a clinician, first offered that a defect in satiation plays a role in the etiology of eating disorders. She inferred that abnormal early socialization in her clients had led to their misperceiving the visceral sensations of hunger and satiety (Smith, 1989, p. 67).

Through preventing normal satiation, sham feeding allows the peptides known to be released when food enters the gut to be studied. Injection of cholecystokinin (CCK) has been shown to reduce feeding in sham fed rats, raising the possibility that CCK deficiency is a causal model of bulimia (Gibbs, Young, & Smith, 1973). Nemeroff, Osbahr, Bissette, Jahnke, Lipton and Prange (1978) suggest that CCK may be useful in the treatment of disorders characterized by overeating; while Smith and Gibbs (1988) conclude that there is, at present, no evidence for the therapeutic use of CCK.

However, as CCK inhibits feeding by signalling satiation, it is not surprising that it has been studied in anorexia nervosa. The converse of its promise as an anorectic agent (intake reducer) in the treatment of bulimia is the possibility that in anorexics it may be implicated as a factor in their self-imposed starvation. Moran and McHugh (1982) demonstrated that gastric emptying is delayed by injection of CCK in monkeys. CCK's role in the inhibition of gastric emptying makes it a model of anorexia, while it is a putative treatment of bulimia.

While sham feeding blocks the satiating effects of eating, it enhances the consummatory and oral factors. It is known that the typical bulimic binges on foods high in carbohydrates (particularly sugar), fat and salt (Neuman & Halvorson, 1983). This has spurred interest in the exploration of palatability (tastiness) and its possible role in overeating. For example, studies of intact rats have shown that high carbohydrate, high fat, and mixed diets containing various sugar- and fat-rich foods (the "cafeteria" or "supermarket" diet) all induce overeating and obesity (Scalafani, 1989, p. 281).

Sham feeding allows these findings to be studied independently of post-ingestive effects such as satiation, nutrient absorption, and sensory experience associated with the stomach. However, the versatility of sham feeding is such that the converse is also possible. The impact of the nutrient value of a certain diet on consummatory and oral experience can be studied. Scalafani (1989, p. 283) described "an 'electronic esophagus' preparation." "In this preparation, rats are fitted with chronic intragastric catheters, and as they eat or drink normally by mouth a nutrient is automatically infused into their stomach" (p. 283). In a variation of this, dogs who had been "prepared" with both esophageal and gastric fistulas, deprived of oral stimulation, and receiving nutrition only through the gastric fistula later ate more in a sham feed procedure than did those not so deprived. They concluded that deprivation of oral stimulation causes binge eating in this animals Lawson, Schiffman, and Pappas (1993).

While Scalafani demonstrated that the post-ingestive effects of nutrients influence food preference in rats, Schneider, Van Vort and others typically use the sham feeding operation to mimic eating without calories and to answer the question: why do monkeys and rats continue to sham feed and, indeed, increase the rate and amount of food ingested, if they are obtaining no calories? Van Vort and Smith (1981) found that rats develop as great a preference for the same food (sweet milk) eaten under sham as compared to real meal conditions. Further, a flavored milk diet in a sham feeding condition leads to eating even after satiation from a real meal (Van Vort, 1988, p. 800). Also, at high concentrations of sucrose, CCK (a satiety signaller), was less effective in reducing volume of sucrose ingested. These findings imply that oral stimulation can overcome the satiation effect. (On the other hand, prolonged experience with sham feeding does have a negatively reinforcing effect [Van Vort, 1988, p. 800]). Schneider also has demonstrated the "relative orosensory/hedonic potency of food" as a determinant of overeating (1989, p. 316).

In his review of animal models of bulimia, Smith concluded that "the major positive reinforcing effect of food occurs in the mouth of the rat.... [This] raises the possibility that the positive feedback effect on eating produced by orosensory stimuli in bulimic patients is exaggerated either innately or, more likely, by previous bulimic experience" (1989, p. 69). On the face of it, this is not a very informative answer to the question of why animals eat without calories and why bulimics are bulimic: nonhuman animals eat without calories because the food tastes good, and bulimics by nature or nurture have a particularly sweet tooth.

However, Schneider and others have inquired further into the physiological mechanisms that sustain nonnutritional eating. It had earlier been shown that dopamine, a neurotransmitter in the brain, was implicated in the orosensory reward of sweet solutions in intact rats. Dopamine systems are known to play a major role as a physiological substrate of behaviors that are rewarding or pleasurable. Smith, Bourbonais, Jerome, and Simansky (1987) found increased dopamine activity during sham feeding of sucrose. Dopamine antagonists such as halperidol and pimozide (both anti-psychotic tranquilizers), have the opposite effect, confirming its role. This suggests that dopamine may be involved in the rewarding power of bingeing in bulimics and, of course, that drugs that block dopamine receptors may be a treatment of bulimia. However, the antipsychotic drugs are ineffective in the treatment of eating disorders (Walsh, 1992, p. 329).

Schneider, Davis, and others have also explored the microstructure of eating behavior and its physiology. Following Wiepkema, Davis (1989) utilized measures of ingestive behavior in rats that advance beyond simple measures of rate of ingestion. "Bout analysis" is a complex of measures of "bursts," a series of 6–7 licks per second. Bouts or bursts in turn occur in clusters. Bout analysis includes measures such as number of licks in a given period and amount of time between licks (inter-lick interval). In a typical experiment, Davis varies the concentration of sugar (palatability) in sham-versus-real fed rats and measures the effects on cluster size. While under real feeding conditions average intercluster interval increases with the concentration of maltose (sugar), in sham feeding this interval is shorter than in real feeding (p. 111). Again, this supports the controlling power of sensory features in eating without calories.

Grill and others carry the analysis further by describing taste-reactivity responses in rats. Following tasting, ingestive responses such as mouth movements, tongue protrusion, and lateral tongue protrusion can be distinguished, as can various aversive responses or behaviors through which a food is rejected including gaping or opening the mouth, chin rub, head shake, and forelimb flail (Flynn & Grill, 1988, p. 936).

Grill, Norgren and others employ a rat "preparation" that can include any or all of the following: intra-gastric cannula to effect sham feeding; intraoral cannula with external leads issuing out of an acrylic headcap and extending into the ceiling of the chamber to allow direct infusion of controlled amounts and concentrations of liquids into the mouth; implants of wire electrodes into various muscles involved in ingestion to record muscle contractions (EMG); and lesions at various levels, such as the caudal brainstem, to locate the neural levels controlling gustatory behavior (decerebrate rat).

Norgren, Nishijo, and Travers (1989) developed a "preparation for chronic recording" that combines the intraoral cannula and EMG procedures with an immobilizing (stereotaxic) apparatus. This allows the recording of individual stimulated neurons in the gustatory cortex in unanesthetized animals. They describe the technology as "permit[ting] near-natural ingestion while providing some stimulus control" (p. 254). Through this technology, these investigators have followed "the gustatory system, synapse by synapse, into the CNS [central nervous system] and use[d] it to probe neural mechanisms..." (p. 246). For other purposes, to measure metabolic rates,

Nicolaidis and Even (1989) developed technology that allows such assessment instantaneously in "freely moving animals" (p. 101). I provide, below, an analysis of the use of technology in animal model research and discuss the aptness of terms like "near-natural ingestion" and "freely moving animals."

As mentioned, there are several families of "eating without calories" animal models of bulimia including feeding of nonnutritional foods, sham feeding, and central brain stimulation. In each of these the rewarding features of orosensory feeding is enhanced while the post-ingestive results of eating are restricted. Schneider describes the reward inherent in intracranial electrical self-stimulation as "less natural" than the ingestion of foods such as saccharine (1989, p. 307).

Hoebel, Hernandez, Schwartz, Mark, and Hunter (1989) developed a technique, the "microdialysis cage," which allows the exploration of intracranial self-stimulation (as well as experimenter-controlled stimulation) as a model of bulimia. "Dialysis" here is a general term for the passage of any solution through a membrane. The apparatus involves implanting in the brain a "guide shaft" into which is inserted a microdialysis probe. Through it, solutions of interest can be assayed while the animal moves about in a standard Skinner box (a cage outfitted to allow and measure the learning of different behavioral responses [operants]). In this way, different parts of the brain and associated neurotransmitters, as well as introduced agonists and antagonists can be assessed as to their role in either the rewarding or the aversive value of eating.

Animal Models of Bulimia: Stress-Induced Eating

We have been reviewing models that mimic the bulimic solution of eating without calories, of eliminating weight gain while promoting oral pleasure. To further indicate the range of models of bulimia, I consider another family of models that builds on a different feature of bulimia.

It is well known from clinical experience that bulimics often report that their binge-purge behavior is preceded by situations they perceive as stressful. Blass, Shide, and Weller (1989) note that both bulimia and anorexia "... reflect developmental and familial tensions, particularly as they surround a meal" (p. 303). Stress-induced overeating is also a common observation made in clinical and research settings (Lytle, 1977). Of course, stress is a precursor to and maintainer of many, if not most, pathological adjustments. It is no surprise, then, that several models of bulimia attempt to exploit the relation between stress and this particular eating disorder. Unlike the sham feeding model, in this group of models there is a direct attempt to get at the cause of bulimia, to ascertain whether and how bulimia arises and/or is maintained as a disordered way of dealing with stress.

As was the case with sham feeding, the models here originate in other areas of research and are tried out as putative models of bulimia. Psychologists have developed and utilized many ways of inducing stress in non-human animals. As mentioned in the discussion of models of obesity, environmental variables that manipulate stress include tail-pinching, immobilization, and isolation. Each of these also has been explored in relation to bulimia and/or anorexia.

In addition, investigators have explored the relation of other stressors to normal and abnormal eating behavior. For example, in their study of hyperphagia, Vaswani, Tejwani, and Mousa (1983) induced "acute mild stress" through deprivation of food and water for 12 to 48 hours and "acute severe stress" through 12 hour food and water deprivation followed by a 10 minute swim in water at 4°C. (p. 1983). They found that both mild and severe stress induce overeating, but that only severe stress induces preferential overeating. Severely stressed rats overeat sugars and fats. As already noted, bulimics tend to binge on foods high in sugar and fat.

Using food deprivation as a high stress inducer, other investigators found that starvation-associated stress induces eating (Vaswani et al., p. 1993). Hagan and Moss (1991) found that rats subjected to a history of three separate episodes of food deprivation (reduction to 75–80 % normal weight through restricted feeding schedules) in the first five months of life later showed an increase in eating when tested at normal weight and when not food deprived. They offered this history of "fasting episodes" as a causal model specifically of bulimia.

Coscina and Dixon (1983) confirmed the findings of earlier investigators demonstrating that severe food deprivation in rats (four days) increases the efficiency of food utilization (metabolism). However, they also found that following weight gain to predeprivation levels, deprived rats gained more weight than nondeprived rats and did so through excessive intake of a sweet milk solution. They concluded that periodic loss and regaining of body weight produces more efficient food utilization and pressure to gain even more weight. They propose that such a deprivation history may reinforce fears of weight gain and be a factor in the occurrence of episodes of the binge-purge behavior often found in anorexia.

Some stressors have the opposite effect, that is to reduce rather than increase the amount of food eaten (hypophagia). Of course, these are explored in relation to the primary symptom of anorexia or severe weight loss. Perhach and Barry (1970) found that immobilization stress is hypophagic. Haslam, Stevens, and Donohoe (1987) found some indication that immobilization also reduces body weight. Further, they found that a serotonin antagonist reverses the effect of immobilization, providing support for the involvement of this brain neurotransmitter in hypophagia and specifically in anorexia. Another example of a stressor that reduces eating is exposure to an activity wheel when food availability is limited in time. I return to the "activity-stress" model of anorexia (Pierce & Epling, 1991) below.

A number of investigators have explored stress induced by tail-pinching as a model of disordered eating (Antelman & Szechtman, 1975; Rowland & Antelman, 1976; Morely, Levine, Murray, Kneip, & Grace, 1982; Bertiere, Mame Sy, Baigts, Mandenoff, & Apfelbaum, 1984). In her review of the literature on tail-pinching, Montgomery (1991) concluded that it is best regarded as a model of bulimia rather than obesity (p. 189).

However, in their study which first identified a "syndrome of eating, gnawing and licking behavior" induced by tail-pinching in rats, Antelman, Szechtman, Chin, and Fisher (1975) suggested that the procedure provided a model for schizophrenia, a family of disorders involving gross deterioration in intellectual and interpersonal functioning. The stereotypical behavior of the "syndrome" is similar to that found in an already existing model of schizophrenia. Further, certain drugs that are effective in the treatment of schizophrenia (e. g., haloperidol) significantly reduced tail-pinch-engendered behavior. In any case, Antelman and Szechtman (1975) announced that "the tail-pinch paradigm provides a new, unusually powerful, and especially simple tool for investigating the neural organization of behavior" (p. 733).

The tail-pinch paradigm involves application of mild pressure to the tail of a rat, employing a ten inch surgical hemostat (a clamp-like instrument used in surgery to stop bleeding) insulated with foam rubber. The hemostat is applied one inch from the tip of the rat's tail in some studies for five 20 second periods, in others for a two minute period. The procedure is considered only moderately stressful, although some rats, in addition to gnawing, eating and drinking, are observed to vocalize, move from pellet to pellet or shred food—indications of greater stress (Antelman & Szechtman, 1975, p. 731). Further, in studies requiring injections of substances into the brain, rats undergo implantation of chronic intracerebral cannulas prior to the tail-pinching procedure.

Antelman and Szechtman (1975) and Morely et al. (1982) found that tail-pinching induces eating in already satiated rats, and results in both overeating and obesity (Rowland & Antelman, 1976). Bertiere et al. (1984) found that tail-pinching results in preferential hyperphagia of sucrose sweetened skim milk. Sahakian and Robbins (1977) showed that one stressor (rearing rats in isolation) enhanced the effects of a second stressor (tail-pinch induced eating behavior). Investigators have also explored the neurophysiological pathways associated with tail-pinching (Robbins & Fray, 1980). Montgomery suggested that there are similarities between behavioral and physiological aspects of tail-pinch induced stress and feeding induced either by deprivation or by electrical stimulation of certain parts of the hypothalamus (1989, pp. 188–9).

Research has also tested the effectiveness of various drugs in offsetting the effects of the tail-pinch stressor. Robbins, Phillips, and Sahakian (1977) explored the effect of the benzodiazepines, tranquilizers used in the treatment of stress and anxiety. They and others have found that these tranquilizers actually stimulate eating. Paradoxically, benzodiazepine enhances the effectiveness of tail-pinching as a stressor that induces overeating. One further complexity is that stress reduction is a common consequence of eating. In their study of ingestion and stress reduction, Blass, Shide, and Weller (1989) found that ingestion of milk reduces the stress of rat pups. In any case, the use of tranquilizers have been found to be ineffective and is not part of the current treatment of bulimia (Walsh, 1992).

Another feature of psychological stressors that has led to a great deal of research is their association with the release of endogenous opiates. Opioids or opiates are naturally occurring neurotransmitters that carry messages within the nervous system relating to pain and stress. They are activated by various stressors, both those directly causing pain and those involving social stress (e. g., isolation). They create decreased sensitivity to pain and stress (analgesia). In addition to this desensitizing role, opioids directly mediate appetite and food intake. The opioids are related to highly addictive substances like morphine (opioid agonists). In recent years, much research has been undertaken to explore the role of the endogenous opioids in addiction, affective disorders such as depression, anxiety disorders, and other disorders.

Tail-pinching induces eating by causing the release of endogenous opiates (Morley & Levine, 1980), as do other stressors generally and food-related stressors in particular (e. g., food deprivation). However, the relations between stress, eating, and the opioids are complex—in part due to the fact that the opioids are also "regulators of feeding" (Levine & Billington, 1989). Here is a sampling of findings from several investigators (Fullerton, Getto, Swift, & Carlson, 1985; Montgomery, 1989; Levine & Billington, 1989; Blass et al, 1989):

- Opioid agonists increase short-term feeding and preference for certain foods such as sweet solutions
- Sugar ingestion increases opioid levels
- Opioid injection into parts of the hypothalamus increases eating in already satiated rats
- Genetically obese rats and mice have high opioid levels in the pituitary system (an endocrine system)
- Opioid antagonists (naloxone) decrease feeding in numerous species (chicks, cockroaches, mice, monkeys, sheep, rabbits, tigers, wolves, deer...)
- Opioid antagonists decrease a preference for sweets
- Opioid antagonists decrease feeding and a preference for sweets after various stressors—tail-pinch, food deprivation, electrical brain stimulation, isolation....

Clearly, eating behavior, including food preference, is intimately related to stress. As protection against stress through its analgesic effects and as a regulator of feeding generally, the endogenous opioids are implicated as a mediator between stress and eating. Stress induces eating and eating reduces stress—both mediated by the opioids. These relations are known to obtain in normal humans and most rats (Marrazzi et al, 1990, p. 1427).

Unfortunately, contradictory findings of research with mice and a certain breed of rats puts in question the generality of some of the findings cited above. In this species and this breed, the effects of administration of an opioid agonist (morphine) has the opposite effect, that is to decrease rather than increase eating (Marrazzi et al., 1990, p. 1427). Further, confirming this inconsistency with the literature on other species, the opioid antagonist (naloxone) has the effect of causing *overeating* in both obese and lean mice (McLaughlin & Baile, 1984). However, as we will see immediately below, at least one team of investigators exploited these findings inconsistent with a positive relation between stress and overeating in bulimics and obese individuals by suggesting that they provide a model for anorexia. For if bulimics respond to stress by overeating, perhaps anorexics respond to it by undereating. Marrazzi et al. (1990) suggest that the "atypical endogenous opioid systems in mice" are a model of a biological predisposition presumed operative in anorexics.

The addictive feature of the opioids plays a role in these relations among stress, eating, and the opioids. Through opioid mediation, stress-induced eating shows features of addiction, specifically, withdrawal and tolerance. Rats subjected to stress-induced eating multiple times each day over a period of ten days exhibit withdrawal symptoms similar to those seen after opiate addiction (Morley & Levine, 1980). Davidson, McKenzie, Tuju, and Bish (1992) found that the analgesic effect of deprivation-induced stress decreases over time, indicating the development of tolerance. These findings have led to addiction models of both bulimia and anorexia. It is suggested that an "auto-addiction" mechanism operates in which an individual is addicted to his or her own opioids, triggered by food deprivation and maintained by that and other stressors.

The stress of dieting (deprivation) results in a drive to overeat, a preference for sweet foods, and induced analgesia, all mediated by opioids. According to Marrazzi, Britton, Stack, Powers, Lawhorn, Graham, Eccles, and Gunter (1990), the "high" associated with the drive to eat is a model of bulimia and the bingeing often found in anorexia. As tolerance increases, more overeating is required to obtain the same high. On the other hand, the investigators offer the "high," associated with the dieting itself and the body's subsequent shift into lower gear to conserve energy, as a model of anorexia (p. 1428). Again, the tolerance feature increases the level of self-starvation necessary to get the same psychological effect.

Despite the suggestion in both animal and human research of the treatment potential of opioid antagonists, investigators and clinicians have concluded that they are not effective in the treatment either of bulimia or obesity. In his recent review of current pharmacological treatments of the eating disorders, Walsh (1992) refers to this literature only briefly and in passing and lumps the opioid antagonist with other drugs for which the data is "negative or inconclusive" (p. 334).

While Jonas and Gold (1988) found that a high dose of an opioid antagonist drug (naltrexone, related to naloxone) reduced bingeing and purging in bulimic humans, in subsequent double-blind studies employing high doses of naltrexone no effects were found. In their review of the role of opioids in eating, Levine and Billington (1989), concluded that the opioids "are not very important regulators of food intake" and that opioid blockade is not an effective form of treatment of eating disorders (p. 214). They argued that the effects of opioid antagonists, particularly naloxone, are not specific to the opioid system and that a mechanism different from blocking opioids is involved. They also suggested that most of the effects of opioids on feeding are short-term and, hence, that the strategy of opioid blockade is not effective for long-term treatment of eating disorders.

Montgomery's conclusion (1989) that the opioid antagonists "hold out little hope" in the treatment of obesity also supports this finding. He cited the ineffectiveness of chronic treatment with naloxone in obese humans, as well as its failure to reduce eating in Zucker rats, and its paradoxical effect of actually producing overeating in mice (p. 192).

An Animal Model of Anorexia Nervosa: Activity-Stress

Before more fully evaluating the animal models of eating disorders selectively surveyed here, I will describe one more model that explores the role of stress, this one specifically of anorexia. The activity-stress model of anorexia differs from the sham feeding and tail-pinch models of bulimia in that it is a more recent development. While the bulimia models allow a clearer evaluation of the effect of animal models on the relevant clinical literature and on treatment applications, a presently evolving model permits comparison between earlier and more recent treatment of animals in psychological research.

In this procedure, rats are housed in an activity wheel cage. They are limited to feeding during one period, varying in different studies from 1 to 4 hours. During the rest of the time they are given free access to the activity wheel.

A brief historical account (Watanabe, Hara & Ogawa, 1992; Lambert, 1993) provides insight into the development of the model. In a footnote to their 1954 study, in which an increase in activity level in rats deprived of food for 23 hours per day was found, Hall and Hanford described that 30 % of their sample exhibited extremely high levels of running, and died. In a methodological note published in 1962, Spear described excessive running in rats housed in an activity wheel, resulting in death in some animals. In 1968, Routtenberg termed this phenomenon associated with rats living in an activity wheel "self-starvation." In 1973, Pare and Houser found that self-starvation was associated with extensive lesions in the stomach. Subsequently, in 1978, Manning, Wall, Montgomery, Simmons, and Sessions offered the activity-stress paradigm as a model for human peptide ulcer. In the mid-80's, Katz reported two case studies of anorexic human males who had a history of high running levels (50–90 miles per week). He proposed that excessive activity could trigger and sustain anorexia nervosa.

It was only at this juncture that Lambert (1993), Watanabe et al. (1992), Pierce and Epling (1991), and others offered the activity-stress paradigm as a model of anorexia nervosa. Watanabe et al. refined the procedure by increasing the period of food availability from 1 or 2 to 3 or 4 hours. Under this feeding condition, female rats did not get ulcers. However, they did greatly increase the amount of running and weight loss, and their estrous cycles ceased (amenorrhea). Weight loss is an essential feature of anorexia; amenorrhea is a common feature; excessive exercise is one means of creating weight loss, reported in 38–75 % of anorexics (Yates, 1989, p. 822). Pierce and Epling cite research in support of their claim that hyperactivity is a central and, in fact, determinative feature of anorexia (1991, p. 299).

In the activity-stress model, the feeding schedule in itself does not deprive the animals of sufficient food. Rats adjust to being fed once per day. Rather, food consumption decreases as "voluntary" exercise increases (up to 6 miles a day in rats). Self-starvation is defined as reduction to 70 % of free-feeding body weight. It is interesting to note that while earlier studies include starvation to death, Pierce and Epling (1991) report that "... for ethical reasons, the[ir] experiment was stopped when they reached 70 % of baseline weight" (p. 271). They also report that younger animals are more prone to the activity-stress effect, and that there is some evidence that females are more susceptible. As indicated earlier, the disorder in humans has a typical onset of age 17 and 90 % of cases occur in females (American Psychiatric Association, 1994, p. 543). This is one of the rare instances in the animal model literature on eating disorders that the sex of the animals studied is taken into account.

Pierce and Epling offer an evolutionary account of how strenuous activity became associated with appetite suppression. Some species obtain a survival advantage through increased activity during times of food scarcity, while others adapt by energy conservation during such times. Monkeys in a free-ranging colony have been observed to dramatically increase food-directed physical activity during a severe food shortage. The authors suggest that "... wheel running is displaced food-seeking behavior" (p. 287). Of course, in terms of their own motivation, those human anorexics who exercise excessively are not consciously doing so to look for food.

Pierce and Epling (1991) also offer a physiological explanation of how strenuous activity grossly suppresses eating. Drawing on the opioid research already reviewed, they suggest that opioids mediate between physical activity and decreased food intake (p. 291). They also refer to research on the "runner's high," arguing, following Marrazzi, that anorexia results from an addiction to the opioids. As we have seen, these relations are complex and apparently inconsistent, as stress also is associated with increased opioid levels and increased food intake. In any case, Pierce and Epling offer a relatively cohesive account of the etiology of anorexia. In it, hyperactivity is a critical determinant of self-starvation, while the various psychological symptoms, such as preoccupation with food and distortion of body image, are secondary consequences.

In a critique of animal models of anorexia, Mrosovsky (1984) argues that there are insufficient data to assert that hyperactivity precedes weight loss and psychological symptoms in the onset of anorexic symptoms (p. 26). She also suggests that the term "self-starvation" is "silly" as the experimenter imposes the feeding regimen on the rats, and, against Pierce and Epling, suggests that these animals have difficulty coping with such restricted schedules. Finally, Mrosovsky believes that the relation between exercise and eating is not firmly established, and that anorexics may in fact feel safer in eating more following exercise than following inactivity (p. 31).

2. EVALUATION

Before providing an evaluative analysis of these animal models, it is helpful to reset the discussion, following this extended and technical foray into selected models of eating disorders.

From many animal researchers' viewpoints, the contribution of their work to the understanding and treatment of human psychology and pathology is significant, even foundational. As we will see, they and their professional associations generally make strong claims about the benefits of animal research. To these scientists, the enterprise of animal research is an important component of scientific psychological inquiry. They identify with and are genuinely committed to what they characterize as the systematic, exhaustive, open-ended, and ingenious intellectual enterprise of animal-based research. Psychologists pride themselves in being able to study and measure anything and everything. In the view of some, it is animal research that enables them to do just that.

On the other hand, from many animal protectionists' viewpoints, the enterprise is unacceptable on ethical grounds, independent of any claims of benefits. Further, it is easy to be dismissive about it on scientific grounds, for it can so readily be caricatured. What could be more far-fetched than studying the peculiar and apparently cultur-ally driven psychology and behavior of bulimia by observ-ing the eating behavior of a rat whose stomach has had a hole cut into it, or attempting to understand the dense and warped body image that apparently sustains anorexia by arranging for a rat to run to death on an exercise wheel?

In the following analysis, I take the enterprise of animal research seriously. For the moment, I suspend dismissal on ethical grounds. I also try to avoid the application of what I consider specious arguments against it. For exam-ple, it is facile to generalize about the enterprise from any one study, or to evaluate one study independent of the context of relevant studies within which it occurs. Also, not everyone would agree on the validity of faulting a study or even a set of studies for simply being limited to any one level of analysis or discourse—for example, for focusing on a individual behavioral level and not address-ing family systems. Finally, it is unfair to criticize any recent study or even set of studies for not yet resulting in beneficial treatment applications.

The immediate question before us, then, is: What is the contribution of animal-based, and, specifically, animal model, research to the larger research enterprise and to the treatment and general understanding of eating disorders?

Ultimately, this evaluation must rest on a philosophical position regarding the value of nonhuman animals. I re-view contemporary ethical positions as they relate to psy-chological research in the next chapter. However, in the other direction, any ethical position must be grounded in the real world, that is in some set of empirical facts. Here I provide data and an evaluation based on those data that are more or less independent of any philosophical commitment. I provide assessments of whether and how the results of animal model research are utilized in other scientific literature and in applied treatment settings, and of whether and to what degree the animals involved suffered. Building on the two prior chapters, we first assess the limits and biases involved in the reliance on experimentalism as defined in laboratory research psychology and on the laboratory animal as socially constructed. Then, we explicate the concept of model implicit in the research surveyed. While animal-based research is only a limited part of the total research enterprise, it may or may not have an impact on it. Its own limits and biases may steer the larger research enterprise and perhaps even shape applied clinical practice.

Two biases are inherent in undertaking this task. I have already declared my points of view as a clinical psychologist and animal advocate. More subtly, I in turn am subjected to any biases present in reviews of the published literature. Indeed, several studies offer evidence that such a bias is substantial. In a study of an earlier research literature, Lederer (1992) found that the editor of the *Journal of Experimental Medicine* during the period 1921–46 adopted the editorial policy of "...altering the presentation, description and illustration of laboratory procedures and results involving animal subjects in efforts explicitly undertaken to placate critics of animal experimentation " (p. 61). For example, "[t]he substitution of objective medical descriptions [for more graphic descriptions of suffering] was intended to convey the idea of minimal animal suffering in the course of laboratory experimentation" (p. 70).

In a study of more recently published research, Birke and Smith (1995) examined 152 articles in eight biomedical journals for the rhetorical strategies employed in the presentation of animal research. They found linguistic devices were used to obscure and minimize death and obscure the experience that living animals undergo, in favor of descriptions of apparati and measures. Any conclusions regarding the procedures undergone by animal subjects are hampered by this rhetorical laundering.

In his study of "animal images" in introductory psychology texts, Field (1993) found a comparable minimizing and obscuring mode of presentation. He concludes his analysis of the treatment of the work of Harlow in 24 popular introductory texts, as follows:

> The graphic and textual material seem to present a sanitized, bland, or comical interpretation of this research. The limited presentation of stressful or confining procedures, the cute photos of baby monkeys, the glowing assessment of the value of the research, and the objective treatment of the results combine to minimize the severity of the procedures used... (p. 200).

As discussed in Chapter 2, these biases in the ways research is presented linguistically, which distance the reader from the actual experience of the animal and focus on technical instrumentation, are part of the ideology of laboratory animal psychology. I should mention in passing here that one study of literature in the animal rights movement has noted a converse finding. In their analysis of the rhetoric employed in the direct mail appeals of three national animal rights organizations, Mechling and Mechling (1991) found a linkage between animal research and death, torture, and cruelty.

The Laboratory-Based Animal Model Strategy: Limits and Biases

The preceding survey of particular animal models of eating disorders suggests several issues and aspects for discussion, some of which were not yet evident from the abstract analysis of models in the last chapter.

Where do models come from? How do psychologists create them, or where do they discover them? The tail-pinch model existed as a procedure to induce stress before it was used to study eating disorders per se. The hypothesis that stress might be an important determinant of eating disorders derived from the clinical literature on eating disorders and from the general theoretical literature on psychopathology. Earlier, it was also suggested as a model of schizophrenia. The observation that stress in animals induced changes in eating behavior antedated the selection of tail-pinching as a model of bulimia.

Sham feeding also was in the animal literature before its selection as a model of bulimia. It was the "standard approach" to "the study of digestive physiology in ruminant animals" as early as the late 19th century (Webster, 1994, p. 239). An account of a study of a gastric fistula of traumatic origin in a human clinical setting was published in 1943 (Wolff).

Hall and Hanford (1954) were studying the effects of food deprivation on activity level as measured in an exercise wheel when they serendipitously (and, given later use, ironically), observed an effect in the opposite direction—increased levels of exercise decreased food intake to the point of starvation. Still, the use of the exercise wheel as a model of anorexia was delayed while it was exploited as a model of ulcers, following the discovery that excessive exercise was a stressor that induced gastric ulceration. Eventually, Watanabe et al. (1988) induced anorexic features in food-restricted rats using the exercise wheel, without ulcer production.

It would appear that animal models typically are not constructed *de novo* as direct efforts to represent the phenomenon of interest. While unquestionably the products of a kind of creative insight, they do not juxtapose two apparently disparate phenomena, as does the poetic metaphor. The process is more prosaic and, fittingly, experimental. It is also more "in-house," as borrowings from and refinements of already existing procedures in the animal lab are tried out. Parenthetically, as already noted, an apparent exception to this is Harlow's borrowing of a metaphor from the clinical literature to arrive at the "intuition" that chambering would induce depression in primates.

In addition to being jury-rigged from existing procedures in the animal literature, rather than directly built or based on an original analogy to the phenomenon of interest, another characteristic of these models is that they often purport to mimic only one or two features of the original. At least in their inception, it is enough that, for example, sham feeding, as a putative model of bulimia, mimics only a single feature of binge-purge eating—eating without calories. There is little concern with capturing, through the model, the full-blown entity as it appears in the context of individual human history, family dynamics, and social customs. Tail-pinching and the exercise wheel mimic relations between stress and eating. The former is a convenient and established laboratory routine for inducing stress. No further claim is made regarding its similarity to the familial and/or culturally induced stress that actually occasion the bulimic's preoccupation with body size and shape. As a form of stress, the exercise wheel does mimic the anorexic's penchant, at least in some cases, to excessive exercise. These modelled features may or may not mimic causality. Sham feeding is an isomorphic rather than a causal model; no one claims that bulimia is caused by a hole in the stomach.

These two characteristics, the limited number or extent of features modelled, and the symptomatic rather than causal mimicry, are in contrast to the examples of earlier biomedical models, discussed in Chapter 3, which were conceptually the precursors of contemporary models of psychological disorders. Animal models of tuberculosis (TB) purported to house this disease or syndrome in its entirety, with its various symptoms and complex course. The germ was the cause of TB and its development mimicked that phenomenon as a whole. This historical precursor gave rise to the contemporary claim that a model mimics "in all respects" the phenomenon of interest.

Further, the one or two selected features modelled are coarse rather than subtle or nuanced. As discussed, animal model researchers generally conceive and operationalize eating disorders in terms that imitate various gross aspects of food intake. Accordingly, they build models that center on food intake arrangements, such as sham feeding, or on general conditions hypothesized to determine food intake, such as nonspecific stressors like tail-pinching. This gross or simplistic basis of model construction is vulnerable to legitimate criticism, and again, it lends itself also to caricature. As noted in Chapter 3, in the discussion of concepts of animal models employed in psychology, the initial choices of models here are not based on a "deeper structure of thought" (Midgley, 1981, p. 332) through which "likeness and unlikeness" are examined rigorously.

I have noted that animal studies of eating disorders rely on a simple algorithm as the basis of the construction of models (bulimia and obesity = excessive intake; anorexia = inadequate intake). This reliance is understandable in terms of the experimentalist ideology that rationalizes animal-based laboratory research. The concept of intake is readily operationalized, embodied in a laboratory procedure that is directly observable, quantifiable, and repeatable. The relation between the operationalized feature and the original of which it is a model is that of a rough and partial metaphor. We are far from the concept of a model which globally presents, in the setting of another organism, all aspects of the original, as in the classic animal models of germ implantation of infectious diseases. We are also far from the idea of a model as a small-scale version of the original, as obtains in the testing of a airplane or rocket in a wind-tunnel.

In constructing their models, psychologists give observability and measurability priority over similarity with or faithfulness to the target phenomenon. These criticisms are not necessarily negative as, in the final analysis, any

model must be judged in terms of its usefulness in furthering understanding of the phenomenon of interest and in
its ability to issue in its effective treatment (again, ethical
considerations being temporarily suspended). However,
it is striking that these models are built on such rough and
limited analogies to the target phenomenon.

Having constructed this analogy built on or borrowed
from extant laboratory procedures, how does the investigator proceed: how does he or she use the model? By far
the most frequent use of the model is to test other relevant
variables. Ideally, such empirical relations within the animal literature would then be compared to the phenomenon of interest and used to confirm the model. Only at this
point is the investigator in a position to cash in on the
alleged benefits of the animal model strategy—he or she
uses the model to generate and then test as yet undiscovered relations within the phenomenon of interest and thus
increase our understanding of it.

In practice, the testing of other relevant variables remains the predominant way in which a given model is
used. Obtained relations already gained in the clinical
setting that are consistent with understanding the disorder are taken as confirming, those at variance as discon-
firming. The discovery and exploration of relations as yet
undiscovered but found in the model are relatively un-
common. Formal testing of such new features of the original in the original are rare. In this way, model construction typically stays in a very early stage of development.
Advances are largely limited to discovering its consistency with other variables and models in the animal literature.

As we have described, the logic of experimentation results in a recursive and self-feeding enterprise. A "new"
model, based on a serendipitous observation or borrowed
from another area of research, produces "new" variables
the relations of which are then explored with other variables from other models. A model that operationalizes eat-

ing without calories is compared to other manipulations that operationalize that same condition (sham feeding is compared to brain stimulation). Or a model of stress-induced bulimia is compared to other models that induce stress (tail-pinching is compared to immobilization or food deprivation or isolation).

From one point of view this is a traditional strength of science, the provision of systematic and exhaustive exploration of all possibilities. From another point of view, echoing Midgley, in practice it often is a surprisingly thoughtless enterprise in which investigators undertake explorations that are not based on careful and incisive analysis of the phenomenon of interest and really have little rationale beyond convenience and availability.

As I argued in Chapter 3, part of the proper function of a model is that it help the investigator to think about and to creatively imagine the object phenomenon. This review of animal models of eating disorders suggests that they function oppositely. Investigators often latch onto a model that is only coarsely and in a limited way analogous to the object of study, and then proceed in a purely empirical way, trying out variables already available in the animal research literature. Rather than providing an object of careful and deliberate reflection through which the investigator is enabled to see the original in a different light, these models provide a more or less arbitrary starting point that ultimately leads away from further thoughtful scrutiny of the object of study. Rather than providing a productive thinking device, in practice, the use of these models truncates thought.

Further, instead of a genuine interaction between an evolving model and the phenomenon as it appears in both its general cultural and clinical settings, the research enterprise is in-grown in this additional sense, as different laboratory-grown models and variables are played off against each other merely to fill out the table of all possible comparisons. The move back to any purported fresh understanding of the phenomenon of interest remains a continually receding goal.

This recursive, omnivorous feature of the enterprise leaves it vulnerable to faddism, as any new promising variable or relation is quickly exploited for its relevance to the investigator's own immediate area of interest. When highly invasive research is involved, the wastefulness and inefficiency of this "explore all possibilities" tactic and certainly of this "grab at the hot topics" inclination clearly raises an ethical question.

Bias toward Physiological Explanation and Analysis

The survey of models of eating disorders confirms another general characteristic of the animal model strategy, though one not limited to it—the bias toward studying disorders at the level of their physiology. As I noted in the description of the ideology of experimentalism, the construction of the laboratory embodies the value of manipulating one or two variables at a time while controlling others. It emphasizes objectifying the phenomenon through distancing oneself from it in both a physical and personal sense. Controlled manipulation and objectification usually involve "reducing" the phenomena to that which is observable and measurable or quantifiable. Given their relative uncontrollability, indeterminateness, and irreproducibility, in practice, this reduction entails a deemphasis of social (cultural and familial), symbolic, and psychological levels of analysis in favor of simple behavioral variables (food intake or preference) and concomitant physiological processes. This produces psychology as brain-behavior relations. With this conception of the field, the task of interpreting meaning-laden and culturally-driven conditions (e. g., woman as body, thinness as attractive), relating these to their expression in family and individual dynamics (e. g., differential roles and valuation by gender) and to the production of symptoms (e. g., bingeing-purging) are all bypassed. Instead of being intelligible in a certain cultural, familial, or individual context, a symptom is understood as a simple, quantifiable behavior more or less directly under the control of a physiological mechanism (e. g., enhanced or decreased hypothalamic activity).

In turn, the emphasis on physiological mechanisms lends itself to the conception of psychological disorders within a biomedical model. It follows that the search for treatments are biased toward medical and, specifically, psychopharmacological interventions. Bulimia is presumed to have a physiological cause and require a drug or other biomedical form of treatment. The search is for physiological dysfunction such as a disordered satiation or appetite enhancement mechanism. This dysfunction may be a direct result of a genetic defect; or a genetic vulnerability (diathesis) that leaves an individual more prone to the deleterious effects of stressful conditions; or a deprived developmental history or acquired eating habits, such as dieting; or it could be a direct result of such conditions of stress or deprivation. As I have described, neurotransmitters and other biochemicals that enhance or inhibit food intake become putative models and treatments for one or another of the eating disorder—as do drugs that are agonists and antagonists to them.

It is an understatement to note that these physiological mechanisms have their own complexities and apparent inconsistencies. Yet compared to the ambiguities, variable interpretations, and complexities in the sociopsychological domain of culture, family, and individual psychology, experimentalism is significantly better equipped to exploit the former. Political and economic considerations enter here, since defining the disorders as biomedical rather than sociopsychological allows psychology identification with the hard sciences and results in a greater likelihood of funding.

For these several reasons, the preponderance of animal-based and specifically animal model, studies of eating disorders utilize a physiological level of analysis and discourse. In their critique of Montgomery's recent (1991) review of animal models of eating disorders, Coscina and Garfinkle (1991) divide the models reviewed into those featuring physiological ("biological") and sociopsychological ("environmental") causes. By their accounting, two-thirds of the models are physiological (p. 241). However, they go on, this breakdown "... underestimates the true representation of this category. If instead one were to tally the actual number of published studies in the animal literature devoted to each, the preponderance of biological models would *far outweigh* the environmental ones" (p. 241, emphasis added).

Despite their preponderance, in Coscina and Garfinkle's view, "... such biological models alone seem to have little direct utility in helping us understand the causal features of clinical eating disorders" (p. 21). They clearly prefer models that would emphasize such psychosocial phenomena as attitudes toward eating and weight, for example "the concept of self as viewed through the body image," and "feelings of self-worth and body size." Their own hypothesis is that psychological conflict is the underlying cause of eating disorders—a conflict between the wish to weigh less and perceived weight. In this conceptualization, food intake, which we have seen is the primary concept upon which most animal models of eating disorders are built, is at most a "symptom" or "sustaining factor" rather than a direct cause (p. 239). While not excluding a role for animal models, Coscina and Garfinkle limit their usefulness, given their emphasis on psychological conflict: "[I]t is not possible to use animal data to learn about the attitudinal dimensions, in part related to societal ideals, of the excessive concern with body weight and shape, that are so characteristic of human eating disorders" (p. 238).

Other investigators support this critique that there is an overemphasis on physiology in current animal models of eating disorders. In an article with the telling title, "Animal models: Anorexia yes, nervosa no," Mrosovsky (1984) argues that psychological aspects of the disorder ("nervosa") are primary and are not captured by animal models. For example, Mrosovsky rejects the idea that hypothalamic dysfunction is a primary cause of anorexia, arguing that there is no evidence for this and that the loss of appetite such dysfunction produces is not a feature of anorexia. Despite the term ("anorexia" = loss of appetite), the anorexic's refusal to eat does not imply loss of appetite. The phenomenology is closer to an individual who, protesting conditions perceived as unacceptable, goes on a hunger strike. Like a prisoner, lacking effectiveness and control, the anorexic asserts him or herself in one of the few ways available. Bruch's titular image of "the golden cage" is apt (Mrosovksy, p. 32). Starvation is rewarding (golden) for the anorexic, for through it he or she effects a mini-rebellion against perceived oppression (cage) even though denying physiological needs.

Obviously, one can not infer this psychological or, even more aptly, existential position from decreased food intake in animals resulting from their physiological manipulation. Like Coscina and Garfinkle, Mrosovsky sees a limited role for animal models:

> Work with animals can help define the course of anorexia nervosa once it is initiated, and some physiological complications and sustaining factors, but can play only a secondary role in combatting this uniquely human disorder (p. 32).

The operation of a bias toward the search for physiological causes of disorders is clear here. While there was a case reported in 1982 of an anorexic girl who was subsequently found to have a tumor in her hypothalamus, "there are thousands of cases of anorexia nervosa where no tumors have been found" (Mrosovsky, 1984, p. 22). "There is no compelling evidence that hypothalamic dysfunction is primary in anorexia nervosa" (p. 22).

However, there is some evidence that anorexia may cluster in families (Strober, 1992). The evidence regarding bulimia is less clear. Twin studies comparing the number of identical versus fraternal twins who are both diagnosable for the same disorder show differential "concordance" for anorexia. (Since only identical twins have the same genetic material, the number of such pairs with the same diagnosis is a measure of genetic transmission of the disorder). This has been interpreted to mean that there may be inherited variations in personality traits that predispose an individual for anorexia, such as obsessional and avoidance tendencies (p. 73).

Other investigators and clinicians who bring a psychoanalytic or psychodynamic perspective to the issue also emphasize the role of conflict in the eating disorders. In her review of psychodynamic concepts, Casper (1992) describes conflicts involving sexuality, body image, gender role, autonomy, personal identity, and control. For example, she notes deficits in meeting emotional needs dealt with by focusing on one's own body and food intake; reactions to the demands of puberty; and reactions to the autonomy and identity demands of adolescence (pp. 289–295).

In addition to the lack of direct evidence of physiological dysfunction as the root cause of eating disorders, an indirect line of evidence also points to the same conclusion: the finding of correlations between sociocultural variables and the incidence of eating disorders. In their review of this evidence, Vandereycken and Hoek (1992) conclude that eating disorders are "culture-bound syndromes." They are disorders "... restricted to certain cultures primarily by reason of distinctive psychosocial features of those cultures" (p. 20).

As an example, both Greek girls in Germany and Arab college students in London are more likely to develop eating disorders than their peers in their respective homelands (p. 21). More generally, the investigators interpret evidence of a higher incidence of eating disorders in "Western" cultures, in middle and upper classes, in certain occupations that emphasize weight or body shape (models, athletes, dancers), among females, among Caucasians, and in increasing incidence in recent times (the effect of "modernity") as supportive of the sociocultural basis of these disorders (p. 22). Conversely, the absence of these disorders in certain cultures also points to their being culture-bound. "There is simply no such thing as anorexia among native peoples in North America," according to Manson, a medical anthropologist (Goldman, 1995).

In her review of eating disorders, Yates (1989) summarizes other evidence along these lines: The incidence of anorexia and/or bulimia is higher in certain religious and ethnic groups (Jews, Italians, Catholics), in upwardly mobile ethnic groups, in individuals undergoing acculturation into less traditional societies, in high achievers, and in university women (pp. 815–6). She concludes:

> The eating disorders are unique because they represent the only common type of psychopathology in which the culture appears to be a major factor in determining the prevalence of the condition (1990, p. 7).

Evidence of the remarkable increase in the incidence of eating disorders over the past 30 or 40 years (Raphael & Lacey, 1992) is also consistent with the view that these disorders are culture-bound. Pate, Pumariega, Hester, and Garner (1992) interpret the increase in incidence rates outside Western countries as the result of changing cultural factors. Finally, reports of newly emerging forms of eating disorders support a cultural rather than a physiological etiology. The "binge eating disorder" involves the typical overeating bouts but without purging; while a "grazing" pattern consists of eating throughout the day, regardless of appetite (Sugarman, 1994).

The evidence of the sociocultural origins of all of these disorders is consistent with a feminist perspective. In a feminist reading, eating disorders "... are a response to the unequal status of women in our society" (Shisslak & Crago, 1994, p. 420). The emphases in modern cultures on "women as bodies," thinness as an attribute of attractiveness, the power of fashion and advertising all make women more vulnerable to disordered eating and problems with body image. A second more recent set of themes is the conflict between traditional and nontraditional gender roles (p. 420). As women struggle to realize the new won freedom to participate in roles for which they have traditionally been excluded, they encounter resistance and discrimination. At the same time, they are still burdened by the traditional roles of housekeeper and nurturer.

These accounts of the social construction of gender roles explain the predominance of eating disorders among women without implicating the physiology of the female sex. However, the discussion in this section is not meant to deny the possibility, in principle, that models based on physiological interventions, such as hypothalamic manipulation, might contribute to the understanding and/or treatment of eating disorders. Although *ideally* built on understanding, treatment is not always so. The point is that investigators who seek to develop animal models of eating disorders seem to have an *a priori* bias or preference for a physiological level of analysis and discourse. They continue to search for a physiological cause despite considerable literature, mostly produced by those in clinical practice, that offers strong evidence of the sociocultural origins of eating disorders.

As noted earlier, a sociocultural origin of eating disorders does not strictly rule out use of the animal model strategy. Animal models can mimic some psychological and behavioral aspects of eating disorders. Certainly both disordered learning and conditions in which not eating is rewarding can be approximated. It remains to be seen, however, if a meaning-laden psychological or existential position such as that symbolized by the golden cage or that shaped by the religion of thinness could be modelled in animal studies and could then yield further insights or effective treatment of a disorder based on that position. What is clear is that while current understanding of these disorders demands that investigators adopt a psychological level of analysis and discourse, few researchers utilizing the animal model strategy are so disposed.

Even models initially built on behavioral and environmental features of a disorder take this physiological turn. The sham feeding model of bulimia mimics a behavioral aspect of bulimia, eating without calories; while the tail-pinching and the activity stress models both mimic environmental conditions that might give rise to eating disorders. Yet all three are used to explore physiological variables that purportedly underlie, that is cause and/or sustain, these disordered behaviors.

The predominant choice of the physiological domain is a bias particularly prevalent in animal model research. That bias is intelligible, first, in terms of a philosophy of science, positivism, and its derivative investigative approach, experimentalism. Their emphases on control, quantification, operationalization, and reductionism (here a preference for proximal or direct causal chains) in turn determine the choice of the lab and lab animal as the site and object of study. As I described earlier, in their construction of the lab, investigators reduced laboratory animals to a physiological mechanism, to a "preparation."

Put another way, this bias is effected through the animal model research enterprise becoming method- rather than phenomenon-centered. Eating disorders both on their face and upon closer inspection are phenomena that arise, are maintained, and presumably can be made most intelligible in a sociopsychological context; however, the constraints and limits of the animal research method in effect force their study through physiological analysis and discourse.

Once embodied in the construction of the lab and lab animal, the ideology emphasizing physiology is institutionalized and perpetuated through training programs and mentoring relations. "Because of the background and training of many of the researchers in this field [human eating research], there has been a tendency to investigate sensory ... and internal physiological mechanisms in control of food intake" (Meiselman, 1992). I have described the distance between the world of the applied psychologist, for example an individual who treats eating disorders, and that of the laboratory animal-based research scientist. Beyond this applied/research distinction, even within the laboratory, psychologists who are trained to do rat surgery do rat surgery, while those trained to measure belief or family systems do just that, and there is little cross-over.

Beyond this sedimenting or conservative effect, other shortfalls in the training and subsequent career of psychologists as nonhuman animal surgeons are important to note. In both training and research settings, these psychologists are conducting surgery involving any and all physiological systems without the benefit of a formal training in veterinary or human medicine. As a result, they typically do not have the sophistication and familiarity with the broad range of interventions pertinent to the treatment of surgical patients. Their project is more specialized, lacking the primary and unrelenting focus on therapeutic ends and continuous patient care that characterizes the practice of veterinary and human medicine. For example, compared to veterinarians, they are relatively lacking in knowledge of anesthesia and analgesia (Phillips, 1993; John Gluck, personal communication, May, 1994).

In that they are performing surgery without a primary and direct therapeutic goal, their intervention lacks the constraints lent by a therapeutic frame. By contrast, both human and veterinary practitioners are required to take an oath that emphasizes allegiance to that frame. The Hippocratic Oath of the Classical period emphasizes the primacy of acting for the benefit of patients, while the Declaration of Geneva adopted by the World Medical Association in 1948 states that the "... health of my patient will be my first consideration." The Veterinarian's Oath obliges practitioners to "... the protection of animal health, [and] the relief of animal suffering" (Tannenbaum, 1989, p. 68).

Although purporting to develop treatment innovations for eventual application in a human setting, animal-based research psychologists work without such immediate personal and institutionalized safeguards. As critically, they typically have little direct experience of the treatment needs and limitations of the human setting. Of course, to effect this indirect therapeutic end the animal model strategy requires that they first induce illness. By contrast to another Classical dictum of physicians—*primum non nocere* (first do no harm)—they are burdened with the Orwellian proposition: sicken to heal.

Preoccupation with Technology

The physiological bias is both partly realized through and reinforced by the preoccupation with technology. As discussed in Chapter 2, in their efforts to achieve objectivity and to enhance and extend the limits of objective observation, psychologists turn to technology. The predominance of the resulting "technophilia" is evident in the review of animal models of eating disorders. The measurement and restraining devices and the apparati that support the experimental procedures are products of technological innovation. Direct observation gives way to elaborate and indirect recording schemes. Instead of being the servant of its presumed focal end—the direct observation of the phenomenon of interest, at least as modeled—this technological development of the lab becomes an ongoing project of primary interest.

These technologies are built around the laboratory animals *and* those animals have been built around them. Through technology, a class of animals, the laboratory animal, was constructed as a preparation, an isolated physiological mechanism. At the extreme, laboratory animals are for all intents and purposes conduits, measurable vessels, parts of the machinery. The line between animal and instrument blurs, as the following progression of three diagrams demonstrates. While the investigators employ descriptives like "near-natural ingestion" (see Figure 1, adapted from Norgren, Nashijo, & Travers, 1989) and "freely moving animals" (see Figures 2 and 3, from Nicolaidis & Even, 1989), the terms "deindividuated, despecified, and deanimalized," developed in Chapter 2, are more apt—as the individual animal becomes indistinguishable from the technology in which he or she is embedded. In the sham feeding model of bulimia, the animal is reduced to a tube with openings on both ends. Rather than providing a creative and productive heuristic, a

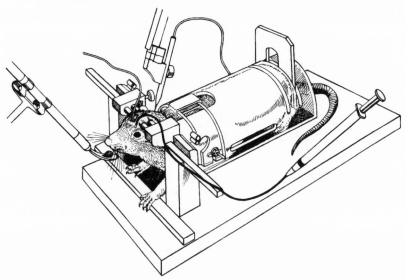

Figure 1. Apparatus for chronic recording of rat's "near-natural ingestion."

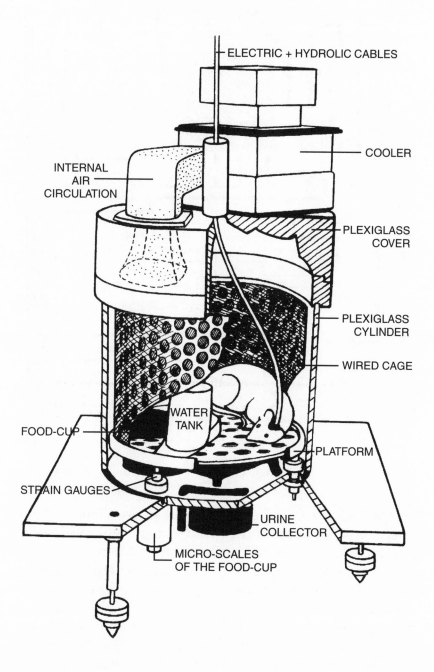

Figure 2. A "freely moving" rat in a metabolic chamber.

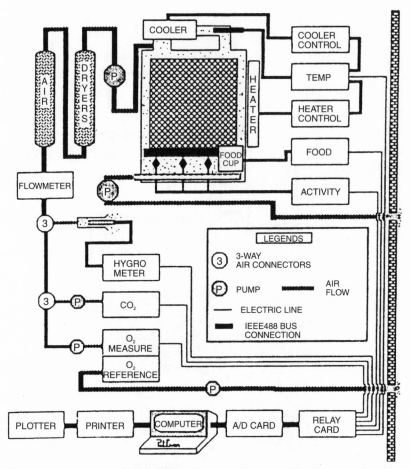

Figure 3. Supporting technology for a rat in a metabolic chamber.

bridge back to the phenomenon of interest, the animal model links up with and leads to other highly technologized and physiologized exploration.

This general character of the animal research enterprise has obvious animal welfare implications. As part of the effort to achieve objective observation, psychologists remove themselves from "the company of animals." They develop high-tech ways of observing and recording without being present. This technology is intended to stand between the investigator and the laboratory animal so that the ideal relationship between investigator and animal "subject," that is nonrelationship, can be attained. Even that distant, impersonal, and attenuated relationship implied by the act of observation is absent. The investigator "observes" metabolic rates as measured in metabolic chambers, not the actual rat. The rhetoric employed to describe his or her studies reflects this distance—certain technical procedures are effected, rather than animals are suffering, or being killed. There is denial both that there is an "inevitable bond" (Davis & Balfour, 1992) between investigator or lab assistant and an animal, and, more generally, that what is going on in the laboratory is only intelligible as a complex social interaction among individuals of different species. As they can not be acknowledged either rhetorically or in fact, these relationships are not given consideration, at least officially.

The emphasis on technological development can subvert an open search for understanding. Some have argued that laboratory research, both human and animal, produces a body of results that is not extrapolable and lacks relevance to the phenomenon outside the lab. Meiselman (1992) reported the result of a survey of studies on "human eating research." He asked the question, "What percentage of research in our field now takes place in 'real life'?" In his 1990 literature search of three major indices, he found that, of 58 studies involving human subjects, not one reported data from a "real-life eating situation." When his search was expanded to include nonhuman animals, he found that there were more than twice as many animal studies conducted on the topic of eating in that year.

In his discussion, he takes to task the more or less exclusive use of "artificial foods and artificial meals," the emphases on sensory and physiological mechanisms and proximate causation, and the reliance on short-term studies in the human-based research. He proposes a shift to a research methodology based on "real meals, real people, real situations."

In Meiselman's view, the lack of studies in "natural eating environments" in human-based research is partly due
to the influence of animal-based research:

> The tradition of animal behavior research has also brought with it
> a tradition of using comparable methods for animals and hu-
> mans.... Inbred rats raised in isolation in cages and fed lab chow
> cannot be used to study natural eating. Human research analogues
> of animal studies cannot achieve any more (p. 53).

Rozin echoes Meiselman's concern about the artificiality
of the laboratory-based research:

> Animals, whenever they eat, are choosing to not do something else,
> and in the typical laboratory situation they basically have nothing
> else to do. This effects enormously how much eating they do or
> their pattern of eating....[I]f you give rats a place to sleep a little,
> the number of meals and the meal pattern change substantially
> simply because they have another alternative" (quoted in Morley,
> 1989a, p. 160).

There is a tension between the technology of the lab and
the study of "natural" conditions. The former pack-
age—lab-based, animal-based, technologized, and physiologized research—delivers a peculiar form of understanding, one that has distinct limitations. Further, its constraints and biases are so powerful that their sphere of
influence extends to human-based research as well, as the
latter takes on the same characteristics—artificial foods,
short-term studies, emphasis on physiology, and so forth.

With this, the official ideal is stood on its head. Instead
of the phenomenon of interest shaping the development
of animal models which generate new hypotheses to be
confirmed in human-based research and then directly in
an applied human setting, we have a (de)formative influence operating in the opposite direction. For these biases
derive directly from this peculiar scientific enterprise
which features the production of animal models in a laboratory setting. They are not inherent in or demanded by

the phenomenon under study: human eating and its disorders. For example, the bias toward technological development is not dictated by the nature of eating disorders. While these phenomena are complex, studying them does not require high technology. As indicated, much of their complexity is of a different order—symbolic, cultural, familial rather than physiological.

In any case, more naturalistic environments both for human and nonhuman animals can be achieved, and achieved without heavy reliance on sophisticated technology. For example, Mrosovsky observes, "Natural anorexias are widespread in the animal kingdom" (1984, p. 23). In more general terms, then, the tension between technology and nature is between the ideology of the lab and the phenomenon itself. Clearly, the typical resolution of this tension is heavily weighted toward the method dictated by the philosophy of science rather than faithfulness to the phenomenon targeted for study.

Treatment as Technological Fix

In the context of the search for effective interventions, both preventative and ameliorative, the partnership between physiology and technology resulted in a focus on a search for medical forms of treatment. If, as it was assumed by most laboratory-based animal researchers, eating disorders have a physiological cause, then it also was assumed that they require a drug or other form of biomedical treatment. It does not follow that a disorder thought to have a physiological cause is most effectively treated through intervention at that level. Even in the simple case of a disorder caused by a germ or toxin, "treatment" can be at the level of removing the environmental conditions that produce that toxin or facilitate its emergence. In the other direction, finding an effective intervention does not necessarily require or imply understanding of the cause of the disorder or that its cause is necessarily at the same level. The project of searching for an effective intervention may proceed more or less independently of the search for understanding. At the extreme, it can displace and distract from the latter project. Technology can be in the service of either the search for intervention or understanding. However, true to its etymology (*techno*, Greek for art, craft, and, by extension, applied science), technology is often found in closer company with applications and practices than theory or understanding.

Discursis on Therapy

In the following evaluation of the effectiveness of interventions in the eating disorders, I begin with a brief overview of therapies as defined and practiced in psychology. We need to understand what characterizes those therapies and to examine their relations, in general terms, to animal-based research. Turning next to the eating disorders, I examine the role of animal models in the development of treatments, and specifically, the emphasis in that enterprise on the search for a psychopharmacological intervention. Has it been effective? What is the actual role of the use of animal models in that search? In what sense do animal models yield drug treatments?

Each basic science has its crowning area of application: As biology has its sophisticated surgical repair and replacement, physics its space travel and moon walk, so psychology has its reconstructive psychotherapies. More than half of psychologists practice some form of therapy. Since Freud gave the seminal therapy of psychoanalysis to the field, numerous other schools of thought have contributed other forms of therapy. At first, these were largely variants on his seminal global theory of personality and pathology. However, soon other approaches appeared, often built on opposition to one or another tenet of psycho-analysis.

By the 1970s, a popular textbook featured 13 "current psychotherapies," including psychoanalytic, gestalt, be-havioral, humanistic or person-centered, cognitive, ge-stalt, transactional, and family systems approaches (Corsini, 1979). By the 1980s, an encyclopedia of psychol-ogy by the same editor included an entry on psychother-apy technique which stated, "Systems of psychotherapy number in the hundreds, ranging from Adlerian psycho-therapy to Zaslow's z-process attachment" (Peyser, 1984, p. 190). A more popularized account described "more than 250 different therapies in use today" (Herink, 1980).

During the height of this proliferation, there was a short-lived hope that these therapies would distinguish themselves by their specificity of effect. As in medicine there are different treatments for different illnesses, so in psychotherapy there would be procedures specific to a syndrome or symptom. When it became clear that in prac-tice this desired parallel to medicine was, with few excep-tions, unrealizable, much research on psychotherapy shifted to the search for features common to many ap-proaches that provided, as it were, the universal active therapeutic ingredients.

This research soon revealed that therapeutic interven-tions by psychologists were distinguishable more by their differences from than their similarities to medicine. In a review article in a special issue of the *American Psycholo-gist* devoted to psychotherapy research, Strupp, the doyen of this investigative area concluded that:

> Psychotherapy is not a form of medical treatment in the usual sense. Instead it is a specialized human relationship designed to facilitate changes in the patient's cognitions, feelings, and actions (1986, p. 128).

The common core of variables found to be therapeutic in this research included therapist qualities such as "personal warmth, understanding, and the ability to guide clients to new perspectives" (Styles, Shapiro, & Elliott, 1986, p. 172); client qualities such as the ability to focus on one's own experience and the presence of positive expectations regarding treatment (pp. 172–173); and therapist/client relationship variables such as a positive bond and a working alliance (p. 173).

These findings of a set of "nonspecific" therapeutic features, those not limited to any one theoretical approach or even modality (individual, group, or family), were consistent with another body of results from therapy research. Most research comparing the relative effectiveness of different psychotherapies (outcome research) showed little or no difference among them (Stiles et al., 1984).

> Psychotherapy works ... All of the more established orientations,– psychoanalytically oriented, client centered, cognitive, and behavioral—have been shown to be effective, but none have been demonstrated to be generally more effective than the others (Raskin, 1984, p. 186).

While some findings tilt toward cognitive or the hybrid cognitive-behavioral therapy as more effective than psychoanalytically oriented and humanistic approaches, this finding is confounded by another finding: the bias of the investigators. In their review, Stiles et al. note that "... the allegiance of the investigators... almost invariably predicted which treatment approach yielded superior results in comparative studies" (p. 167).

In general, then, most psychotherapies have been found to produce positive effects beyond the natural progress which is seen in most disorders over time (spontaneous remission) and which offsets certain demonstrable negative effects, i. e., results from psychotherapy that worsen or aggravate the presenting condition (Strupp, Hadley, & Gomes-Schwartz, 1977). On the other side, those many disorders which remain recalcitrant to treatment do so in the face of all approaches.

As in other endeavors lending themselves to taxonomy, there are always the "splitters" and the "lumpers." However, at present in the field of psychotherapy the lumpers, those that emphasize more the similarities than the differences between approaches are in the fore. Consistent with this, practitioners are often eclectic. However, their choices of what therapies to combine reflects more personal preference than any evidence that a specific modality or mixture of modalities are the preferred treatment of a particular presenting problem. The general view is that certain general skills of the therapist are therapeutic. Strupp states, "The therapist's skills consist in the ability to create, maintain, and manage a specialized human relationship toward therapeutic ends" (1984, p. 128). This overview has important implications for the issue of animal research.

Therapies and Animal Research

There is a limited relation between the development of psychotherapies and animal-based laboratory research. The fact that effective features of therapy are common to most approaches implies that unless the creation of all those therapies were dependent on it, animal research has made no indispensable contribution. In fact, I will show, to the contrary, that nearly all of the major therapies developed outside of and independently of the animal laboratory.

Further, the particular character of the documented active therapeutic ingredients, that they revolve around the establishment of a specialized human relationship, also suggests that the study of nonhuman animal behavior played a limited role and, in any case, an unnecessary one. This is not to assume that nonhuman relations are inferior to or radically different from human relations. The point is that if effective therapy necessarily includes "skills" like warmth, understanding, and forming of a trusting working alliance, surely these can be studied directly, whether in the clinic itself or an analogue setting using human subjects. To reach such insights, animal research is, on its face, a long way around, if not, indeed, a wrong turn.

More subtly, and more critical to the present monograph, the animal model strategy would seem a poor wager. With respect to its role in contributing to effective therapy, it presumes that an "understanding" of a particular disorder will inevitably yield a treatment peculiarly tailored to that disorder; or, more specifically, that an understanding of the etiology of that disorder is necessary to the discovery of its treatment. The thrust of both outcome and process research in therapy strongly belies these assumptions. For there are few disorder/treatment fits, and effective treatment is a function of the presence of general factors, not derived from the understanding of a pathological process peculiar to a given disorder.

The analysis to this point oversimplifies a complex set of enterprises and their interaction. For the moment, it also omits evaluation of pharmacological therapies and their relation to animal research. This is justifiable since, as indicated, psychotherapy is the predominant activity of applied psychology. Still at a general level, I will first look at the relationship between animal research and particular approaches to psychotherapy, and then at current therapies of the eating disorders, including drug treatment.

As indicated, there are many classification schemes for describing the array of available psychotherapies. Under the "major field" of clinical psychology, the APA membership directory lists about 30 therapies (American Psychological Association, 1989, pp. xlviii-l); while a national register of applied psychologists distinguishes only 7 orientations (National Register of Health Service Providers in Psychology, 1993, pp. l-13). For the purpose of this informal overview, I will be a merciless lumper and distinguish the following 5 therapies: psychodynamic (including psychoanalysis), behavioral, humanistic (client-centered and experiential), cognitive (including cognitive-behavioral), and systems (including structural).

Clearly, psychoanalysis together with its later developments, referred to most inclusively as psychodynamic psychotherapy, have a provenance which owes virtually no debt to animal research. They were conceived and developed in the human consulting room and clinic. One exception to this is the attempt by Dollard and Miller (1950) to recast the psychoanalytic concept of neurosis in terms of learning theory. While this effort was important in the emergence of behavioral therapy, it had little impact on psychoanalysts, the great majority of whom continued to follow the Freudian tradition. The relation of learning theory and behavioral therapy to animal research will be considered in a moment. In psychoanalysis, any role of animals shrank to a metaphoric allusion to that aspect of humanity which Freud offered as the motor force of individual behavior and personality, the unconscious. With its reservoir of instinctive yearnings, Freud's unconscious was the "animal" side of humans, as distinguished from the peculiarly human rational and deliberative side. While laboratory psychology featured the white rat, that socially constructed icon of sterilized control, "psychoanalysts stalked the dark rat scurrying through the obscure shadows" of patients' dreams, as in Freud's seminal case study of the "Rat Man" (Wertz, 1986, p. 152). My focus in this monograph is the effects on psychology of the former, the white rat of the laboratory. However, ecopsychologists and feminist psychologists have developed a critique of the dark rat, of animals as symbolizing instinct-dominated irrationality, and the influence of this association on our views of nonhuman animals, nature, and women (Roszak, Gomes, & Kanner, 1995)

Humanistic therapy included Rogers' seminal client-centered approach, experiential and existential therapy, the sensitivity training group approach, the human potential movement, and even a precursor of cognitive therapy (Ellis' rational-emotive therapy). In a sense, this influential "Third Wave" distinguished itself from psychoanalysis and behaviorism precisely by leaving behind nonhuman animals, both those in the lab and those, symbolically, in the dark recesses of our minds. Reacting against both behaviorism's stimulus-response mechanics and psychoanalysis' instinctive drive theory, humanistic psychology built its theory and therapy on the presumed higher potentials of human being—"the farther reaches of human nature" (Maslow, 1972). It had no use for white or black rats, for laboratory animal models or animal symbols, as its concept of self-actualization was for humans only (Shapiro, 1990a).

Systems theory also is independent of laboratory animal psychological research. A development of engineering science, systems theory is now found in computer technology, cybernetics, automation, and systems engineering (von Bertalanffy, 1968, p. vii). For psychology, the important shift in this approach is from a focus on the individual, whether on the anatomy of his or her psyche or on behavior, to a consideration of interindividual structures. These include rules, communication styles, and interpersonal interactions that maintain a family, couple, or, in its most ambitious application, a nation. More than any other set of concepts, systems theory supplied the impetus for the emergence of family and couples therapy.

The relation of both the cognitive and the behavior therapies to animal research is more complex and difficult to sort out than the three approaches just considered. In part, cognitivism was a reaction against behaviorism, that psychological theory most associated with laboratory animals. Against radical behaviorism's denial that mental events play any role in a science of psychology, cognitive psychology reinstated the determinative role in individual behavior of structures and processes of "mind," and, to a lesser extent, of consciousness. However, a legacy of behaviorism retained by cognitive psychology was the focus in research on observable behavior. Cognitive psychology is, then, methodologically but not ontologically behavioristic; it is behavioral, not behavioristic. In place of an explanation in terms of observable environmental contingencies, cognitive theory emphasizes "mental" structures and processes.

The resulting investigatory enterprise is thus predominantly human-based. As quoted in Chapter 1, a popular text on cognitive psychology included virtually no animal-based research. In fact, the influence is in the other direction: this human-based cognitive psychology has affected the study of animal behavior itself, at least that part that, unlike the animal model strategy, investigates animal behavior as an end in itself. This comparative psychology is now becoming cognitive ethology as the newly dominant paradigm of cognitive psychology "re-minds" nonhuman as well as human animals (Shapiro, 1992).

The cognitive therapies, then, are largely independent of animal research. In fact, in the view of two critics, the development of certain techniques in cognitive therapy, such as the use of imagery, were delayed precisely because the dominant influence of behaviorist psychology discouraged consideration of such mentalist phenomena in a scientific psychology (Drewett & Kani, 1981).

To be fair, this reading of the history of psychology would be strongly opposed by those psychologists who believe that radical behaviorism and with it, animal research, provided the foundation of all subsequent developments in the field of psychology. To them, the various relations between stimulus and response provided psychology with its periodic table, with its basic elements and the relations among them. However, this is a minority view. For most psychologists the accomplishment of the behaviorist program was mixed and much more modest. Rather than delivering the basic principles or laws of the field, it provided a method (methodological behaviorism) grounded in observable behavior.

Finally, I will consider the role of animal research in behavior therapy itself. From the early work of Pavlov and Watson, through that of Hull, to the more recent efforts of Skinner, psychologists used nonhuman animals to work out what were, in their view, the basic governing principles of all learning—the understanding of how organisms, human and otherwise, acquire, maintain, and change behavior. On the face of it, these learning theories gave rise to several therapeutic techniques (e. g., systematic desensitization and response contingent reinforcement). As importantly, particularly in the Skinnerian version, behaviorism provided an important form of thought that clearly had a strong influence on psychotherapy. The behavioristic emphasis on the immediate, observable, and concrete factors that control behavior shifted therapy away from the long-term reconstruction of personality, that is from "depth psychology," toward a focus on defining pathology in terms of concrete behavioral problems that are more readily specified and more immediately accessible to treatment.

However, there are qualifications to the centrality of the role of animal-based research in the development of behavioral therapy. While it is a historical fact that the seminal behaviorist theorists relied heavily on the use of laboratory rats and pigeons, the necessity of their having done so is arguable. As I will discuss in Chapter 6, one of the pivotal issues in the current ethical and policy debate regarding the use of laboratory animals in psychology is whether that use is or ever was "necessary," that is, indispensable.

Secondly, the exact nature of the contribution of animal-based learning theory research to behavior therapy is a matter requiring extensive analysis and interpretation of the historical record. Did animal-based research provide a "point-to-point correspondence" to specific human ther-

apeutic interventions, as one of its proponents implies
(Miller, 1985, p. 433); or did it provide only a strategy of
analysis, a general way of formulating clinical problems
and framing interventions? This is not to suggest that this
last is a trivial contribution; to the contrary behaviorism
provided an important shift in this regard. However, even
a superficial examination of the history of behavioristic
research reveals that that enterprise proceeded at a level
of detail, of preoccupying proliferation of variables, that
rivaled medieval scholastic argumentation about angel
transportability (how many angels can dance on the head
of a pin?).

Restricting his critique to Skinnerian (operant) animal-
based research, Neuringer notes that "a number of critics
... have remarked that even behavior modification [ther-
apeutic] procedures have, in fact, derived little from basic
operant conditioning research" (1984, p. 399). He speculates, "The lack of influence of operant research may be
due in part to its *oft-noted ingrown nature*" (1984, p. 399,
emphasis added). Neuringer implies that investigators do
not frame their research to answer questions directly
raised in applied settings and that, in any case, they do
not test their own hypotheses in applied settings.

Current use of behavioristic-based methods does not
reflect the niceties of the animal laboratory enterprise,
which is largely an ingrown enterprise. Those variations
that are apparent are later developments of experience in
the clinic rather than direct extrapolations of "laboratory-
bred" parameters. In fact, most contemporary behavior
therapy is a mix of cognitivism and behaviorism: "Virtually all current procedures in behavior therapy involve
some cognitive influence" (Franks, 1984, p. 141).

Evaluation of Therapy of the Eating Disorders

Before examining current approaches to the therapy of bulimia and, to a lesser extent, of anorexia, it is worth noting the status of therapy of the related but distinct condition of obesity. The prevalence of this condition "has doubled since 1900 and has increased even in recent years (Brownell & Rodin, 1994, p. 781). Obesity is known for its recalcitrance to treatment and high relapse rates (1994, p. 781). The extensive use of animal models in its study has not altered these facts. Interestingly, there may be a complex reciprocal influence between cultural stigma associated with obesity and the prevalence of the bulimia and anorexia. For the epidemiology of eating disorders indicates that the cultural interest in dieting, of which the scientific study of diet and dieting is part and parcel, contributes to that prevalence. However, while "Dieting often precedes the development of these problems [eating disorders], . . . a direct link has not been proven (Brownell & Rodin, 1994, p. 786). Although the empirical relation is not yet demonstrated, the conflicting roles of dieting in obesity and the eating disorders is clear:

> The debate over dieting is due in part to a collision of philosophy in two fields. In the eating disorders field, chronic, severe dieting is a central feature of the disorders and may be etiologic.... In the obesity field, dieting represents a potential solution to a serious medical problem (Brownell & Rodin, 1994, p. 781).

Is there effective treatment of the eating disorders, bulimia and anorexia? The answer is yes and no. In terms of immediate and short-term effects, results are comparable to the level of effectiveness of therapy in general, around 70%. In their review of 19 controlled studies involving the treatment of bulimia using cognitive-behavioral therapy (CBT) and other therapies, Mitchell and Raymond found decreases in the frequency of bingeing and purging, two definitive symptoms, of between 70 and 80% (1992,

p. 316). Depressive symptoms were significantly abated in 16 of the 19 studies. Similarly, Johnson and Sansone (1993) found that for both bulimia and anorexia approximately two thirds of patients treated with brief to moderate length interventions had favorable responses.

But there are two serious qualifiers. First, the levels of abstinence found immediately following the termination of treatment are "disappointingly low" (Mitchell & Raymond, 1992, p. 325). Subjects are still bingeing and purging but less frequently. Second, these levels diminish when remeasured at the end of a follow-up period varying from six weeks to one year. Reduction in frequency of bingeing at follow-up is closer to 50%; while abstinence rates are even lower (pp. 316–320). In his review of nine studies with at least a one year follow-up, Hsu found that about 75% of clients treated are "not diagnosable for a bulimic disorder" (1992, p. 140). (This is a less stringent criterion than that employed by Mitchell and Raymond). But review of four studies with a follow-up period of more than two years showed that 16–50% of the subjects were still diagnosable (p. 140). Rorty, Yager, and Rossoto (1993) found that those individuals who do have a recovery lasting at least a year attribute their success to the presence of caring, empathic relationships provided by family and friends. Mitchell, Raymond, and Specker (1993) conclude their review of the literature on outcome studies by underscoring the uncertainty about the long-term effectiveness of most current treatments. As is obesity, bulimia is clearly "difficult to treat" (Yates, 1990, p. 1).

Anorexia is even more difficult. The prognosis is worse, as are relapse and mortality rates (Yates, p. 6). In his review of seven outcome studies at 4–12 years after onset of the disorder, Hsu found "about 50% had a good outcome..., about 5% had died, about 20% were still anorectic, and the remainder (about 25%) were in various stages of recovery" (p. 129). Yates concludes, "Eating disorders tend to become chronic and to resist treatment"—although she adds, "On the other hand, a number of untreated women seem to improve spontaneously" (p. 6).

Given these limitations in the effectiveness of eating disorder therapy, which approaches are most effective? The findings again roughly reflect those for the general literature: Most therapies are relatively effective when compared to no treatment. There is no clear treatment of choice and, in practice, it is typical to employ several approaches concurrently (Yates, 1990, p. 3).

Comparative evaluation studies, those pitting one therapy against another, vary in their results. Some show no difference, while some give a qualified nod to a particular approach. For the treatment of bulimia, cognitive-behavioral therapy has received the most attention in treatment studies (Mitchell & Raymond, 1992, pp. 307–308). In their review, Mitchell and Raymond conclude that it is "as effective or more effective when compared with other types of psychotherapy" (p. 325). For example, compared to interpersonal therapy (ITP; within the present scheme, most directly a derivative of humanistic psychology), both ITP and CBT initially resulted in symptom reduction; CBT had more effect on modifying disturbed attitudes, and at one year follow-up treatment differences had washed out (p. 320). Several studies found CBT to be more effective than behavioral therapy (Wolf & Crowler, 1992; Thackwray, Smith, Bodfish, & Meyers, 1993; Fairburn, Jones, Peveler, Hope et al., 1993). Both Wilson and Fairburn (1993) and Leitenberg, Rosen, Wolf, Vara, et al. (1994) found that CBT was more effective than anti-depressant drug therapy and that treatment combining the two approaches concurrently was more effective than either alone.

As applied to the treatment of bulimia, CBT is a multifaceted approach which attempts to alter attitudes toward body shape, weight, and food; to reinstate normal eating habits, and to develop coping skills to undercut bingeing and purging (Wilson & Fairburn, 1993). Clients learn about various aspects of bulimia, and learn to monitor and reframe their own thoughts, feelings, and behaviors about eating and their bodies (Mitchell & Raymond, 1992, pp. 322–324). While some of the specific techniques employed clearly show the stamp of behaviorism and behavioral therapy, the approach keys on cognitive psychology. "Central to the CBT approach is the emphasis on understanding one's one *cognitions* about shape, weight, and other problems" (p. 324, emphasis added). Further confirming this, Yates notes that CBT applied to bulimia is a development of Fairburn who based it on Beck's cognitive approach to the treatment of depression (1990, p. 3). CBT "attempts to change the patient's system of beliefs ... through a semistructured, problem-oriented approach (p. 3).

As discussed, cognitive psychology and its application, cognitive therapy, are largely independent of animal research, as is the specific form of cognitive therapy developed for the treatment of bulimia. Further, with its emphasis on attitudes, restructuring of thought, and sensitivity to distortions in body image, CBT clearly owes no debt to that area of animal research under scrutiny here—animal models of eating disorders.

With regard to the behavioristic components of CBT, their relation to animal research is closer. However, the influence of the animal lab is general, indirect, and diluted by mixture with a basically cognitive therapy.

A more pure form of behavioral therapy, behavior modification, has played an important role in the first phase of treatment of anorexia (Yates, 1990, p. 2). Anorexics are often hospitalized to gain control over their self-imposed starvation regimens. A behavioral therapy approach provides an emphasis on careful monitoring of weight gain and its linkage to behavioral rewards. Again, these general principles owe their development to animal research only as qualified in the several ways already indicated.

Beyond this important initial symptom control, the treatment of anorexia relies heavily on family (Russell,

Dare, Eisler, & Le Grange, 1992) and group (Harper-Giuf-fre & MacKenzie, 1992) therapies, approaches which developed independently of animal research. The use of the first is compelling in that anorexic clients are in a struggle with their parents; while the second facilitates dealing with the issue of body image distortion through the social reality check provided by a group of peers. However, hasten to recall that neither these nor any other current treatment is very effective in the treatment of this severe disorder.

While I will deal with claims about the benefits of animal research more fully in the following chapters, it is worth noting here that Miller gives a very different impression of behavioral therapy, both as an effective treatment of anorexia and in its relation to animal-based behavioristic research. Accompanying it with graphic pictures of an anorexic person before and after treatment (1985, p. 428), he states, "If your daughter had a problem like this, would you want to have prevented the behavioral research on animals that led to the treatment that cured her (p. 427)?" The hysteroid form and content of this rhetorical question notwithstanding, there is currently no cure for anorexia or even the less severe disorder, bulimia; and there is rarely a "point-to-point correspondence" (p. 432) between the results of animal-based behavioral research and their purported application to therapy.

Pharmacological Therapy and Animal Research

While applied psychology largely entails the practice of psychotherapy, or "talking cures," animal-based laboratory research in psychology is heavily directed to a search for effective drug treatments of the various psychological disorders. As described, this follows from a predilection toward a physiological explanation, which, in the case of the eating disorders, is arguably a bias since there is little evidence of primary physiological ausation and considerable evidence that incidence rates correlate with sociocultural variables. The search for drug treatments also is intelligible in terms of a preoccupation with technology directed toward the instrumentalization of the laboratory and its animal "subjects." In addition to nonhuman animal research on the eating disorders, this peculiar brand of experimental investigation also has influenced human-based research toward utilizing artificial conditions and narrowing the search for causes to those that are proximal, typically, physiological mechanisms.

In the context of therapy, these physiological and technological bents are consistent with a focus on the development of medical, notably pharmacological, intervention. This trend toward the medicalization of psychological disorders has been challenged by the sharply contrasting view that such disorders are "problems in living" rather than disease entities. According to this view, effective "treatment" is more likely to require therapies that are socio-psychological and psycho-educational rather than medical. However, the former position is strongly held in the clinic and, clearly, has prevailed in the laboratory study of the eating disorders. This is ironic in that, in a major review, one investigator asserted that the incidence of these disorders, even more than others, are attributable to culture not physiology (Yates, 1990, p. 7).

How has this search for the silver bullet, the cure for bulimia and anorexia, fared? What drugs have been studied, how effective are they, what is their relation to animal models of eating disorders?

One review of drug treatment studies begins, "The pharmacological treatment of eating disorders remains problematic" (Morley, 1989b, p. 22). Contrasting them to relatively successful drug therapies of schizophrenia and the affective disorders (depression and mania), Morley characterizes the "pharmacological manipulation of the eating disorders" as "disappointing" (p. 22). Yates states "there is no single medication which has been proven effective for patients with anorexia nervosa or bulimia" (p. 3).

Two other reviewers, Walsh (1992) and Montgomery (1991), restrict these gloomy conclusions to anorexia. Walsh notes that anorexia "remains relatively refractory to pharmacological intervention" (p. 329). Montgomery states that while "[a] variety of drugs have been investigated as treatments of AN [anorexia], ... none [has] yielded clear evidence of enduring efficacy" (p. 179). Regarding anorexia only and taking their three reviews together, Yates, Walsh, and Montgomery list the following drugs as ineffective or of uncertain effectiveness: antipsychotics, antidepressants, tranquilizers (antianxiety), antimanics (lithium), opioid blockers, an anti-convulsant (phenytoin), a serotonin antagonist (cyproheptadine), a drug that hastens gastric emptying (metoclopramide), a drug used in the treatment of Parkinson's disease (L-dopa), zinc, and that panacea of the 1960s, marijuana.

With the exception of one class of drugs, the antidepressants, the list of drugs found ineffective in the treatment of bulimia is comparable and largely duplicative. One additional drug, fenfluramine, initially showed promise. Walsh notes two "encouraging" studies exploring its effectiveness with bulimic clients. However, a more recent study of fenfluramine offers conclusive negative results (Fahy, Eisler, & Russell, 1993). Fenfluramine is an appetite suppressor and also is unsuccessful in the treatment of obesity.

The opioid antagonists, naloxone and naltrexone, while also initially showing promise (Jonas & Gold, 1988), subsequently were shown to be ineffective (Levine & Bullington, 1989). Similarly, CCK, a peptide that inhibits eating by signalling satiation, did not prove to be helpful in the treatment of bulimia. Finally, antipsychotic, antimanic, anticonvulsant, and antianxiety drugs also proved ineffective.

A large number of studies in the 1980s consistently found that drugs in the several classes of antidepressants were effective in the short-term treatment of bulimia, when compared to no treatment (Walsh, 1992, p. 334). Recently, an advisory panel of the Food and Drug Administration recommended approval of the antidepressant Prozac for bulimia, which would make it the first drug in the United States specifically recognized as a treatment ("Prozac as Bulimia," 1994).

Despite association with this highly touted medication ("the pill of pills") (Nuland, 1994), use of antidepressant medications in the treatment of bulimia is clearly limited. According to some studies, short-term use merely reduces symptoms, and long-term effectiveness has not been demonstrated. Walsh reported a study in which half the subjects who had responded positively to antidepressant treatment relapsed over a four-month period, although still taking the medication. In its short-term usage, antidepressants are less effective than cognitive-behavioral (Leitenberg et al., 1994) or group (Walsh, 1992, p. 337) therapies, which, as described, have their own limitations in effectiveness. Although some therapists use antidepressants in conjunction with other interventions, it "should not be considered an adequate or first-choice treatment for bulimia nervosa" (Walsh, p. 338). Yates makes the interesting additional observation that medication itself as a treatment of bulimia is problematic given the bulimic symptom of vomiting, which can prevent the full absorption of the drug (1990, p. 2).

As I turn to the relation of these drugs, both the clearly ineffective and the relatively effective, to specific animal models of eating disorders, it is helpful, first, to review the range of possible relations. In the earlier discussion of concepts of models, I described an idealized notion of the model as virtual identity, as stand-in, for the phenomenon of interest, indicating how this was suggested historically by a loose reading of the nature and use of animal models of certain infectious diseases in the 19th century. According to this ideal, since an animal model virtually reproduces the disease process, understanding of the determinants of that process at a physiological level can lead directly to the discovery of a drug with action specific to that process. I offered a more realistic notion of the model as heuristic, as providing a generative context in which to think about the phenomenon of interest. On the far side of even this more limited function, I noted various degenerative uses wherein the model is further reduced from identity, and pragmatic tool, to a rhetoric device which has only a vague analogic relation to the phenomenon of interest.

Investigators have devised many animal models of the eating disorders. To date, none of these has led to the discovery of a drug effective in the treatment of those disorders. Even those drugs at one time investigated in studies involving these animal models and subsequently found *ineffective* in the treatment of the eating disorders did not originate therein. In no sense can they be said to have been discovered under the auspices of those models.

This is not surprising since there was no claim that the tail-pinch model of bulimia, for example, is a condition that reproduces the particular context and conditions which give rise to that disorder in humans. The tail-pinch model was already in use as one of many models that elicit stress in laboratory animals. Its use as a model of bulimia is an adaptation to test the possible role of stress as a cause of that disorder. As noted, it also has been explored as a model of schizophrenia. In its application to the study of the eating disorders, researchers employed it only as a general model of stress to investigate the relation of stress to appetite, eating, and other phenomena apparently related to the eating disorders rather than as a model specifically tailored to these disorders.

Drugs tested on the tail-pinch animal model of bulimia, such as the tranquilizers and the opioid antagonists, were already available as treatments of other disorders. Their examination as treatments for bulimia were part of the "development" of animal models of eating disorders, not the result of that development.

While accompanied by the activity-stress theory, a relatively cohesive account of the cause of anorexia, the activity-wheel model has not led to the discovery of any effective drug treatment of that disorder. The model itself was serendipitously discovered, first developed as a model of ulcer, and, only later, used as a model of anorexia.

A procedure initially used to study gastric functioning, the fistula was adapted by investigators to create the sham feeding model of bulimia. While ingenious, sham feeding is, at best, a coarse analogy to the bulimic strategy of eating without calories. The procedure did provide a way of exploring the role of satiation in the disorder. However, the hypothesis that a defective satiation mechanism caused bulimia issued first from a clinical setting, the brain-child of Bruch. Further, well before its study in the sham feed model, investigators had identified CCK as an important agent in satiation (Morley, 1989b, p. 24). In any case, CCK proved ineffective in the treatment of bulimia and not to be a cause of anorexia.

Fenfluramine was already marketed in Europe in 1985 as an appetite suppressant with promise as a treatment for obesity (Guardiola-Lemaitre, 1991, p. 304). Its development predates its exploration in any of the several animal models under examination. It is no longer believed to be an effective treatment of bulimia.

Several families of antidepressant drugs were already available for the treatment of other disorders and did not originate in animal models of eating disorders. Further, it was clinical observation, not animal models research, that suggested their use in the treatment of bulimia nervosa: "The starting point for these trials [of antidepressant medications] was the observation made by a number of clinicians in the early 1980s that many patients with bulimia nervosa exhibited significant mood disturbance" (Walsh, 1992, p. 334). Many investigators believe that much of this depression is secondary to the binge-purge cycle, a concomitant of which is considerable discouragement and lowering of self-esteem.

I am not making any claim as to whether or not other animal research played a role in the initial discovery of these antidepressant drugs. That would require a separate study. However, the general conclusion I do reach has significant scope. The models under scrutiny made no contribution to the development of significant pharmacological treatment of eating disorders. Clearly, animal models of eating disorders are of limited heuristic value in generating effective drug treatments. I have already shown that this conclusion also obtains in regard to treatment with psychotherapy. There is every reason to believe that the results of this exercise involving animal models of these disorders would also extend upon examination of models of other psychological disorders.

This relation between animal models of eating disorders and therapeutic drugs is not what one would think, or may have been led to believe. It does not consist in the relentless search for specific causal mechanisms which, in turn, suggest specific drugs which are then tested in the model: the model leads to the cause which leads to the cure. The models do not function as a constructive heuristic.

Rather, the models I have examined are only rough stand-ins of the phenomenon of interest. They typically mimic one or two coarse features of the disorder—sham feeding models the condition of eating without calories, tail-pinching models the stress associated with an eating disorder. This is a far cry from developing a model of tuberculosis by infecting an animal with the relevant bacterium. Given a relatively low fidelity version of an eating disorder, the strategy consists of trying all extant drugs. There are only a limited number of classes of drugs available for the treatment of psychological disorders. The *Physicians' Desk Reference* (1994) lists six categories of psychotropics (p. 218). In practice, then, it has been a matter of "rounding up the usual suspects." Any tranquillizer can be tested with the tail-pinch model and any appetite suppressor can be tested with the sham feed model.

While there is much sophisticated exploration of the physiology of the eating disorders, the function of the animal model devolves into a vehicle for testing the array of drugs that already exists. The function of these animal models, thus, is to test drugs, not to generate or facilitate their discovery or development. This is a degenerative use of models. Despite claims to a more seminal role, the function of the animal models have been reduced to mere drug evaluation—in a context in which by only the greatest stretch can it be argued that the disorder of interest has been induced in the animals tested.

Survey of Clinicians Specializing in Eating Disorder Treatment

Animal models of eating disorders have not resulted in direct forms of treatment. However, one might argue that the knowledge gained from the explorations involved— the mapping of physiological pathways concomitant to eating behavior, the microanalysis of the topography and physiology of eating, digestion, and satiation, and the like—has added to the clinician's store of knowledge in ways which, at least indirectly, make their interventions more informed and effective.

It is a relatively simple matter to test this proposition. If research involving animal models of eating disorders has had any impact on treatment, whether direct or indirect, those psychologists in the trenches, those actually devoting a significant portion of their efforts to clinical treatment, would have to be knowledgeable of it. Even if the

Table 6: Survey on Research in Eating Disorders

The following informal survey is intended for psychologists whose practice includes working with people with eating disorders.

Results from the survey will be incorporated into a monograph in progress on psychology's use of animals in research. Results will be treated anonymously.

Your name has been suggested to me by . . . .

Please return completed survey to that person or to me: Dr. Kenneth Shapiro, PO Box 1297, Washington Grove MD 20880.

1. What percent of your practice involves working with people whose diagnosis is an eating disorder—anorexia or bulimia? . . . .
. . . .

2. In your view what is the best method of psychological intervention for anorexia; for bulimia? . . . .
. . . .
. . . .

3. What journal(s) or other resource do you find most helpful for clinicians that specialize or work with eating disorders? . . . .
. . . .

4. Did you know that there are animal models of eating disorders? .
. . . .

5. Can you name or describe an animal model of an eating disorder? If yes, please describe it briefly. . . . .
. . . .

6. Do you know what sham feeding is? If yes, please describe it and what you think its relation to bulimia is. . . . .
. . . .

7. Do you know that putting animals on a 23 hour food deprivation cycle and housing them in an activity wheel is offered as an animal model of anorexia? If yes, please describe what you think its relation to anorexia is. . . . .
. . . .

8. Do you know what fenfluramine is or what it is used for? . . . . .
. . . .

9. In your view, have animal models of eating disorders had any influence on your method of psychological intervention for anorexia; for bulimia? . . . .
. . . .

influence of the animal lab on the clinic is limited to the rhetorical one, discussed in Chapter 3, that of providing language or graphic images of the phenomenon, the clinician presumably would have some awareness and rudimentary understanding of these animal models.

To assess how informed clinicians are in this regard, I devised a survey questionnaire (see Table 6). I employed two approaches to identify clinicians specializing in the treatment of the eating disorders, the selected target population of the informal survey: a list of clinicians suggested by but not themselves members of **PSYETA**, and clinicians listed in the *Directory of Eating Disorders* (1992). Following an initial screening by telephone to establish that the individual specialized in the treatment of eating disorders (defined as a practice 20% of which involved working with people whose diagnosis is an eating disorder) and willingness to participate, individuals were sent the questionnaire by mail. Both rates of refusal to participate and of unreturned questionnaires were low and the process continued until 30 questionnaires were in hand.

The percentage of practice involving treatment of eating disorders ranged from 20–90% with a mean of 55%. The most commonly mentioned "best method of intervention" in the treatment of these disorders was cognitive behaviorism, followed by multi-modal (combinations of approaches). Other methods mentioned by more than one respondent were behaviorist, cognitive, group, psychoanalytic, and insight therapies, and hospitalization.

More than half of the clinicians (60%) indicated that they were not aware that there were animal models of eating disorders; 37% were aware, and one individual (3%) answered that she was "vaguely" aware. When asked if they could name and describe an animal model of eating disorders, 67% said they could not. Of the 33% who said they could, most gave inadequate or vague descriptions. When asked to identify and describe sham feeding, an animal model of bulimia, 87% could not. Of the 13 % who indicated they could, none gave a description of the model which showed that they understood the basic experimental set-up. The results with respect to the activity wheel model of anorexia were similar, with 80 % indicating they could not identify it and no one providing an adequate description. With regard to fenfluramine, a drug used for appetite suppression in the treatment of obesity and subsequently tested in animal models for its effectiveness in the treatment of the true eating disorders, 60 % could not identify it.

When asked their view of whether animal models of eating disorders influenced their treatment approach to these disorders, 87 % replied in the negative. Of those replying in the affirmative, one indicated that the research was useful for conceptualization but not for intervention, one indicated that it was "indirectly" an influence, and one stated, "only helpful in reinforcing my explanations to patients about how what's happening to them is a natural physiological response to food deprivation."

These clinicians listed the following journals and other sources of information as most helpful in their work, beginning with the most frequently mentioned: *International Journal of Eating Disorders* (*IJED*), none [no journals listed as "most helpful"] (tied); conferences on eating disorders; *Handbook of Psychotherapy for Anorexia Nervosa and Bulimia* (*HPANB*)(1985), psychoanalytic journals (tied); *Journal of Consulting and Clinical Psychology* (*JCCP*), newsletters (tied).

It is apparent from this survey that clinicians specializing in the treatment of eating disorders generally are unaware both of the existence of and of the particular results of research efforts by researchers in their own and related fields that utilize animal models to understand and develop effective treatment of eating disorders.

If they don't know, why don't they know? I have already suggested one answer to this question: They do not know because this research enterprise has been unproductive in providing effective treatments. They do not read this literature because it is not helpful to them in their practices. But how would they know that without reading it? By and large they read an applied literature—*IJED*, *HPANB*, and *JCCP*. The first of these is a journal exclusively devoted to eating disorders, while the last covers the field of applied psychology—at least, clinical and consultative interventions. Is the literature on animal models of eating disorders published or even cited in these applied publications? More generally, where and how often is this literature cited? To answer these questions, I undertook a citation analysis of selected investigators of animal model research in eating disorders.

Citation Analyses of Selected Animal Model Researchers' Studies

Citation analysis is a tool that provides quantitative indices of the extent to which particular studies are cited in the scientific literature. It can yield an evaluation of "scientific performance" of an individual, institution, subfield, or even of the development of science as a whole based on the frequency, publication site, and quality of those citations (Garfield, 1979, p. 359). While issues about the technique itself and the possible misuse of results in some contexts, particularly the evaluation of an individual in promotion and hiring decisions, have generated considerable discussion (Garfield, 1985), citation analysis is the recognized centerpiece of the field of scientometrics—the science of the analysis of the "process and development of science" (Garfield, 1987, p. 9).

With the advent of this sophisticated technique, assessment of the scientific contribution and impact of a particular research investigation, set of studies, or subfield advanced beyond reliance on a simple count of the number of publications by a particular investigator. It is important to understand the degree to which research projects vary in the contribution that they eventually make, in both basic research and applied settings. At one extreme of this spectrum of impact are investigations never completed, in the middle are the large number of published studies, at the other extreme are the few published studies that profoundly change the field. Citation analysis provides a powerful tool to measure these and other very different possible scenarios.

As is true in other fields, in psychology not all studies are completed and not all completed studies are published. Journal rejection rates of submitted manuscripts in psychology are between 70 and 80%, a rate which is higher than that in the biological sciences (Rotton, Levitt, & Foos, 1993). While researchers often submit a study to a second journal, some unknown percentage of studies remain unpublished.

Of those studies published, more than half are never cited in subsequent studies. For example, 55% of the papers published between 1981 and 1985 in journals indexed in the *Science Citation Index (SCI)*, the primary publication providing data for such analyses, received no citations in the 5 years following their publication (Hamilton, 1990, p. 1331). To give some idea of the number of possible citation sites, there are over 108,000 scholarly (including nonscientific) journals published (p. 1332).

Further, of those studies cited, about 10% are self-citations (Garfield 1979, p. 362), citations by an investigator of his or her own work. An effective citation analysis distinguishes between citations which are indicative of actual impact on others in the field and those for which that inference is unwarranted—self-citations, review articles, publications not subjected to peer review, and published abstracts. Finally, even within the citations of scientific studies, it is important to assess the quality of the citation by distinguishing among its more or less significant uses or contexts. For example, the investigator may use an earlier study to interpret additional animal or human data or to provide an innovative method; or, of less significance, he or she may mention the earlier study only in passing, in a generalized discussion that simply provides an introduction to the present study. Analysis of the significance of use of the cited study requires an interpretation of the context in which the citation occurs (Garfield, 1983).

One caveat regarding the inference of impact from number of citations is that a high citation rate more reliably implies high level of impact than does a low citation rate imply minimal impact. Garfield describes two phenomena which can conflate the latter inference. "Premature discovery" is a study that is significant but not cited because it is a "work ahead of its time." "Obliteration by incorporation" refers to a process whereby a significant study is relatively uncited because its impact was so profound that it became part of "common understanding" and citation was unnecessary (Garfield, 1987, p. 9). This last is unlikely to obtain where insufficient time has elapsed for such incorporation to occur, as in the citation analysis of relatively recent studies undertaken here.

The present citation analysis attempted to take the above considerations into account. The procedure involved first selecting a sample of nine investigators from among those publishing studies relating to at least one of the three major animal models of eating disorders discussed—sham feeding, tail-pinch, and activity wheel. An individual experienced in the technique was then enlisted to conduct the actual citation analysis (McArdle, 1990).

McArdle searched Medline, a database of the National Library of Medicine, for publications since 1968 authored or coauthored by the nine investigators. For all nine, he included only those publications involving the use of laboratory animals and related to the topic of eating disorders. These animal-based publications were then examined using the CD-ROM version of the *SCI*, which includes all citations from 1986 to 1994.

Since the intent was to identify citations only in original scientific studies by other researchers, the investigator eliminated from the citations examined those that appeared in editorials, review articles, meeting abstracts, and all self- and co-authored studies. Finally, for each citation so identified, he examined the citing study to determine the context of the citation. He judged as significant those citations that used the earlier study to interpret additional animal or human clinical studies, or for its innovative method.

Table 7 lists the number and annual frequency of citations and of citations judged significant, for the nine selected investigators. Taken together, the studies on eating disorders published by the nine investigators were cited .69 times per year in the 9 years following their publication (1986–1994). By comparison, the average annual frequency of all the references in the *SCI* is 1.87 (Garfield, 1980b, p. 317) or more than two and a half times the rate of those examined. While some of this discrepancy may reflect the more stringent criterion for inclusion employed, on the face of it, this is a low overall frequency.

When only those citations judged significant are counted, the overall annual frequency rate is .31. This means that, on average, in a given year seven in ten of the studies examined received no significant citations in the scientific literature.

Table 8 lists the frequencies by journal in which these citations occurred, in order of descending frequency. Comparing this list to those journals indicated in the survey of clinicians as "most helpful for clinicians that specialize or work with eating disorders," there is no overlap! Not one of the journals in which the studies of the nine investigators are cited is mentioned as helpful by these practitioners specializing in the treatment of eating disorders.

Incidentally, the list of journals in which citations appeared reinforces my earlier point that investigators using animal models of eating disorders disproportionately em-

Table 7: Number and Annual Frequency of Citations and Citations Judged Significant, for Nine Selected Investigators

Reference examined	No. of citations*	Annual freq.+	No. of sign. citations#*	Annual freq.+
M.M. HAGAN				
Hagan, MM & Moss, DE 1994	0	0	0	0
Hagan, MM & Moss, DE 1993a	0	0	0	0
Hagan, MM & Moss, DE 1993b	0	0	0	0
Hagan, MM & Moss, DE 1991	5	1.7	1	0.3
T.L. DAVIDSON				
Davidson, TL 1993	0	0	0	0
Davidson, TL & Carreta, JC 1993	0	0	0	0
Davidson, TL & Jarrard, LE 1993	0	0	0	0
Davidson, TL, McKenzie, BR, Tujo, CJ, & Bish, CK 1992	0	0	0	
Davidson, TL, Flynn, FW & Jarrard, LE 1992	1	0.5	0	0
Breslin, PA, Davidson, TL & Grill, HJ 1990	0	0	0	0
Davidson, TL, Flynn, FW & Grill, HJ 1988	3	0.5	1	0.2
H. SZECHTMAN				
Szechtman, H & Hall WG 1980	2	0.2	1	0.1
Szechtman, H 1980	3	0.3	1	0.1
T.W. ROBBINS				
Cole, BJ, Robbins, TW & Everit, BJ 1988	0	0	0	0
Mohammed, AK, Callenholm, NE, Jarbe, TU, Swedberg, MD & Robbins, TW 1986	5	0.6	1	0.1
A.G. PHILLIPS				
Phillips, AG, Atkinson, LJ, Blackburn JR & Blaha, CD 1993	2	2	0	0
Blackburn, JR, Pfaus, JG, & Phillips, AG 1992	12	6	4	2
K.G. LAMBERT				
Lambert, KG, Kinsley, CH 1993	0	0	0	0
Lambert, KG 1993	0	0	0	0
Lambert, KG, Porter, JH 1992	0	0	0	0
Lambert, KG, Peacock, LJ 1989	3	0.6	0	0
S.M. ANTELMAN				
Caggiula, AR, Epstein, LH, Antelman, SM, Saylor, SS et al 1991	4	1.3	1	0.3

Reference examined	No. of citations*	Annual freq.+	No. of sign. citations#*	Annual freq.+
Rowland, NE, Antelman, SM & Bartness, TJ 1985	9	1	2	0.2
Rowland, NE, Marshall, JF, Antelman, SM & Edwards, DJ 1979	0	0	0	0
Antelman, SM, Caggiula, AR, Black, CA, & Edwards, DJ 1978	2	0.2	1	0.1
Eichler, AJ & Antelman, SM 1977	6	0.7	2	0.2
Antelman, SM, Black, CA & Rowland, NE 1977	5	0.6	4	0.4
Antelman, SM, Rowland, NE & Fisher, AE 1976	6	0.7	0	0
Rowland, NE & Antelman SM 1976	12	0.6	5	1
Antelman, SM, Szechtman, H, Chin, P. & Fisher, AE 1975	36	4	20	2.2
Antelman, SM & Szechtman, H 1975	34	3.8	13	1.4

Reference examined	No. of citations*	Annual freq.+	No. of sign. citations#*	Annual freq.+
D.G. MOOK				
Mook, DG, Yoo, D & Wagner, S, 1993	0	0	0	0
Mook, DG, Atkinson, B, Johnston, L & Wagner, S, 1993	0	0	0	0
Mook, DG, Wagner, S, & Hartline, DF, 1991	1	0.3	0	0
Mook, DG, 1992	0	0	0	0
Mook, DG, & Wagner, S, & Talley, CE, 1992	2	1	0	0
Mook, DG & Wagner, S, 1991	0	0	0	0
Przekop, P, Mook, DG, & Hill, DL 1990	0	0	0	0
Mook, DG & Wagner, S, 1989a	1	0.2	0	0
Mook, DG & Wagner, S, 1989b	1	0.2	1	0.2
Mook, DG & Wagner, S, 1988a	1	1.7	1	1.7
Mook, DG, 1988a	0	0	0	0
Mook, DG, 1988b	7	1.2	7	1.2
Mook, DG, Wagner, S, & Schwartz, LA, 1988	0	0	0	0
Mook, DG & Wagner, S, 1988b	0	0	0	0
Mook, DG & Wagner, S, 1987a	1	1.1	1	1.1
Mook, DG & Wagner, S, 1987b	0	0	0	0
Mook, DG & Dreifuss, S, 1986	4	0.5	2	0.3
Mook, DG, Dreifuss, S & Keats, PH, 1986	3	0.4	3	0.4
Mook, DG, Brane, JA, Gonder-Frederick, L & Whitt, JA, 1986	2	0.3	2	0.3

Reference examined	No. of citations*	Annual freq.+	No. of sign. citations#*	Annual freq.+
Rushner, JR & Mook, DG, 1984	8	0.9	1	0.1
Mook, DG, Gonder-Frederick, L, Keats, PH & Mangione, RL, 1984	3	0.3	2	0.2
Mook, DG, Brane, JA & Whitt, JA, 1983a	1	0.1	1	0.1
Mook, DG, Brane, JA & Whitt, JA, 1983b	0	0	0	0
Mook, DG, Culberson, R, Gelbart, RJ & McDonald, K, 1983	9	1	2	0.2
Mook, DG, Brane, JA, Kushner, LR & Whitt, JA, 1983	3	0.3	3	0.3
Mook, DG & Brandsey, SA, 1982	2	0.2	1	0.1
Mook, DG, Cseh, CL, 1981	3	0.3	1	0.1
Mook, DG, 1981	0	0	0	0
Mook, DG, Fisher, JC & Durr, JC, 1975	5	0.6	5	0.6
Mook, DG, Walshe, DZ & Farris, PR, 1975	0	0	0	0
Kenney, NJ & Mook, DG, 1974	1	0.1	0	0
Redick, JH, Nussbaum, AJ & Mook, DG, 1973	4	0.4	1	0.1
Roberts, S, Kenney, NJ & Mook, DG, 1972	0	0	0	0
Mook, DG, Kenney, NJ, Roberts, S, Nussbaum, AJ & Rodier, WI, 1972	25	2.8	9	1
Burke, GH, Mook, DG & Blass, EM, 1972	5	0.6	3	0.3
Mook DG, 1969	13	1.4	6	0.7
Mook, DG & Blass, EM, 1968	0	0	0	0
Mook DG & Kozub, FJ, 1968	5	0.6	2	0.2
J.D. DAVIS				
Davis, JD, Perez, MC & Kung, TM, 1994	0	0	0	0
Davis, JD, Perez, MC, 1993	0	0	0	0
Davis, JD, Smith, GP & Meisner, J, 1993	0	0	0	0
Davis, JD & Perez, MC, 1993	0	0	0	0
Davis, JD & Smith, GP, 1990	7	1.8	3	1
Davis, JD, 1989	12	2.4	6	1.2
Davis, JD & Smith, GP, 1988	4	0.7	3	0.5
Davis, JD, 1988	0	0	0	0
Breif, DJ & Davis, JD, 1984	50	5.6	25	2.8
Breif, DJ & Davis, JD, 1982	1	0.1	0	0

Reference examined	No. of citations*	Annual freq.+	No. of sign. citations#*	Annual freq.+
Davis, JD, Wirtshafter, D, Asin, KE & Breif, DJ, 1981	21	2.3	15	1.7
Collins, BJ & Davis, JD, 1978	2	0.2	1	0.1
Davis, JD & Levine, MW, 1977	23	2.6	11	1.2
Davis, JD & Collins, BJ, 1978	1	0.1	0	0
Davis, JD & Booth, DA, 1974	2	0.2	1	0.1
Campbell, CS & Davis JD, 1974	5	0.6	0	0
Average annual frequencies =	0.69			0.31

* In the years 1986–1994
+ Based on the number of years since publication in 1986–1994
# Those citations that used the earlier study to interpret additional animal or human clinical studies, or for its innovative method.

phasize physiological processes and pharmacological treatments. *Physiology and Behavior* receives more than twice the number of citations of any other journal; while *Psychopharmacology* has the third highest frequency of citations. Of the seven journals containing ten or more citations only *Appetite* does not have a heavy emphasis on physiology and pharmacology.

An earlier study is relevant to the finding here that clinicians do not read and presumably are not influenced by the research literature presenting animal models of human disorders. Kelly (1986) examined two applied clinical journals to see the extent to which studies published in them cited laboratory animal research. While not limiting himself to animal model research, his results bear on the question of the impact of animal-based research on clinical interventions in applied human settings. He selected two applied journals, *JCCP*, one of the journals mentioned by the clinicians in my survey as most helpful, and *Behavior Therapy* (*BT*). As discussed, behavior therapy is one form of intervention that, with some important qualifications, was reliant on animal-based research for its development. Studies in *BT* might be expected to refer generously to such research.

Table 8: Citation Frequency by Journal for Nine Selected Investigators, 1986–1994

Journal	Frequency
Physiol. & Behav.	76
Brain Research	29
Psychopharmacol	27
Appetite	23
Amer. J. Physio.	21
Behav. Neurosci.	19
Pharmacol. Biochem. Behav.	18
Int. J. Obesity	7
Amer. J. Clin. Nutri.	6
Psychobio.	6
Br. Res. Bull.	5
Anim. Learning & Beh.	4
Develop. Psychobiol.	4
J. Nutri.	4
Peptides	4
Alcohol	3
Annal. NY Acad. of Sci.	3
Annales de Endocrinol.	3
Beh. Br. Res.	3
Br. J. Pharmacol.	3
Eur. J. of Pharmacol.	3
J. Neurochem.	3
J. Pharmacol. Exp. Ther.	3
Life Sci.	3
Toxicology	3
Chem. Senses	2
Endocrin.	2
Exp. Clin. Endocrin.	2
Exp. Neurology	2
J. Neural Trans.	2
J. Exp. Psychol. Anim. Beh. Proc.	2
Med. Clin. N.A.	2
Neurosci.	2
Neuroscience Letters	2
Proc. Nutri. Soc.	2
Psychosomatic Med.	2
Aggress. Beh.	1*

The following journals were also cited once: Am. Soc Nephrol., Beh. Pharmacol., Beh. Neuro. Bio., Behav. Brain Sci., Behav. Process, Biochem. Biophys. Res. Com., Br. J. of Cancer, Br. Poultry Sci., Bull. de Soc. Chimique de France, Can. J. Zoology, Cancer Res., Cell & Tissue Res., Chem. Letters, Clin. Neuropharm., Dairy Sci., Diabetes, Drugs, Endocrin. Exper., Envir. Res., Eur. J. Neurosci., Fed. Proc., Int. J. Peptide & Protein Res., Int. J. Neurosci., J. Pharm. Pharmacol., J. Neurosci. Methods, J. Exp. Anal. of Beh., J. Chem. Neuroanatomy, J. Clin. Endocrin. Metab., J. Clin Psychiat., J. Pharm. Exp. Ther., J. Clinical Gastroen., J. Endocrin., J. Anim. Sci., J. Comp. Neurol., J. Endocrin. Invest., Letters Appl. Micro., Med. Hypotheses, Metabolism, Mol. Cell. Neurosci., Neuropharmacol., Neuroreport, Proc. Nutri. Sci., Proc. NAS, Prost. Leukot. Ess, Fatty Acids, Reprod. Nutri. Dev., Science, Thrombosis & Haem.

Of over 3,000 references in *JCCP* in 1984, "only 10 (or less than one third of 1% of the total) were citations of laboratory animal studies" (p. 840). Of over 1,100 references in *BT* in 1984 "only 23 (or 2% of the total) were references to animal studies" (p. 840). From these empirical findings, Kelly concluded that "(c)linical researchers who publish in these two high-quality journals rarely cite animal studies" and that "most current clinical interventions... depend far more closely on previous behavioral research with people rather than animals" (p. 840).

To conclude, the finding of the present citation analysis is that studies of animal models of eating disorders are less frequently cited than the average scientific study in the literature and that their contribution to basic understanding has been relatively insignificant. In addition, the context of most in which those citations do occur further establishes that this research typically does not provide significant or substantive advances. Combining the data from this citation analysis with the survey of clinicians, it is clear that the animal model literature is rarely cited in those journals consulted by clinicians specializing in the treatment of eating disorders. They do not know, for instance, what sham feeding is because it is not discussed in the literature which they have found helpful in their work—the treatment of eating disorders.

Plous' attitude survey of nearly 4,000 psychologists, discussed in the first chapter, provides findings that are consistent with the results of the present citation analysis and survey, while placing them in a broader context of all animal research. Of those psychologists in his sample who are mental health providers (clinicians and counselors), 92.2% indicated that they never, rarely, or only occasionally use findings from psychological research on animals (1996a, p. 1172). Similarly, only 5.7% of such applied psychologists felt that a ban on animal research would seriously hamper their work, while 47.8% indicated that a ban would have no serious effect whatsoever (1996a, p. 1172).

While the present findings and Plous' add to the conclusion, reached in Chapter 1, that animal research is in decline in psychology, they must be tempered by the fact that clinicians are less supportive of animal research than are psychologists who are primarily teachers and researchers. Huskey (1991) found a significant difference between the attitudes of members of the American Psychological Association (APA) and the American Psychological Society (APS). APS members, who are predominantly research psychologists, showed more "pro-animal research attitudes" than did APA members, who are primarily applied or clinical psychologists.

Level of Invasiveness of Selected Animal Model Researchers' Studies

To complete this evaluation of animal models of eating disorders, I shall provide some data on the levels of invasiveness typically involved in these studies. Recall that several scales offer measures of the suffering attendant to experimental procedures on laboratory animals, suffering being defined as in Chapter 1—the emotional response to pain or distress, including that distress associated with harm. The Scale of Invasiveness (Field & Shapiro, 1988) specifically identifies and measures procedures utilized in psychological research. Utilizing this scale, studies of trends in level of invasiveness have found that levels continue to be moderately high.

Of course, the initial selection for study of this particular area of animal models was critical in the levels subsequently found. As noted, I attempted to avoid areas in which the nature of the phenomenon, inherently painful or depressive conditions, would require creating high levels of invasiveness in models with any degree of fidelity—also noting, however, that by definition virtually all disorders involve harmful and/or distressful conditions. Further, I avoided disorders that are predominantly held to be biologically caused, as physiological procedures often involve more invasive procedures than do environmentally or psychologically induced disorders.

While still largely bracketing the question of ethics, the following data arguably stretches beyond the relatively neutral question that has framed the evaluation to this point: What is the contribution of animal models of eating disorders to the larger research enterprise and to the treatment and general understanding of these disorders? Here, we factor in the costs to the animals. As I will suggest in the final chapters, the issue of costs is critical to a utilitarian ethic and is also relevant to a rights theory. However, although not ethically neutral, it is obviously an important parameter of the current debate over the use of animals in research.

To this end, I will organize the presentation around application of the invasiveness scale to the models considered. This provides the requisite overview of the general level of invasiveness involved in animal models of eating disorders while largely avoiding singling out individual studies or researchers.

The sham feeding model of bulimia involves a surgical procedure from which an animal is allowed to recover for at least some period. A surgery that causes an extended period of pain/distress or moderate long-term harm is scored 4 on the six-point scale (0–5, with 5 most invasive). An animal that has a fistula fitted with a cannula in his or her stomach has been significantly harmed. According to Webster, in addition to the distress during recovery from the surgery, a permanent fistula disrupts peristaltic movements and is, functionally, chronic indigestion (1994, p. 239). Further, many of the variables explored in conjunction with this model increase this base level of invasiveness, as a study is scored for the most invasive procedure involved. Some of these involve additional surgical procedures such as brain lesioning, fitting with intracranial cannula, and implanting wire electrodes into muscles involved in ingestion. Most of these are scored 3 or 4 even without the intragastric cannula requisite to sham feeding. Others involve deprivation of food, physical immobilization, and other stress inductions such as tail-pinching and cold-water immersion.

As discussed, these last procedures, particularly tail-pinching, are utilized in the stress-induced eating models of bulimia. Depending on their extent or duration, they are in the 3 or the 4 range. Within this family of models, level of stress itself is typically a variable. For example, Vaswani, Tejwani, and Mousa (1983) induced "acute mild stress" through deprivation of food and water for 12 to 48 hours and "acute severe stress" through 12 hour food and water deprivation followed by a 10 minute swim in water at 4°C. (p. 1983). While often limited to the 3 level, some deprivation studies operationalize such stress at the 4 level (reduction to between 70 and 80% of free-fed body weight). Hagan and Moss (1991) subjected neonate rats to three episodes of deprivation defined as between 75 and 80% free-fed weight. Coscina and Dixon (1983) and others utilized severe food deprivation in rats (four days).

As described, researchers differ in their assessment of the level of stress involved in tail-pinching. In their study utilizing tail-pinching as a stressor, Antelman and Szechman observed several behaviors associated with significant stress (1975, p. 731). In the terms of the Scale of Invasiveness, tail-pinching is an "inescapable noxious stimul(us) that cause(s) moderate pain/distress" (Table C, Chapter 1). Further, tail-pinching typically is combined with other procedures, either surgical (implantation of intra-cerebral cannula) or explicitly stress inducing (rearing rats in isolation). Sahakian and Robbins (1977) combined tail-pinching and social isolation; this latter, as in this instance, when lasting for a period of days is scored 4. Finally, as noted, stress-induced eating shows features of addiction, such as tolerance and withdrawal (Morley & Levine, 1980). Forced addiction and addiction with withdrawal are procedures involving an extended period of pain/distress or moderate long-term harm, and are scored 4.

Another procedure involving stress is central to the activity-stress model of anorexia. Placing a rat in a cage fitted with an exercise wheel and limiting the availability of food to 2–4 hours a day results in excessive exercise to the point of self-starvation. In effect, this procedure induces food deprivation resulting in reduction to 70 % of free-fed weight, which is scored 4—in fact, a weight below this percentage is scored 5. This procedure also results in cessation of the estrous cycle in females. As noted, earlier uses of the activity wheel with a more restrictive schedule of food availability (1–2 hours/day), result in extensive ulcers and even death.

Clearly, animal models of eating disorders typically involve moderate to high levels of invasiveness. The basic procedures of the models reviewed involve invasiveness in the 3 and 4 range. These studies rarely are limited to procedures scored 0–2, those involving only mild, escapable pain, or mild distress and no long-term harm. Further, because the scale only scores for the most invasive procedure in a given study and because the studies under review often combine more than one invasive procedure, this general result must be considered an underestimate of the amount of pain/distress and harm involved. The level of invasiveness found here for animal models of eating disorders is consistent with those found in studies of trends of invasiveness in the larger field of psychological research, which also are at the 3 and 3 + level.

In this section, I have assessed these models with respect to costs to the animals, using the Scale of Invasiveness. Several other scales attempt to score a broader range of parameters in a given study. For example, Porter (1992) described a system that combined scores from eight different factors into a single score of ethical concern. Three factors of immediate interest here are "aim of the experiment" (alleviation of substantial human or nonhuman pain = lowest ethical concern; fundamental research with no clear alleviation intended = highest ethical concern); "realistic potential of the experiment to achieve objective;" and "quality of animal care" (p. 102).

Using Porter's scheme, the findings reported earlier (the review of the effectiveness and research sources of current treatments of eating disorders, the survey of clinicians specializing in the treatment of eating disorders, and the citation analysis of published studies of selected animal model investigators) allow me to go beyond the assessment of the "realistic potential" of the experiments under review here and indicate whether they, in fact, realized their aim. These three sets of findings strongly indicate that they did not and that, therefore, scores from this factor are of the "highest ethical concern." While I have no direct data on the issue of quality of animal care (although see Phillips, 1993, noted earlier), the shortfalls in the training of psychologists in surgery and the absence of constraints lent by a therapeutic frame (no Hippocratic or Veterinarian Oath) discussed earlier, suggest the likelihood of relatively low quality of care. The high scores of ethical concern for low treatment contribution (low alleviation of pain, in Porter's terms) and the likely high score for low quality of care, combined with the high invasiveness scores, in effect, constitute a cost/benefits analysis. Thus, animal models of eating disorders have high costs to the animals and low benefits to humans.

Conclusion

In his discussion of the complexities involved in assessing the benefits of animal research, Rowan (1993) employs the metaphor of an "endless circle." That circle is formed by "insights flowing from the clinic to the laboratory to the theoreticians and back again" (p. 11). In a related context, Zurlo, Rudacille, and Goldberg (1994) employ a similar geometric metaphor, an "infinity circle," to describe their view of the relation among three types of research—*in vivo* (animal-based), *in vitro* (test-tube based), and clinical (human patient-based). "Progress depends on these three strands of investigation flowing into and feeding each other in an infinity circle of inquiry and information" (p. 7).

The clear and, I think, compelling thrust of the present extended presentation and evaluation of animal models in psychology is that these metaphors are not apt. While perhaps appropriate or at least attractive as ideals, a better metaphor, one descriptive of the actual practice of animal research, requires a very different geometric concept: one representing separateness or discreteness rather than reciprocal interaction.

For the enterprise of animal models of human psychology is a "separate world." I borrow this image from Garfield (1980a, p. 103) who used it to characterize a narrower instance of the general finding reached here, specifically, the lack of interaction and communication between animal researchers using cats and those using rats. A related image already discussed is also descriptive, the "oft-noted *ingrown* nature" of operant research (Neuringer, 1984, p. 399, emphasis added), preventing it from productive application to behavioral therapy. Finally, an image implied by Stephens in his study of maternal deprivation studies, mentioned in Chapter 3, while less critical is also related—a one-way street. Quoting Kraemer and McKinney, Stephens noted, "'It must be admitted that the primary flow of information, to date, has been from human clinical research into the animal modelling area,' not vice versa" (1986, p. 66). While not quite ingrown, this is far from the endless circle.

Rather than constructively interactive with other parts of the research enterprise or with work being done in treatment settings, research involving animal models of eating disorders is ingrown in several ways. Although related, I divide them into the scientific or investigative process itself, its relation to applied settings, and the role of animals in the laboratory.

The animal model research under scrutiny here is insulated from the target phenomenon of interest, the eating disorders. Rather than arising from extensive familiarity with these disorders in its human settings, the models build on procedures already in the scientific research repertoire of unrelated experimental procedures. More critically, once an animal model is defined, its development proceeds largely through further research consisting of recursive and often duplicative investigation of already studied variables and of other models. Rather than continually going back to the target phenomenon for validation to form that vaunted endless circle, it relies on confirmation by the insular criterion of consistency with other comparably insulated research.

The logic of experimental discourse allows and fosters this separateness. The model is often based on one or two features that are only coarsely analogous to the target phenomenon. In the instance of animal models of eating disorders, I showed that an algorithm is constructed so elementary as to omnivorously incorporate an inexhaustible supply of variables, hypothesized as either etiological explanation or treatment. The presence of any aspect grossly analogous to the target phenomenon is taken as a hypothetical etiology, while its absence suggests that a possible treatment is lurking. Insidiously, the rough analogic basis inspiring models and the use of already operationalized variables for their further investigation truncates rather than productively generates thought. The enterprise does not issue in fresh understanding and insight; everything is tried and nothing works. The resultant opus is relatively infrequently cited even within the scientific, as distinguished from the applied, literature.

On the applied side, it is even more strikingly clear that practitioners and laboratory-based researchers operate in separate worlds. The animal models have contributed virtually nothing toward the effective treatment of eating disorders. Clinicians specializing in their treatment read a literature that only rarely cites the purportedly relevant research. They are unaware even of the names and basic operations that identify several of the more fully investigated animal models. They believe that animal models have not influenced their method of treatment of the eating disorders. Consistent with this, a sample of all clinicians indicate that they rarely use findings from psychological research on animals (Plous, 1996a).

Most animal model research pursues a physiological etiology and correlative psychopharmacological treatment of the eating disorders despite the fact that the preponderance of evidence from cross-cultural and epidemiological studies suggests that the phenomenon is culturally determined. This physiological bent is also at variance with the predominant view of practitioners and clinic-based researchers. The perennial split between practitioners and lab-based researchers described earlier as a leitmotif in the history of modern psychology is borne out in this particular corner of the field.

Another aspect of the separate world of animal model research is the relation of the investigators involved to their animal subjects. Unlike the separateness resulting from the failure of animal models to form a circle of reciprocal and productive intercourse with the target phenomenon and practitioners treating it, this aspect was purposively designed. The investigators live in a separate world in that they have intentionally worked to construct animals for the laboratory to prevent sharing (being biased by) a common world with them. While I have reviewed evidence that this desideratum was never realized, the preoccupation with technology that would reduce animals to preparations, physiological part-processes, conduits, and instrumentation—in effect, to technology—stands between the investigator and any intercourse with his or her animal subjects.

In the contemporary pluralistic world, the phenomenological possibility of living in a separate world strikes a deep and troubling chord. Our modern world is so complex, dense, and varied in language, beliefs, and values that each of us primarily lives a world apart, as a member of one of countless distinct subcultures, neighborhoods, professional specialties, and the like. Yet the development of electronic and computer technology (the information highway) and of the environmental movement (the web of life) are strange bedfellows in underscoring the converse truism. For it is also true that there is only one world, and that we all live, enjoy, and suffer in it together, human and nonhuman animals alike (Roszack, 1995). What each of us does, through our individual and as well as our institutional identities, impacts on all inhabitants of this one world. In the final two chapters I turn to a review and discussion, first, of the ethical obligations and, in the final chapter, of the policy obligations that follow from that common membership.

Chapter 5
Ethical Issues
in Psychology's
Use of Animals

Less than two decades after the publication of Singer's *Animal Liberation*, the first serious modern philosophical treatment of ethical issues involving nonhuman animals, there are already several distinct ways in which philosophers address these issues. For virtually all these discourses, a starting point is the argument that animals are "objects of moral concern." They count morally for their own sake. Unlike in an earlier humane ethic, our concern about being "kind to animals" is not limited to the effects that cruelty to animals might have on us. On the other side, to say that animals are now the direct objects of our moral concern does not imply or require that they must also be moral agents, as distinguished from moral objects. While hurting animals can be the occasion of blame, only we can be blameworthy.

To say that animals, or at least much of the animal kingdom matters ethically means that when we act in any way that affects them we must take their interests into account. In the language of ethics, their and our interests and welfare are competing claims. As we will see, the two leading philosophical discourses differ in the way they talk about these claims. For Regan (1983), the claims are individual rights that in most ordinary circumstances cannot be abridged; for Singer (1975), they are part of an assessment of costs to and benefits for all those affected.

Scholars point to several different factors occasioning this admission of animals into the moral universe. During the 1960s reforms directed at institutionalized discrimination against classes of people based on race and later on gender led to increased sensitivity to and strategies for addressing injustice to nonhuman animals (Jasper & Nelkin, 1992). In this period, critiques of science and of over-reliance on technological fixes also crystallized, lending themselves to reconsideration of the use of lab animals as instruments—as a kind of technological fix. More recently, concern about violence in society has included consideration of how our treatment of animals contributes to the maintenance of a "culture of violence" (Lockwood & Hodge, 1986; White and Shapiro, 1994).

Within science itself, the Tuskegee affair led to the need to oversee the use of human subjects in research. In the early 1970s it was revealed that studies undertaken by the United States Public Health Service over a period of decades had involved withholding known effective treatment (penicillin) for syphilis from Southern African-Americans who sought help at a clinic at Tuskegee Institute in Alabama. The development of institutional research review committees resulting from this affair provided an opening for a comparable mechanism to oversee animal-based research.

Many scholars point to the development of the modern notion of animals as companions or pets, itself a product of urbanization and loss of contact with nature, as another important factor in the inclusion of animals on our ethical agenda (Thomas, 1983; Serpell, 1986). When surveyed, most Americans indicate that their pet animals are members of the family (Cain, 1985). It is a small step from that membership to the idea of giving moral consideration to animals.

Finally, and somewhat ironically, animal research itself has been an occasion of this development. While mostly derived from nonlaboratory ethological research, the description of sophisticated intellectual and social capabilities in many different species of animals, from chimpanzees (Goodall, 1990) to bees (Griffin, 1992), has occasioned their placement on our moral agenda. With these discoveries, it becomes more difficult to maintain the reductionistic construction of laboratory animals as deindividuated, despecified, and deanimalized instruments. Animals begin to emerge as beings who have minds; who take in and process information, or think (Griffin, 1992); who have subjectivity—form intentions and have feelings, or experience the world (Noske, 1989; Cheney & Seyfarth, 1990); and who have a social life—form relations with each other and with us (Goodall, 1990; Davis & Balfour, 1992).

Given these several historical factors and the strength and robustness of the several philosophical discourses, no doubt animals are on our moral agendas to stay. As Garner notes, "[o]ur treatment of animals is now taken seriously as a mainstream branch of applied ethics..."(1993, p. 2). However, the changes in practice that should follow from this development have only begun to be realized. As we will see, continued resistance to these changes is a function of institutional vested interests and inertia, of psychological mechanisms that allow the continued exploitation of animals, and of popular attitudes toward animals that, in practice, still exclude them from moral consideration or, as social psychological research refers to it, from the "scope of justice" (Opotow, 1993).

Spectrum of Ethical Positions

The number of feature-length popular U.S. magazine treatments of the animal issue increased from two in 1980 to ten in 1990 (Bott, 1993). In general, the articles were positive or at least balanced in their presentation of an animal rights perspective. The impact of this coverage was mixed: the issue was now on the social agenda and people were beginning to be educated to some of the conditions in question. However, as it does for most contested social issues, the press was inclined to limit coverage to oversimplified, polarizing, and extreme positions that it defined as newsworthy (Gitlin, 1980).

This should not blind us to the fact that there is a broad spectrum of positions on "both sides" of the issue. Jasper and Nelkin (1992) divide the contemporary animal advocacy movement into welfarists, pragmatists, and fundamentalists, while Orlans (1993) divides animal-related organizations on "both sides" into exploiters, users, welfar-

Table 9: A Spectrum of Contemporary Ethical Views on the Use of Animals in Research

Ethical skepticism: "there is no such thing as objective right and wrong," a view taken by many scientists in the positivist tradition

Ethical relativism: right and wrong is simply a reflection of a particular society's current values

Absolute dominionism: humans have no ethical obligations to animals, as they are not objects of moral consideration

Anthropocentric consequentialism: wrong treatment of animals is only that which harms humans

Non-malevolence: it is wrong to have evil motives with regard to animals

Humane beneficence: it is wrong to cause unnecessary pain to animals

Reverence for life: it is wrong to kill animals except for important purposes

Permissive utilitarianism: it is acceptable to harm and kill animals if there is a likelihood that the benefits will outweigh the costs

Restrictive utilitarianism: it is wrong to harm and kill animals as, in most instances in which their interests are given equal consideration, the costs to them outweigh the benefits to humans

Rights philosophy: it is wrong to exploit animals because doing so violates their rights as individuals

ists, rightists, and liberationists. Kellert (1978) finds evidence for ten distinct attitudes toward animals in American society: naturalistic, ecologistic, humanistic, moralistic, scientistic, aesthetic, utilitarian, dominionistic, negativistic, and neutralistic. Finally, Tannenbaum and Rowan (1985) define a spectrum of contemporary ethical views on the use of animals in research (Table 9).

Similar or Different: An Organizing Concept

What kind of being is an animal? For philosophers to argue that animals count ethically, they must answer this question. If they can describe the qualities or attributes of humans that clearly require that we treat each other ethically, then the question becomes: do nonhuman animals also have these attributes? If they do, there is an obligation to consider them ethically. More generally, in what ways are animals similar and in what ways are they different from us? We take this last as an organizing concept that is helpful in understanding the various philosophical positions and their application to the use of animals in psychological research.

Obviously, human and nonhuman animals are similar in some ways and different in others. We are similar in that we are all animals and different in that we are a distinct species of animal. Historically, some cultures have emphasized the similarities and some the differences. Of those that emphasize the similarity, some emphasize how humans are animals and others how animals are human. At their respective extremes, the former is dehumanizing while the latter is anthropomorphizing. Those that emphasize the differentness typically do so by valuing humans at the expense of other animals: they are beasts while we are god-like. But it is also possible to emphasize the differentness and derive from it an obligation to treat animals humanely. The early humane movement in the United Kingdom was built on the view that humans (at least humans in certain social classes in English society) are different from nonhuman animals (Tester, 1991, pp. 94–120). The obligation to be kind to animals derived in part from the view that only we can master our animal impulses and be humane to other beings. We can and should be kind to animals because unlike them only we can be humane, humanitarian, human.

In philosophy, the question of similarity/differentness is typically couched in terms of continuity or discontinuity between human and nonhuman animals. Continuity implies not identity but an absence of important qualitative differences, while discontinuity implies that such radical attributes as rationality, language, soul, mental life or self-awareness do, in fact, separate us from other animals.

The ideas of Descartes are a clear and influential example of the insistence on discontinuity. For this 17th century philosopher, humans are distinguished from nonhuman animals in that only humans are rational and have a mental life. By underscoring discontinuity, Descartes affirmed a radical categorical distinction between two kinds of beings: humans are conscious, experiencing, and spiritual, while other animals are complex and mindless machinery.

On the other side, Darwin is a clear and influential example of the insistence on continuity. The theory of evolution emphasizes the continuity among species, as they have common ancestors and humans have only recently diverged from other species. Genealogical lines between species are blurred, complex and continually shifting. The broad canvas of evolution reveals the continuity, relationship, and similarity beneath the only apparent differences among species. In any case, it allows no place for any special differences between human and nonhuman animals. It departs both from the Cartesian idea that only humans have minds and experience and from an earlier

Judeo-Christian tradition featuring a special creation that elevates humans above the rest of creation.

Each in his own way, both Descartes and Darwin provided part of the conceptual framework of contemporary science and, in particular, of laboratory animal research in psychology. By depriving animals of the capacity for a mental life, Descartes laid the ground for behaviorism, an animal-based enterprise in which behavior rather than the experience of it is the exclusive focus of study. On the other hand, by building a theory on the continuity of evolution among species, Darwin justified the assumption that any law or principle governing human behavior could also be found in animal behavior.

This dual influence from exemplars of discontinuity and continuity helps clarify the philosophical background to the contradiction which Singer described in contemporary scientific research involving animals:

> So the researcher's central dilemma exists in an especially acute form in psychology: Either the animal is not like us, in which case there is no reason for performing the experiment; or else the animal is like us, in which case we ought not to perform an experiment on the animal which would be outrageous if performed on one of us (1975, p. 47).

Singer's "dilemma" is limited to a critique of animal research that has as its primary goal understanding humans, that is primarily to animal model research. By the way, his assertion that there is "no reason for performing the experiment" if animals and humans are different applies only to the strong analogy concept of animal models. As we have seen, under the weak analogy concept, animal models can still serve a heuristic function in helping us to understand human pathology and behavior even if they are different from us. More importantly for the discussion here, it is clear that the inconsistency which Singer has articulated has roots in the joint Cartesian-Darwinian legacy of contemporary science: we can study them to understand ourselves because of the continuity between us which the theory of evolution implies and its later scientific demonstration in genetic biology confirms, and we can subject them to even the most painful procedures because they are mindless machines, certainly not the kinds of things that require moral consideration. In this best of all possible worlds, animals are like us (continuity) on biological grounds while unlike us (discontinuity) on ethical grounds.

However, Singer's challenge to the research enterprise to get its practice and ethics together can also be mounted against the animal protection movement. As I described, an earlier humane movement underscored the discontinuity between humans and animals. By contrast, the contemporary animal rights movement builds on the idea of continuity. Newkirk, cofounder of People for the Ethical Treatment of Animals, asserts, in a quip which she justifiably complains is often misquoted, that when it comes to feelings like pain, hunger, and thirst, "...a rat is a pig is a dog is a boy" (Corrigan, 1990, pp. 171–172). More philosophically, both Singer and Regan underscore similarity or continuity, Singer through concepts of suffering and interests common to all animals and Regan through the notion that all animals (at least adult mammals) are "subjects of a life."

While the charge of the animal rights movement that laboratory animal research is unethical is based on continuity, its most prevalent critique of that research on scientific grounds is based on an assumption of discontinuity. We cannot learn anything about ourselves from the study of nonhuman animals because we are so different from them. Rats are so unlike us that we cannot learn from them about the development of cancer or the psychology of learning in humans. So, while pro-animal research scientists inconsistently assert continuity to justify the use of animals on scientific grounds and discontinuity to justify use on ethical grounds, anti-animal research activists reverse that: they assert discontinuity to disqualify the use of animals on scientific grounds and continuity to disqualify that use on ethical grounds.

Still, as the following discussion of different philosophical discourses will show, it is the pro-animal research advocates that are out of stride with contemporary developments. On the ethical issue, most philosophers agree that traditional Western philosophy and cultural values were overly human-centered at the expense of nature and other animals, and that in the modern industrial era their loss is, and increasingly will be, our loss. The inclusion of non-human animals in a widening circle of compassion, the reevaluation of their use as tools for our ends, and the acknowledgment of them as objects of moral consideration are all needed correctives to this anthropocentrism. They are consistent with a progressive movement of history which increasingly distances itself from the myth of an earth- and human-centered view of the universe.

On the scientific issue, an earlier naive view that other animals can serve as disease containers which would allow us to directly observe and study human diseases is no longer viable. As I argued earlier, it is not accurate to conceive of animals as models that can directly (isomorphically) reveal the causal relations underlying psychological or even biological phenomena.

Consistent with these trends, a growing consensus (Midgley, 1989) comes down on the side of emphasizing similarity and continuity. When we emphasize similarity, we blur the line between human and nonhuman and no longer take it as the fundamental cleavage. When we give up the categorical scheme in which humans are given special standing, we dismantle the framework within which justifications for using nonhuman animals to promote human welfare have traditionally operated. We are then open to draw lines elsewhere, say between animals and plants (de Chardin, 1959); or between living and nonliving matter; or, between the Great Apes (humans, chimpanzees, gorillas, orangutans) and all other animals

(Cavalieri & Singer, 1993). When we do blur the line between human and nonhuman animals, we more typically treat those other animals better.

Yet, logically and philosophically, differentness or discontinuity could be the basis of an ethic of respect. In fact, the contemporary philosopher Levinas (1969) makes what he calls "otherness" the foundation of his moral philosophy. For Levinas, the simple observation that we can never fully know the experience of another being and that there is always distance between us is the foundation of our moral obligations to each other. "Otherness," not similarity or togetherness, is the basis of respect.

However, the literature of social psychology strongly suggests the opposite—that in our daily dealings with each other some "principle of similarity" more often provides that basis:

> In general, people give more consideration to others who are perceived as similar to themselves than to those who are perceived as dissimilar. For example, people are more willing to help similar others, more attentive to the pain and suffering of those who are similar, more attracted to similar others, more punitive when the victim of an aggressive act is perceived as similar, and less punitive or aggressive when the offender is similar to them (Plous, 1993, p. 32).

With respect to other animals, degree of concern about a particular endangered species corresponds to the perception of how similar those animals are to us (p. 34).

I conclude that similarity/differentness has been and is an important organizing concept in our treatment of other animals and that, while recognizing differentness, emphasizing similarity is a preferred attitude on scientific, historical, ethical and psychological grounds.

However, I offer one final counter example which will direct us to the need for an additional organizing concept. The history of hunting reveals that it is a complex phenomenon that has been justified through many different views of animals and nature (Cartmill, 1993). Here also, it is helpful to organize these views into those emphasizing similarity or differentness between humans and other animals. Biblical language underscores differentness by placing us nearer to God, alone being created in his image, and giving us dominion over other animals. In the more secular terms of modern times, this role of steward allows us to "manage" other animals as a natural resource for our own use. We are different in that only we have the capacity to be rational managers. Dominion, stewardship, and wildlife management are all apologies for hunting other animals based on ideas of discontinuity.

However, recent studies indicate that hunters often perceive their kill as similar to them. A study of contemporary Dutch hunters reveals that the "pleasure of hunting" increases to the degree that the hunter attributes presumedly human characteristics to the game-species, such as cleverness, unpredictability, and courage (Dahles, 1993). Hunted animals are constructed as similar to humans. However, other investigators have emphasized how similarity is achieved as the human hunter becomes like other animals. "Others like to hunt because it dissolves that [animal-human] boundary for them and lets them know that they themselves are beasts" (Cartmill, 1993, p. 235). Relying on the animal rights position, those who are anti-hunting also typically emphasize the similarity between human and nonhuman animals. So, while the issue of human/animal similarity or difference is salient in attitudes of hunters and anti-hunting activists, it does not cleanly sort them out.

Cartmill notes a distinction that does:

> One important difference that separates nature-loving hunters from their opponents is that the antihunting activist worries about the lives and welfare of individual members of an animal species, whereas the hunter-ecologist regards the species as the enduring entity and sees the hunted animal chiefly as an ephemeral sample of it (p. 236).

This brings us to a second organizing concept in contemporary philosophical discourse on how and whether animals matter ethically: individual- and nonindividual-based philosophies. The following brief presentation of the different philosophies divides them into those which make the individual the focus of moral concern and those which build ethics on broader bases such as relationship, community, and the ecosystem itself. The discussion keys on the implications of several philosophies on the ethics of psychological research using animals.

Individual-Based Philosophy: Regan's Case for Animal Rights

Philosophies that take the individual as the primary unit of consideration form the foundation of Western moral and political tradition. By contrast, in certain Eastern traditions the individual is secondary and primary consideration is given to a global process of which the individual is only a part. In these holistic philosophies, such Western goals as self-development are turned upside down. Rather than to fulfill or "actualize" oneself, the "goal" is to forget the self, to give up a preoccupation with "ego" and individual goals. Such moral philosophies are, arguably, more consistent with political philosophies which take the society as a whole as primary and promote political systems such as communism and other forms of statism (cf. individualism of Western liberalism). Historically, while intending to foster cooperation for the greater good of the group and community, these have been vulnerable to totalitarian means of controlling and limiting individual freedom. However, more recent efforts at nonindividual-based philosophies are emerging which may avoid such pitfalls.

The modern expression of the Western emphasis on the individual dates from the Enlightenment which made rationality the basis of individuality and held, following Descartes, that animals are not rational. By virtue of their rationality, only human beings are free and self-determining. Only they are objects of moral consideration for their own sake and only they have rights.

In a sense, Regan's seminal theory of animal rights (1983) merely extends this individualism to nonhuman animals. His is an individual-based philosophy solidly within the Western tradition. By contrast, as I will discuss, certain current environmental philosophies claim that ethical considerations should be extended beyond individuals to ecosystems, or that rights can be attributed to levels of a system that even an animal rights philosopher would not accept as individuals. In his discussion of its implications, Regan notes the "central importance of *the individual*" (p. 395) in animal rights philosophy and the difficulty of reconciling it "with the more *holistic* view of nature emphasized by many of the leading environmental thinkers" (p. 361, emphases in original).

For Regan, an individual has rights if he or she is a "subject of a life" (p. 243). While clearly broadening beyond it, this notion can be seen as a modernized and more psychological version of the traditional Enlightenment criterion of rationality. At least some nonhuman animals are subjects of a life in that they have beliefs and desires and the ability to satisfy them through action and anticipation of results. In terms of the organizing concept of continuity/discontinuity, here Regan opts for continuity or similarity. Nonhuman animals are like humans in certain ways that are the basis of the attribute "individual." Animals are similar to humans in that they also are individuals.

By virtue of this, they have "inherent value," that is they have "value in themselves" (p. 235) and "in their own right" (p. 237) and are not merely "receptacles" or "replaceable resources." For example, their value is not reducible to their use as animal models or carriers of disease.

The fact of their inherent value means that they have rights and obliges us to treat them *"in ways that respect their inherent value"* (p. 248, emphasis in original). Respectful treatment does not allow harming one individual so that other individuals or groups of individuals can receive benefits. This distinguishes an individual-based rights philosophy from a utilitarian theory such as that of Singer, discussed below. According to Regan's critique, in a utilitarian philosophy individuals are mere receptacles of values, for the goodness of any act is the sum of value or satisfaction gained or lost for all involved. One individual's rights can be overridden for the sake of this greater value to the group.

Regan's philosophy has generated an extensive debate within moral philosophy. I will discuss Singer's critique on utilitarian grounds, denying any overriding or first principle such as rights. Other efforts borrow from other major philosophical theories: Rawls, Davidson, and the later work of Wittgenstein. Taking on both Regan and Singer, Carruthers (1992) argues that animals do not have moral standing as they are not rational agents or contractors. If they cannot represent their own interests, they cannot participate in the development of a social contract which, following Rawls, is the basis of ethics. Following Davidson, Frey (1980) reasons that since rights presuppose interests, which presuppose, in turn, belief and language, then nonhuman animals do not have rights. Leahy (1991) also asserts that their lack of language means that our talk about them, our "language games" (a term from Wittgenstein), are radically different than our talk about ourselves. For example, even when we say that "the dog thinks, or believes ... ," we mean it in a much more limited sense, one that is not consistent with the attribution of rights.

Application to Psychological Research

The implications of the rights view for the use of animals in research, including psychological research, are straightforward:

> Scientific research, when it involves routinely harming animals in the name of possible 'human and humane benefits,' violates [the] requirement of respectful treatment. Animals are not to be treated as mere receptacles or renewable resources. Thus does the practice of scientific research on animals violate their rights. Thus ought it to cease, according to the rights view (Regan, 1983, p. 385).

While in the rights view the harm of one individual cannot be justified on the basis of benefits to others, Regan does recognize that there are exceptional situations where any action taken will harm one or another individual and we must choose between competing harms. Regan analogizes these to the situation where several individuals share the risks of being in a lifeboat which can not accommodate the survival of all its passengers. In such a circumstance where we must choose between, say, the death of a dog and a human, Regan argues that the death of a dog is not as great a harm as is the death of a human. This is not because the dog does not have inherent value but because the loss of his or her life "is not comparable to the harm that death would be for any of the humans [on the lifeboat]" (p. 324).

For Regan this extreme circumstance where harms must be compared is decidedly not the situation in the research laboratory. The differences between the situation in the laboratory and that in the lifeboat are several: the benefits in the lab are only possible results; they are not benefits to the individuals, human or animal, immediately involved; the individual laboratory animals are not there voluntarily; their value is being reduced to a receptacle or resource for the interests of others; and such harm would not be allowed if done to a human.

Regan clarifies that his is not an anti-science or anti-research philosophy. It only prohibits research that routinely harms individuals and research the possible benefits of which is limited to individuals not directly involved in the investigation. Since by its very nature experimentation is the testing of a hypothesis that may or may not be found to obtain, no research can guarantee benefits. However, it is possible to conduct research that has the possibility of benefiting the individual to which it also subjects harm. This would seem to allow research on sick animals and humans in which efforts are made to develop and test potential treatments. In the case of the human, such a procedure would require their consent or the consent of a guardian. It is not clear how this would be dealt with an animal who can not give direct consent. Dawkins (1980; 1990) has suggested ways in which behavior can be taken as indication of a preference and, by implication, of a consent to allow a certain condition.

It is also possible to conduct research that does not routinely harm the objects of study. For example, certain kinds of research involve merely observing animals and minimize any disturbance of them. Such field-research is done in naturalistic or semi-naturalistic settings where the individual animals are essentially free to live out their lives. These are potentially very significant exceptions to the prohibition against research in the rights view. There is already a considerable enterprise in ethology and comparative psychology that conducts such noninvasive research in naturalistic settings. Through it, we have demonstrated scientifically the considerable social, communicative, and cognitive abilities of animals. Presumably, then, Regan would not oppose noninvasive, naturalistic animal research.

However, it is clear that using animals as models of human phenomena is the paradigmatic case which the rights view does prohibit. In it, animals are explicitly used as stand-ins for our interests rather than as individuals in their own right. As we have seen, such research is typically highly invasive and/or harmful and occurs in a setting which is anything but naturalistic. The basis of the animal model strategy is to help generate ideas about the actual object of study. Benefits for humans are only an indirect possibility and one that, arguably, might be reached by other means requiring less extrapolation. Any consideration of benefits for the animals involved is extraneous and incidental.

For Regan, laboratory-based animal research as currently practiced is not an instance in which the harm of one individual can be simply weighed against the relief from harm of other individuals. In the laboratory situation, the rights of an individual animal trump the value of any benefits to others and cannot justly be overridden. The simple human intuition about humans—that we would not, except in extraordinary circumstances (the lifeboat situation), condone the sacrifice of a human being for the sake of other human beings—is carried over to nonhuman animals. Their inherent value is given equal consideration to our own.

As we will see, the great majority of animal research psychologists do not accept this position. On those rare occasions when they do employ a language of ethics rather than of science, they use language that is closer to Singer's. Through utilitarian discourse, they attempt to justify rather than curtail current research practices involving animals.

However, British psychologist Heim's (1978) concept of "intrinsically objectionable means" can be derived from an individual rights philosophy. Heim argues that certain experimental procedures (and, I add, certain housing conditions) involving animals are inherently offensive on ethical grounds independent of any benefits to others that might be obtained. As examples, she refers to "... experiments which demand the infliction of severe deprivation, or abject terror, or inescapable pain...". Clearly, the implication of this concept is that there are ethical limits to what an individual can be required to suffer for the sake of other individuals. Bateson includes this limitation in his proposed schema of considerations necessary in deciding whether a research study is justifiable. "...[C]ertain levels of animal suffering would be unacceptable regardless of the quality of the research or its probable benefit" (Bateson, 1992, p. 33).

The APA considered making this principle part of its policy on animal research. A version of its Guidelines for Ethical Conduct in the Care and Use of Animals included the following statement, eventually deleted in a later draft, "It is recognized that certain extreme procedures may be inherently objectionable on ethical grounds" (APA, 1984, section 8). Despite the serious consideration of this principle, when discussing highly invasive procedures the latest revision of the APA Guidelines allows their use "when the objectives of the research cannot be achieved by other methods" (APA, 1992, section 5, D). This language clearly refuses the intrinsically objectionable means principle by giving absolute priority to the "objectives of the research"—there are no limits to what can be done to an individual to benefit other individuals (almost always human) not involved in the research. The only exception to this is the prohibition against the use of "muscle relaxants or paralytics alone during surgery, without general anesthesia..." (APA, 1992, section 5, G), which merely echoes the prohibition in the Animal Welfare Act.

Other professional organizations also have listed procedures that are unacceptable independent of potential benefits to others. Orlans (1984), then director of Scientists Concerned for Animal Welfare, suggested several such, including unrelieved restraint of primates in mechanical devices for extended periods of time. In addition to a prohibition against muscle relaxants in place of anesthetics, the Canadian Council of Animal Care prohibits "traumatizing procedures involving crushing, striking or beating in unanesthetized animals or animals allowed to recover from anesthesia," and use of Freund's Complete Adjuvant, a procedure used to stimulate antibody production through an injection that inflames tissue (Orlans, 1993, p. 122).

Again, however, it is clear that neither the substance nor the language of Regan's rights philosophy has found its way into establishment ethics codes and policy statements. A former president and prominent spokesperson of the APA, Miller explicitly rejects a criterion that would recognize any limits on animal suffering in the enterprise of animal research: "... setting a limit on the degree of suffering that may be produced in an animal experiment is likely to halt the understanding, prevention, or cure of the very conditions that produce the greatest animal and human suffering" (1984, p. 8). In the profession of psychology, animals do not have inherent value and do not have rights. We will see below if Singer's utilitarian philosophy has fared better to date in its impact on the practice of psychological animal research.

Nonindividual-Based Philosophy

We will discuss three philosophies that differ from Regan's animal rights view in not resting on the primacy of the individual. We emphasize Singer's utilitarian account as it deals most fully with animal research in psychology; as the publication of *Animal Liberation* is, arguably, the major event leading to the emergence of the contemporary animal rights movement; and as proponents of animal-based research also utilize a version of utilitarian theory or at least borrow its language.

First, two other theories are described briefly: the first is an application of feminist theory, while the second extends a concept of community to nonhuman animals and nature. Although neither is fully developed as yet, they are important for their conceptual and political promise as well, being the possible basis of alliances with feminism and environmentalism, respectively. The demographics of these latter two movements are also favorable for such alliances as 78.3% of animal rights activists are women and 98.4% indicate involvement or identification with the environmental movement (Richards & Kranich, 1991).

Relation-Based Ethics

Feminist theory is primarily a critique of male-centered ways of thinking and acting and an exposé of discriminatory and oppressive applications of their influence and power (Donovan, 1985). It is readily shown that male-centered or androcentric thinking features the power of reasoning applied to the dominance and control of nature. Enlightenment philosophy made rationality the basis of individual autonomy. The resultant free individual was then the primary unit of morality. As we have seen, nonhuman animals provided a convenient categorical foil—presumedly lacking rationality, they were neither free, nor individuals, nor, it followed, objects of moral concern. Feminist theory "challenge[s] the primacy of reason and autonomy of the individual" (Riger, 1992, p. 730), and faults androcentrism as the root cause of that error.

In place of this individualistic philosophy, feminists give a primacy to relationships. The primary unit is not an individual but the *relationship between* individuals. Further, in place of the primacy of the rational, they offer the importance of the affective. While it is nonindividual, feminist philosophy is not yet holistic (although ecofeminism decidedly is [Gaard, 1993]). Immediate, concrete relations are critical, not some global natural or historical process.

It follows from this emphasis on immediate, concrete relations that, for the feminist, ethics cannot be a set of rationally derived principles that are universally applicable independent of social and historical context. Ethics can not be a set of absolute rules applied by and to individuals, but rather must be a set of flexible ways people in relation work things out. Those ways recognize social and historical context and utilize empathic and emotional styles of understanding. They build on and take as the basis of morality the "emotional bond" (Donovan, 1990, p. 351) between individuals rather than the power of pure thought within individuals. "What makes our fellow beings entitled to basic consideration is surely not intellectual capacity but emotional fellowship" (Midgley in Donovan, p. 351).

Nonhuman animals also must be given moral consideration not because they are rational (although few now deny that they are) but because they exhibit "social and emotional complexity of the kind which is expressed by the formation of deep, subtle and lasting relationships" (Midgley in Donovan, p. 351).

Some feminists are critical of Regan's rights philosophy as male-centered in that it preserves the traditional emphasis on individuality and rationality and then extends these to nonhuman animals (Donovan, p. 353). They see in it an abstract theory built on absolute and universal rules rather than on an openness and empathic sensibility to the complexities of particular relations and situations. As the basis of ethics, they prefer talk of caring and responsibility for one another over that of individual rights (Luke, 1992).

As applied to psychology, feminist theory is a critique of the field generally and of animal research in particular. In terms of gender bias on a superficial level, the critique goes, too much psychological research has included predominantly male (human and nonhuman) subjects; only 25% of psychology faculty members are female; much research is biased in using a male experimenter and avoiding topics of particular relevance to women (Riger, 1992). For example, while earlier male primatologists claimed that male nonhuman primates play the major role in mate selection, with the advent of more female primatologists research findings now reverse that, indicating that females play a major role. Apparently for primates, evolution does not proceed predominantly through male preferences or choices.

Or, another example more relevant to this discussion, Gilligan (1982) notes that the original sample upon which Kohlberg based his widely cited description of the stages by which children develop moral behavior consisted of 84 boys. Subsequently, Gilligan has found that girls differ from boys in the way they make moral judgments. Consistent with the critique of Regan by feminist philosophers, Gilligan's study of the developmental psychology of morality suggests that there is a "different voice," a typically female voice, which emphasizes responsibility and relationships rather than rights and rules (p. 21).

At an even deeper level, feminist psychologists argue that the nature of psychology as a science reveals a male-centered bias and ideology (Weisstein, 1971; Riger, 1992). Positivistic-based scientific method emphasizes (1) control which is related to dominance, (2) objectification which is related to interpersonal distance or the refusal of the importance of relationships, and (3) pure logic and rationality which refuses the affective. The science itself is built on male ways of thinking and acting.

In this view, the construction of the experimental lab is a reflection of a male style of dominance and control through a narrow notion of rationality as technology. The idea that the lab is a place where the investigator can somehow isolate behavior from social and historical context is an extension of the patriarchal notion that we can radically control nature. The social construction of the laboratory animal is a caricature of this ideology which reduces animals to instruments fitted into a highly technologized, mathematized, and, recently, physiologized setting. By removing animals from their natural settings, by selectively and genetically breeding animals away from their natural behavior, and by making them part of the instrumentation of the laboratory psychologists realize the androcentric experimentalist ideal of detached objectivity and control.

In her extended critique of his work, Haraway (1989, pp. 231–43) quotes Harlow's own description of the extent to which investigators perceive the laboratory as providing more or less unlimited control of phenomena. A psychologist who developed a series of nonhuman primate models to study the effects of early maternal deprivation and social isolation on later development, Harlow describes his technological innovations in a factual but self-parodying tone:

> In devising this surrogate mother, we were dependent neither upon the capriciousness of evolutionary processes nor upon mutations produced by chance radioactive fallout. Instead, we designed the mother surrogate in terms of modern human-engineering principles. We produced a perfectly proportioned, streamlined body stripped of unnecessary bulges and appendices. Redundancy in the surrogate mother's system was avoided by reducing the number of breasts from two to one (Harlow & Mears, quoted in Haraway, p. 232).

In the following statement, Skinner, psychology's foremost behaviorist, shows these themes of control and denial of relationship:

> We study the behavior of animals because it is simpler. Basic processes are revealed more easily and can be recorded over longer periods of time. Our observations are not complicated by the social relations between subjects and experimenter. Conditions may be better controlled. We may arrange genetic histories to control certain variables and special life histories to control others- for example, if we are interested in how an organism learns to see, we can raise an animal in darkness until the experiment is begun. We are

also able to control current circumstances to an extent not easily realized in human behavior- for example, we can vary states of deprivation over wide ranges (1953, p. 38).

In *The Inevitable Bond: Examining Scientist-Animal Interactions*, Davis and Balfour (1992) show that this social construction of the laboratory animal is a failure even in its own terms. The common theme in this selection of essays by animal psychologists studying a wide range of different species is that human and nonhuman animals form stable, affectively based relations, even in the highly artificial setting of the lab (Shapiro, 1993). An implication of this finding of an "inevitable bond" between investigator and subject is that we can only understand animals through and within that relation. Animal behavior in the lab is not understandable as socially isolated or asocial phenomena. It is certainly not reducible to the detached construction of animals as test tubes that are somehow models of human disease and behavior. If some form of bond or relation between investigator and investigated is inevitable, there is no sense in expending all one's effort in minimizing and denying that relation in the service of a misguiding ideal. Since in any setting which humans share with animals, to understand them we will have to understand the relations and social structures that we form with each other, and there is no justification for the deprivations which Skinner attempts to legitimize.

As feminist theory emphasizes, the ideal that individual investigators are detached, rational individuals, divorced from any relation with their object of study, reveals an androcentric bias. Some feminists conclude from this that a feminine style of research is possible that "emphasizes cooperation of the researcher and subjects, an appreciation of natural contexts, and the use of qualitative data" (Riger, p. 733). In any case, it is clear that the masculine style of traditional laboratory animal research has delayed the recognition of the "inevitable bond" between human and nonhuman animals. In feminist terms, that delay is the result of the predominance of a male-centered hyper-individualistic ideology in psychology.

Community-Based Ethics

Extending beyond a relation-based ethic, there is also available the beginnings of a community-based ethic. Clark (1977) suggests that, "We, dogs, cats, rabbits, sparrows... may, variously, share quite enough of a common perception of the world, common curiosities, ... common affections for the small and defenseless... *for a sense of community to be entirely possible* (pp. 25–6, emphasis added). And Clark again, "... let us at least acknowledge as an ideal a community not merely of many races, many cultures, but one of many species" (p. 179).

With her concept of a "mixed community," Midgley (1983, pp. 112–125) joins Clark in bypassing the individual and their immediate relationships as the basis for defining the class of beings to whom we owe moral consideration. According to Midgley, all human communities have been "mixed" in that they have included nonhuman animals (p. 112). Animals are members of and not merely objects in our communities because both we and they are "social beings" (p. 112). Incorporating the work of Midgley, Callicott states, "Since we and the animals who belong to our mixed human-animal community are coevolved social beings participating in a single society, we and they share certain feelings that attend upon and enable sociability—sympathy, compassion, trust, love, and so on" (1992, p. 253). Further, whether or not animals share this capability, we have the capacity to extend our sympathy beyond our own species. Through that "extended sympathy," we realize a sense of community which, in turn, provides the emotional matrix of an ethic that includes other life forms (Midgley, p. 119).

Here sympathy, sociality, and other affective-based motives and dispositions replace the primacy of rationality,
while the emphasis on shared community replaces that of
individuality. In the resultant ethic, animals can be given
moral consideration even if they are not individuals (although by most contemporary accounts of the defining
criteria for individuality, many species of animals do consist of individuals (see, for example, Dennett, 1981,
pp. 267–286).

Callicott suggests that by combining Midgley's notion
of a mixed community with Leopold's concept of a biotic
community, "we have the basis of a unified animal-envi-
ronmental ethical theory" (p. 254). The foremost ethic of
the contemporary environmental movement, Leopold's
"land ethic" provides that, "A thing is right when it tends
to preserve the integrity, stability, and beauty of the biotic
community" (Leopold, 1970, p. 262). The term "biotic
community" refers to the interdependence among all life
within an ecosystem.

The background to Callicott's suggestion of a unifying
theory is an earlier essay in which he strongly argued that
the animal rights and the environmental movements are
incompatible and require very distinct ethical foundations (1980). In that earlier essay he argued that the envi-
ronmentalist's concern with the integrity of natural systems conflicts with the animal rightist's concern with the
suffering and life of the individual constituents of that
system.

Widening the gap between the two movements, Regan
responded with the argument that any moral concern for
natural systems and for plants constitutes "environmental
fascism" for it attempts to justify overriding the rights of
individual animals for the sake of groups of animals of
certain species (1983, p. 362). In Regan's individual-based
rights ethic, it is clearly wrong and wrong-headed to extend ethics in such a way that "the individual may be
sacrificed for the greater biotic good" (p. 361).

In his more recent essay, then, Callicott seeks to mend the conceptual and political fence separating the two movements through two concepts of community: the biotic community which aims primarily at animals in natural settings, the traditional area of concern of environmentalists; and the mixed community, directed more at domesticated animals, the traditional bailiwick of animal rightists. In the terms of this promising but as yet only outlined unified theory, we are members of a series of communities, extending out from family to neighborhood to civic state to natural state. We have different duties to the different classes of animals in these "nested overlapping" communities (p. 258):

> So the acknowledgment of a holistic environmental ethic does not entail that we abrogate our familiar moral obligations to family members, to fellow citizens, to all mankind, *nor* to fellow members, individually, of the mixed community, that is, to domesticate [sic] animals. On the other hand, the outer orbits of our various moral spheres exert a gravitational tug on the inner ones (p. 259, emphasis in original).

It is debatable whether these two nonindividual theories or Regan's individualistic rights theory present more or less difficult hurdles in the effort to gain acceptance of the idea that nonhuman animals deserve moral consideration. On the one hand, the community-based ethic, for example, requires less conceptual upheaval than an individual-based rights view because it sidesteps the powerful barrier in our tradition which categorically excludes animals from being individuals and rights-bearers.

On the other hand, Nash (1989) has argued that the less difficult and more conservative path is to retain rights talk but extend it to animals and to natural systems or nature itself. In his view, the history of ethics is the story of the extension of moral consideration from a group of male, white, propertied humans to all humans and from there, inevitably, to nonhuman animals and to other parts of or all of nature (p. 5). Earlier, in an influential essay entitled,

Should trees have standing?, Stone proposed that "we give legal rights to forests, oceans, rivers and other so-called 'natural objects' in the environment" (1972, p.9). His arguments were cited by Supreme Court Justice William Douglas in his minority opinion in *Sierra Club v. Morton*. With the agreement of two other justices, Douglas went beyond the Sierra Club's claim of legal standing in the case against a proposed Disney ski resort in the Sierra Mountains of California to proclaim that the mountain itself has legal rights.

However, according to Hargrove, "environmentalists are nearly unanimous in rejecting rights for nature... " (1992, p. xi). This is an overstatement, as Nash is not alone in extending rights talk to natural systems. Nonetheless, it is clear that in our tradition, being an individual is the prerequisite to having rights (although compare the rights of a corporation). For many, it is a considerable stretch to think of a river or mountain as being an individual and so having rights (although compare Hartshorne's Whiteheadian notion of the individuality of a cell [Dombrowski, 1988] and "thinking like a mountain" [Seed, Macy, Fleming, & Naess, 1988]).

Should the animal rights movement stay with the traditional basis of ethics centered on the individual, or will the environmental movement and environmental science with their emphases on interdependent systems and the feminist movement with its emphasis on relations between individuals be powerful enough to establish a non-individual-based ethic? For the moment, the animal rights movement is hedging its bet. In any case, clearly, the two nonindividual-based ethics sketched here are promising on political as well as on conceptual grounds.

Singer's Utilitarianism

It is important to understand that while the publication of *Animal Liberation: A New Ethic for our Treatment of Animals* (1975, first edition) is the immediate occasion for the emergence of the contemporary animal rights movement, Singer's is not a rights- or individual-based philosophy. Singer writes in the tradition of utilitarianism, a moral philosophy that emphasizes using the consequences of an act to all affected by it to determine whether it is right or wrong. Consequences are analyzed exclusively in terms of satisfaction or pleasure and dissatisfaction or suffering. There is no set of rights preserved by an individual in the sense that they preempt or override consideration of this calculus of benefits and costs. While each individual has his or her own interests, the interests of all individuals or of the group are the primary focus in judging the rightness or wrongness of an act. In contrast to Regan's view in which rights cannot simply be summed across individuals (except in extraordinary circumstances—the lifeboat), Singer holds that such individual-centered rights talk is too "absolutist": "It will not do to say: 'Never!' In extreme circumstances, absolutist answers always break down" (p. 77). "If it were possible to save many lives by an experiment that would take just one life, and there were *no other way* those lives could be saved, it might be right to do the experiment" (p. 78, emphasis in original).

Singer argues that the analysis of the act should be extended to take into account the consequences or utility to nonhuman animals as well as humans. Singer's philosophy is a "new ethic" primarily in providing this extension rather than a radically new basis for an ethic. Animals deserve moral consideration because they are sentient, in particular, because, following Bentham, they have "(t)he capacity for suffering—or more strictly, for suffering and/or enjoyment..."(p. 8).

Invoking the traditional principle of equality found in the American Declaration of Independence, Singer argues that the capacity for suffering implies the possession of interests and that, to be fair, the interests of all involved must be given equal consideration. For any act, its rightness or wrongness depends on the sum total of interests served or violated for all affected, independent of race, sex, or species membership.

His general critique of biomedical and psychological research involving animals is that, in his view, researchers treat animals as "mere tools" (p. 44). They develop a "callousness" toward them and a "detachment" reinforced by the use of technical jargon which belies the suffering involved (p. 45). In his own terms, this means that researchers themselves simply do not attribute interests to animals. Rather, they subscribe to the social construction that we have described—laboratory animals are instruments exclusively for our use and benefit. We can not and should not form a relation with them and we owe them no consideration of their interests for they have none. Singer cuts through this social construction and the research justified under its auspices for, in his view, animals can suffer, do have interests and, therefore must be included in the figuring of satisfactions and dissatisfactions.

Application to Psychological Research

Research involving nonhuman animals, then, must be judged by the same consequentialist standard as research (or any other activity) involving humans. Singer, unlike Regan, believes that animal-based research is not wrong in principle, for example it is not inherently disrespectful of the individuals involved. According to Singer's view, for any particular experiment we must calculate the sumtotal of all the interests served and violated in order to make a judgment about it.

However, Singer leaves no doubt that his own utilitarian analysis finds the great majority of studies in psychology unjustifiable. They are wrong, first, because "[m]any of the most painful experiments are performed in the field of psychology" (p. 34) and, second, because "the results obtained are very often trivial and obvious" (p. 40). He clearly singles out and takes to task psychological animal research as an enterprise in which the costs are great and the benefits minimal.

The major implication of Singer's theory is that we must conduct a cost-benefits analysis of any proposed experiment to decide if it is right or wrong. While Singer himself is clear about his view of the results of that analysis in the case of psychology, he conducts no such analysis in a formal sense. This leaves an opening for similarly informal assertions that the costs to the animals are minimal while the benefits to humans and even to other animals are great. As we will see when I discuss the official ethics of the professional organizations and the claims of certain individual psychologists, there is no shortage of such claims. Fortunately or unfortunately, depending on your point of view, the calculation of the sum-total of interests served and violated in a given proposed study is complex and requires both scientific and historical considerations. I will discuss advances and limits in their assessment in Chapter 6.

In practice, Singer employs a different form of argumentation against animal research, and other forms of animal exploitation as well, which at least partly bypasses the need for a formal utilitarian analysis of any particular experiment: "The core of this book is the claim that to discriminate against beings solely on account of their species is a form of prejudice, immoral and indefensible in the same way that discrimination on the basis of race is immoral and indefensible" (p. 255).

Following Ryder (1975), Singer defines speciesism as "a prejudice or attitude of bias toward the interests of members of one's own species and against those of members of other species" (p. 7). By this argument, any claim holding that the value of a study that sacrifices even one animal for the benefits of even many humans can be justified if and only if we would find it acceptable in the case where the animal sacrificed was human. For Singer, the hypothetical substitution of human for animal is the acid test that reveals any bias on the basis of species. As we would rarely allow an experiment which sacrificed one human for the benefit of many humans, so, while he invokes no principle prohibiting such, we can rarely accept an experiment which sacrifices one nonhuman for many humans.

By continually challenging research through the test of speciesist bias, Singer obtains a leverage as powerful as Regan does with his case for individual animal rights— but with, arguably, lesser requirements than those necessary for the attribution of rights. The application of the charge of species-based discrimination is in the service of a utilitarian, not an individual-based, philosophy. At the same time, through the appeal to a discriminatory bias paralleling that of racism and sexism, Singer deftly negates the need for a more direct application of a utilitarian accounting.

This is an important accomplishment as utilitarianism is open to criticism on philosophical grounds (e. g., Regan, 1983; DeGrazia, 1992) as well as on the grounds that application of the costs-benefits analysis it requires is difficult. As I will show, the animal research community has not adopted this test of speciesism. However, it has adopted a form of utilitarianism and does give lip-service to a cost-benefits analysis which it never really delivers.

By the way, the argument of speciesism itself is not immune to criticism. Arguably, the feminist emphasis on both concrete present relationships in the rendering of moral judgments and the emphasis in the community-based ethic on multiple spheres of moral concern provide some justification for giving more consideration to individuals with whom one has a close relation or who live in a community closer to home than the animals in the laboratory. That is, they justify as ethical differential treatment of individuals that would effectively at least partially sort them out by species. For example, in the community-based ethic, it might be justifiable to be more concerned about a companion animal living in your home than about a "wild" animal in a nature preserve.

Smith and Boyd take on the premise of the charge of speciesism by claiming that there is a "relevant moral difference" between human and nonhuman animals which justifies the discriminatory treatment of them that Singer and Ryder define as speciesism (1991, p. 319). That difference is that only humans are self-conscious. It is a morally relevant difference because it, for example, adds to suffering and death the "extra dimension[s]" of threatening one's self-image and sense of one's own future—dimensions not available to nonhumans (p. 322).

However, most philosophers side with Singer in giving priority to the capacity to suffer, whether experienced self-consciously or not. Obviously, self-consciousness can diminish as well as augment suffering, as when, in pain, we know that help is on the way. Conversely, lack of self-consciousness can mean that no such diminution occurs. In Superintendent of Belchertown State School v. Saikewicz, a Massachusetts court ruled that treatment could be withheld from a severely retarded man in a terminal stage of cancer, since the proposed treatment is painful and he was judged incapable of understanding that it would be administered in the interest of his own welfare (Goodkin, 1987, p. 281).

In practice, at least one psychologist and one professional group use the concept of nondiscrimination against species to establish a criterion for assessing whether a particular treatment of animals in a lab setting can be justified. Menzel (Menzel & Johnson, 1978) suggests that one criterion for judging whether a procedure is acceptable is to limit procedures to those which the investigator is willing to try out first on him or herself. The guidelines of the International Association for the Study of Pain (Covino et al., 1980) also suggest this cross-species trial of acceptability, but limit its use to "most non-invasive stimuli causing acute pain" and only "when possible" (p. 142).

Conclusion

There are several distinct and evolving moral philosophies that address ethical issues involving animals. All agree that animals are objects of moral concern, but they disagree on how to count them in sorting out competing ethical demands. Most also agree that the anthropocentrism of traditional moral philosophies exaggerated the differences and discontinuity between human and nonhuman animals, and that contemporary ethics need to provide a corrective on the side of similarities and continuity.

Both Regan's individual-based rights theory and Singer's nonindividual-based utilitarian theory take a strong position against most laboratory animal research in psychology. However, as I will show in more detail in the final chapter, neither is embodied in any meaningful way in current ethic codes and policy statements in psychology or in regulations governing psychology.

A relation-based ethic, the feminist ethic of caring, provides a critique of psychology as male-centered and hyper-rationalistic, while a final nonindividual-based ethic takes community as the primary concept and includes both "domestic" and "wild""animals in nested overlapping communities.

Chapter 6
Psychology's Ethics
The Official Positions

Before describing two distinct ethical positions currently taken by the field of psychology, I will briefly relate an anecdote which reveals an ethical position or, really, an attitude toward ethics itself which I found commonly and explicitly a decade ago and which still often lurks in the shadows of the official stances.

In the early 1980s on the occasion of a symposium which I organized at Bates College on the issue of the ethics of the use of animals in research, I approached many of my colleagues in both academic and applied psychology with a straightforward inquiry about their views of psychology's use of animals in research. Fresh from my own initial reading of Singer, I would frame my question, in retrospect rather naively, in terms of the ethical issues raised by the practice. I quickly discovered that the majority of psychologists had, to me, peculiar notions of what is meant by ethics. Many relegated ethics to a purely subjective region of personal judgment outside of the objectivity and rationality of science. Ethics is up to an individual's personal choice for it is reducible to personal preference. There is no gain in systematic discussion or debate, and certainly no possibility of a rigorous justification of a particular set of positions for there are no ethical truths beyond personal opinion. In effect, ethics is not science but is part of those subjective and speculative ways of thinking from which science historically had and continually has to carefully distinguish itself. The ethics of psychology's use of animals, then, is a matter of each individual's personal conscience.

Others confused ethics with science itself. They believed that acting scientifically, that is within the then customary scientific method, is itself acting correctly. Rather than relegating ethics to an unscientific personal preference or bias, they believed that the rules of good science are an ethic and that following them assures the goodness of an act. To make objective observations and to form and test hypotheses based upon them is to impartially and fairly arrive at the truth of the matter, and to do that is to do good. By this notion of ethics, psychologists who are scientifically rigorous act ethically. Whether or not they use animals as subjects raises no particular ethical dilemma. Like the first notion, this also is a conversation-stopper as no further discussion is constructive.

The first position is known in ethics as nihilism (Nozick, 1981, p. 400) or, to use Tannenbaum and Rowan's more generous term mentioned earlier, ethical skepticism. Since there are no objective values but only our own personal opinions, ethics is reduced to "various subjectivistic or relativistic positions which hold that thinking or agreeing makes it so, or that ethical statements simply are expressions of emotion or preference having no independent objective true content" (p. 400).

The second position is a form of scientism, an inflated view of the scope and application of science and the scientific method. An example of scientism especially pertinent to the present discussion is found in the work of Gallup and Suarez (1980a; 1987). These two psychologist animal researchers argue that ethical systems are themselves naturally evolved phenomena and that they can be explained in terms of the theory of evolution. Since science claims exclusive jurisdiction over the study of such natural phenomena, it follows that only science can describe ethics and that ethics is properly a subfield of science (Shapiro, 1987).

As an example of an insight from this scientific ethic, they argue that all ethical systems derive from altruistic behavior that is evolved and is "highly species-specific" (Gallup & Suarez, 1980a, p. 217). This means that altruism, such as "cooperation and reciprocal helping behavior," and the "human ethics and morality inextricably tied to [them]... may simply be irrelevant when applied to species other than our own" (p. 217). Gallup and Suarez seem to suggest that according to the scientific study of ethics, human ethical concerns need not include nonhuman animals. As we have noted, this flies in the face of the near consensus view that we extend moral consideration to nonhuman animals.

Gallup and Suarez notwithstanding, most moral philosophers agree that, "Ethical truths find no place within the contemporary scientific picture of the world. No such truths are established in any scientific theory or tested by any scientific procedure—microscopes and telescopes reveal no ethical facts" (Nozick, 1981, p. 399). Of course, scientific facts are often useful in arguing ethical positions, and, certainly, scientific practices have ethical implications. The recognition that scientific findings and ethical values are different orders of things is known in philosophy as the fact/value or is/ought distinction.

The Humane Ethic

In the decade since that informal survey of psychologists' attitudes toward ethics, largely as a result of the animal rights movement, many individual psychologists, and establishment pronouncements have become more sophisticated and moved beyond notions of ethics that either devalue it or conflate it with science. (As an exception that proves the generalization, Bekoff recently took White to task for the latter's claim that "animal usage is not a moral or ethical issue" [Bekoff, 1991, p. 45]). Having already discussed several current and emerging progressive ethics, I can place the official positions of the field of psychology in that context. I will show that they utilize language from the humane beneficence and permissive utilitarian views, but that, in both cases, in such a way as largely to provide apologies for the status quo.

Of course, the field of psychology is not a monolithic entity and there is no one official position on the animal research issue. Burghardt has observed a number of incidents that "...indicate a splintered and incoherent response by the APA to issues of importance to animal researchers" (1992, p. 1334). However, while there is more than one professional organization of psychologists, the APA is by far the largest and most powerful. A number of its recent publications can fairly be taken as representing its official position [e.g., APA Backgrounders (1984, 1985a), APA Guidelines (1985b), APA Science Directorate Research Ethics Officer (Baldwin, 1993)].

The humane ethic or humane treatment "is the most commonly cited standard in Federal legislation concerning animals," according to a Congressionally mandated report published in 1986 (U.S. Congress, Office of Technology Assessment, p. 79). Without defining the term explicitly, the APA's "Guidelines for Ethical Conduct in the Care and Use of Animals" (1992) relies heavily on such terms as "humane consideration" and "humane manner." That "humane" talk is still currently the dominant discourse among animal researchers and administrators of Federal agencies charged with regulating animal research is attested to by a personal observation at a recent National Institutes of Health supported conference entitled, "Ethical Issues of Animal Use in Academe and Industry" (June 1993, Philadelphia). In that setting the terms "ethical" and "humane" were commonly used interchangeably. While, understandably, scientists primarily use scientific language, when they do use the language of ethics, these are the two terms which they tend to employ. What do they mean by "humane" and does it deserve to be a synonym for "ethical"?

As described by the director of the NIH's Office for the Protection of Research Resources, Gary Ellis, both in his presentation at the conference and in the Office of Technology Assessment (OTA) report of which he was then project director, the humane ethic refers to a "proscription against unnecessary suffering" (U.S. Congress, OTA, 1986, p. 80). As Garner points out, far from being a new conceptual development, the notion of unnecessary suffering is the "framework provided by the moral orthodoxy" and has been since its consolidation in Britain as early as the turn of the century (1993, p. 3). In their discussion of "the principle that animals ought not to be made to suffer unnecessarily," Hurnik and Lehman state that "it has been used as the ethical basis for many laws... " (1982, p. 132).

Parenthetically, a recent use of the term "humane" in another context highlights by unintended caricature the extent to which some interests utilize this concept of unnecessary suffering for grossly exploitative ends. The International Organization for Standardization (ISO) is developing standards to justify the use of steel-jaw traps to capture and kill animals for their fur ("Pro-steel jaw," 1993). It is currently considering a scale of painful injuries, such as cut tendons, fractured ribs and other broken bones—all of which would be consistent with and, in fact, define "humane" trapping standards. Through the imprimatur of "humane" the ISO technical committee on trapping hopes to convince the European Community to reconsider a ban on pelts and manufactured products obtained from animals caught in a leghold or other, by most other accounts, inhumane traps.

As I discussed in Chapter 1, "suffering" refers to the emotional response to pain and distress, and does not include death itself. For the humane ethic, if an animal is

killed without unnecessary suffering, for example, anesthetized before a surgical procedure and then not allowed
to gain consciousness, there is no ethical cost associated
with the fact of the loss of life. Only his or her suffering
while living, not an animal's life, count.

In this ethic a person's act is good if, in the presence of
pain, the act relieves suffering—unless the suffering is
necessary. So what is necessary suffering? Unfortunately
we discover that in the case of animal research the claim
is made that necessary suffering is that suffering custom-
arily associated with experimental procedures and the
housing and husbandry conditions associated with those
procedures. As Silcock notes, "... [N]ecessity is in the eye
of the researcher, and this view may diverge considerably
from society's view of what is necessary..." (1992, p. 32).

Let us first clarify what is meant by necessity apart from
its use in the term "necessary suffering." In logic, necessity has a strict and restrictive meaning, as in the following
example: To have an automobile, it is necessary (although
not sufficient) to have an engine. Closely related, semantic
necessity is the meeting of a strictly definitional condition:
A sister-in-law is necessarily the person married to one's
brother (or sister, as we increasingly recognize the rights
of gays and lesbians). And likewise for a third restrictive
usage of the term, it is a physical necessity that if two
objects of certain mass are a certain distance from each
other, there is necessarily a certain gravitational attraction
between them.

It is apparent that as used in the question—is the suffering inflicted in this particular animal study necessary?—the term necessary is not meant in any of the restrictive senses of logic or semantics or the laws of physics. In what less restrictive sense is it used and how do we
answer the question of necessary suffering (and who answers the question)?

As we have described, tens of thousands of psychological experiments are conducted each year. Of these, 8–10%

involve animals. On its face, within this broad context of the collective output of psychological research, inflicting suffering on animals is obviously not "necessary" as the great preponderance of research gets along without using animals or inducing suffering in them. It is not necessary in the sense that the research enterprise as a whole obviously finds neither the use of animals nor the infliction of suffering on animals indispensable.

For example, still within this broader perspective, since the 1970s there has been a dramatic increase in the number of psychologists conducting research in neuropsychology, "the study of brain-behavior relationships in humans" (Butters, 1993, p. 3). *Neuropsychology*, a primary journal in this subfield that recently has been taken over by the APA, publishes studies using human subjects and encourages the use of highly sophisticated electrophysiological and neuroimaging techniques "that allow us to assess ongoing cognitive processing in normal and brain-damaged patients" (Butters, p. 4).

Yet, one year before becoming the publisher of *Neuropsychology*, APA published a bibliography of over 2500 studies of animal models of human pathology (Overmier & Burke, 1992). Its index reveals that many of the topics studied and questions explored (e. g., relations between brain and memory function in various pathological conditions) are the same as those studied in the human-based research to which I just referred. At least from this broad vantage point of the output of a particular subfield, it would seem difficult to argue that the suffering inflicted on the laboratory animals to induce presumed models of various forms of human brain-damage (Parkinson's, epilepsy, Alzheimer's, alcohol-induced brain-damage) is necessary since these pathologies are also studied in human-based research.

But let us consider the question of necessary suffering in the narrower context in which it is more typically raised, as exemplified by the inquiry of an institutional animal care committee. It asks, "In what sense is it necessary to conduct this particular proposed animal study?"

One way to answer the question is to define necessary with reference to the consequences of the study. But to do this we must invoke another ethic, such as Singer's utilitarianism. According to Singer, it is "necessary" if the resultant benefits outweigh the costs to all affected by the study. I will discuss the complexities involved in making this assessment below under permissive utilitarianism. Here I only point out that by its very nature the consequences of an experiment are unknown. In any case, it is clear that the humane beneficence ethic by itself offers no guidance in judging necessity by reference to consequences.

In fact, in judging a given study, application of the humane ethic is limited to consideration of the necessity of the experimental procedure described. Since Russell and Burch's (1992) seminal description in 1959 of the concept of alternatives as the "3 Rs" (replacement, refinement, and reduction), the question of necessity has come to hinge largely on the question of the availability of alternatives that would induce the same effect as the experimental procedure. (Other considerations are repetitiveness, poor design, inapplicability to the human condition, triviality.) If there is no alternative method that induces the required experimental condition with less pain, then the suffering so inflicted is judged necessary. The APA "Guidelines" adopt this criterion: Procedures involving pain "should be undertaken only when the objectives of the study cannot be achieved by other [less painful] methods" (1992). This reliance on the notion of the "3 R's" is helpful and has resulted in reduction in suffering and encouraged scientists to think about the development of alternatives. However, when used to probe the issue of necessity in this way, it largely reinforces the status quo.

The alternatives criterion assumes that the proposed study is necessary or has already been judged to be necessary; it inquires only if there is a less painful way to do it. However, any proposed study is only a hypothesis about relations between phenomena. Is frustration a cause of aggressive violence? We may agree that it is necessary, in the sense that, in the present "culture of violence," it is increasingly critical to our welfare to study the causes of violence. We may even agree that it is necessary to examine the possible role of frustration or deprivation in its incidence. But it does not follow that it is necessary to induce any and every particular form of painful deprivation on the off-chance that it is uniquely or peculiarly causative, or that it may further our understanding of the general relation between deprivation and aggression. As a society, we cannot afford to fund all conceivable experiments. Just because there is no less painful way to study a certain form of deprivation does not mean it is necessary to do so and, therefore, humane to conduct the study. In an article entitled, "If it can be studied or developed, should it be?," Sarason, a psychologist, argued that scientists should be governed by societal ethical criteria and that these place restrictions on freedom of inquiry (1984).

This line of argument is particularly clear for research using the animal model strategy. As I have discussed, much animal research in psychology is an effort to generate hypotheses about relations within human phenomena and, therefore, must eventually be validated in humans. Properly understood, the function of an animal model study is limited to a generative one. It is difficult to imagine that there is only one way, a painful one, to generate a hypothesis which, in any case, must eventually be tested on humans. Any relation hypothesized is important only if it obtains generally in many different settings and forms (Midgley, 1981). And if that is the case, then there are many places to find it and alternative ways to induce it.

Put another way, limiting the criterion of what is ethical to finding a less painful alternative procedure forgets the true relation between the laboratory animal and the intent of the study. The use of laboratory animals within the models strategy is already an "alternative" in several ways. In the first place, nonhuman animals have been substituted for the use of humans. Second, in that the animals used are a social construction engineered to adjust to laboratory life and to serve as vehicles of human conditions of interest, they are alternatives to the use of naturally evolved species. Finally, an animal model is already an alternative in the third sense that a condition typically found in humans is artificially constructed and only approximately duplicated in laboratory animals.

By the alternatives criterion, we are, then, seeking an alternative to what is already that three times over, being three times removed from the particular human pathology under investigation. At this extended remove where, at best, the animal model is one of many means of generating a hypothesis regarding the true object of interest, the suffering is not necessary. The criterion of "no alternative less painful procedure" forgets that and reinforces a status quo in which constructing animal models has become an unexamined *modus vivendi* of the research enterprise.

Further, as currently employed, the absence of an alternative as a criterion of necessity is applied in a context that is much too narrow. It is not sufficient to require demonstration of a good faith search for a less painful alternative to the experiment as proposed. The prior question is whether it is necessary to pursue this particular hypothesis. This question is not asked, at least within the humane ethic. Rather, any experimental procedure that has been done in the past provides a strong prejudice to accept as necessary any proposed study employing a further variation on it. In practice, the unrestrictive or loose use of what is "necessary" is even more elastic—any procedure a researcher can devise is by that fact necessary, providing only there is no available alternative to that exact procedure.

Garner suggests that the very difficulty in defining unnecessary suffering, its conceptual elasticity, provides an opportunity to "extend the range of activities which humans regard as *un*necessary" (1993, p. 246, emphasis added). For example, in recent times, the use of animals for fur coats, has become more widely condemned as unnecessary (p. 247). While an interesting twist, the more typical use of the term is to justify practices involving extensive institutional suffering. For example, defenders of factory farming often adopt the rhetoric of necessary suffering, despite the fact that in a world where a large proportion of people do not or rarely eat animal flesh it requires a great stretch to assert that to do so is necessary. The concept "unnecessary" is a rubber fence used within the humane ethic to rationalize contemporary practices involving animals. As applied to practices involving scientific research with laboratory animals and as currently utilized by legislators and professional organizations of researchers, the humane ethic functions largely to permit all procedures that investigators generate.

The alternatives criterion as currently applied clearly effects a prejudice favoring research proposals that utilize already established animal-based procedures. All too often, showing that the suffering inflicted is necessary is reduced to requiring only that the investigator argue that that specific procedure cannot be done in an alternative way. The humane ethic is relatively blind to the larger question of the necessity of continuing animal research in subfields where there exist nonanimal research enterprises that apply highly sophisticated techniques to the direct study of the relevant human populations. Finally, it does not allow ethical considerations to play any part in what are, in the final analysis, social policy decisions as to what hypothesized relations are worth exploring.

This assessment does not imply that researchers and institutional animal care committees do not sometimes address questions of outcome, general significance, and broader context; nor does it imply that a more robust and progressive humane ethic is not possible. Rather, the point

is that the humane ethic, as the prohibition against unnecessary suffering, does not provide an ethical framework
adequate for or conducive to these considerations.

Yet, it is often presented as if it did. While the term
"necessary" is applied loosely in a narrow context as I
have described, it readily is extended to support a general
position about animal research in the form of the following syllogism: animal research is necessary; the suffering
inflicted under its auspices is necessary; therefore, animal
research is humane, which is to say that animal research
is ethical.

I began this section with the observation that the term
humane is often used interchangeably with the term ethical. The analysis presented here clarifies how this equiv-
alence constitutes a very narrow construal of the ethical
issues involved in psychology's use of animals and one
that is highly disposed to retain the status quo.

Recalling the critique of exclusively human-centered
ethics discussed earlier, it is not surprising that this version of a humane ethic gives relatively short-shrift to consideration of animal suffering and exploitation. Like other
humanistic philosophies, it emphasizes the differences
more than the similarities between human and nonhuman
animals, more in the tradition of Descartes than of Darwin. This is ironic in that at least one group of animal
researchers in psychology, the comparative psychologists,
are strong proponents of evolutionary theory. Regrettably,
they have had little influence (Dewsbury, 1992, p. 213), in
part, no doubt, because they typically make less strong
claims to be revealing the nature of human pathology
through their study of nonhuman animals.

For the humanist, humans are radically different from
other animals and must be given priority (Shapiro, 1990a).
In the tradition of scientific humanism predominant since
the Enlightenment, the scientific enterprise itself is the
example *par excellence* that shows that difference—only
humans can do science. It follows that the scientific enter-

prise deserves priority over the suffering of animals; that, specifically, the scientific experiment is sacrosanct; and, finally, that the welfare and lives of the animal subjects it utilizes must be sacrificed before its altar (Lynch, 1988). It is really in this sense that scientific humanism justifies the suffering of animals in the laboratory as necessary, humane, and ethical.

In our discussion of Regan's case for animal rights, I described how the APA, after some consideration, decided to exclude the principle of inherently objectionable means from its guidelines. Instead they adopted language close to the alternatives criterion of necessary—"When the objectives of the research cannot be achieved by other methods..." then any suffering is justifiable as necessary and humane. In principle, there are no limits on the suffering that can be inflicted on animal subjects for the sake of furthering human welfare and scientific knowledge. As indicated earlier, the APA's Miller takes this position explicitly, and, I add here, provocatively. He offers his condemnation of the acceptance of any limits on animal suffering in the enterprise of animal research as a moral imperative. Adopting suitably humane talk, he rhetorically chides those who would accept such limits: "Would this [setting a limit] be humane?" (Miller, 1984, p. 8).

It is only in the context of this allegiance to a human-centered ideology that we can understand a humane ethic that reduces the criterion of necessary suffering in nonhuman beings from that which is indispensable to that which is expedient. "Breathing is necessary. Sleeping is necessary. Eating and drinking are necessary. Vivisection is a *choice*" (Giannelli, 1985, p. 150, emphasis in the original).

Permissive Utilitarianism

The second ethical position taken by the field of psychology employs talk of benefits and, to a lesser extent, of costs. For example, the APA "Guidelines" states in its preamble, "...ethical concerns mandate that psychologists should weigh the probable costs and benefits of procedures involving animals" (APA, 1992). Cost/benefits (C/B) language is an application of a utilitarian theory of ethics.

Permissive utilitarianism is related to Singer's ethic in that both are consequentialist theories. In moral philosophy, this distinguishes them from deontological theories that, like Regan's ethic, offer guiding principles that preempt or trump consideration of the consequences of an act. In this regard, the humane ethic just discussed is more related to Regan's animal rights ethic. As I have described, the guiding principle of the humane ethic is that animal suffering judged necessary to promote human interests always takes precedence over the interests of the animals involved. A primary task of Regan's theory is to question that priority by emphasizing the relevant similarities rather than the differences between nonhuman and human animals. Thereby, he justifies extending these powerful, preemptive individual human rights to animals as well.

A utilitarian theory questions that priority by building an ethic substituting the analysis of consequences for any and all preemptive principles. Given this feature, one would expect a utilitarian-based ethic to level the playing field: suffering is suffering whether it involves human or nonhuman animals; minimize it and maximize satisfactions. However, as we will see, the form of utilitarianism adopted by official psychology is only slightly more progressive than the humane ethic. Tannenbaum and Rowan refer to Singer's utilitarianism as "restrictive," and the variant establishment form we are about to examine as "permissive" (1985). As we will show, "lip-service" utilitarianism is more descriptive.

Acceptance of a utilitarian ethic allows animal researchers interested in maintaining customary and current practices various openings whereby they may override a prohibition against suffering inflicted on animal subjects. These openings are not immediately apparent as the utilitarian account requires consideration of the consequences for all, human and nonhuman animals, affected by the research. How does official psychology and its several prominent spokespersons sidestep this egalitarian potential in utilitarianism and make the account into an apology for the status quo?

Their major claim is that the benefits and value of animal research are great, while the costs to the animals are minimal (Adams, 1981, 1984; APA, 1984; Baldwin, 1993; Feeney, 1987; Gallup & Suarez, 1987; King, 1984a, 1984b; Miller, 1983, 1984, 1985).

On the benefits side, an additional supporting claim is that an accounting of the benefits of a particular proposed study cannot and, therefore, need not be provided because the immediate results are unknown (Miller, 1983, p. 1). Further, most research is "basic" rather than applied (King, 1984b, p. 6), and the possible eventual beneficial applications "lag" significantly, more so in psychological research than in medical research (King, 1984a, p. 57).

On the costs side, supporting claims are that only a small percentage of psychological studies utilize animal subjects (APA, 1984, p. 2; Miller, 1985a, p. 423); that most of the animals used in laboratories are rodents and birds rather than dogs and primates (APA, 1984, p. 2; Miller, 1984, p. 8; Gallup & Suarez, 1987, p. 82); that few animals are used relative to the number of animals exploited in other human activities (Miller, 1984, p. 9; Gallup and Suarez, 1987, pp. 82–83); that most animals used are bred for that purpose (APA, 1984, p. 12; Gallup and Suarez, 1987, p. 86); that those few animals used do not experience much pain (APA, 1984, p. 10; Miller, 1984, p. 7); that the pain that they do experience is less than that they typically experience outside of the lab (Gallup & Suarez, 1987, p. 85); that the pain is not intended (Gallup & Suarez, 1987, p. 90); and that, in any case, pain is already being minimized because there are no alternatives available. The latter is particularly so in psychology which is more dependent on studies using the intact animal than is medical research or product-testing (APA, 1984, p. 14; Miller, 1984, p. 6).

Before examining some of these arguments, it is worth noting a prevalent attitude adopted in their presentation. As described elsewhere (Bowd & Shapiro, 1993, p. 139), the spokespersons often adopt a tone that is indignant, adversarial, and defensive. Recall Phillips and Sechzer's (1989) finding of a significant increase in defensiveness between the 1960s and the 1980s, generally, in the psychological literature treating these issues; and Gluck and Kubacki's (1991) description of a "strategic defensive posture" assumed by researchers. Even an APA spokesperson, refers to the "early [80s] defensive posture of scientists" (Baldwin, 1993, p. 124). In a comment published in the *APA Monitor*, APA's chief executive officer, Raymond Fowler, called for psychologists to "come to its [animal research's] defense" (1992). In a subsequent letter to the editor, entitled "In defense of animal research," 25 prominent psychologists "applauded" APA's defense (Presidents, APA Division 28, 1992). As the animal rights debate heated up, this posture, while understandable, no doubt itself increased the temperature and added to the turbulence.

The primary criticism of this second ethical position assumed by psychology is that neither psychology position papers, nor spokesperson articles, nor published studies involving animals actually present rigorous costs/benefits (C/B) analyses. Yet the APA "Guidelines" recommend these analyses and several major spokesperson pieces feature claims about the benefits of animal research and, generally, adopt the language of utilitarianism. It is a rarity for a published study to address the issue of relative C/Bs. An exception is Benus, Koolhaas, and Van Oortmerssen (1992) which includes a brief section under the heading

"Ethical considerations." To be fair, as I have already pointed out, Singer himself more often uses the criterion of species discrimination than he does provide substantive C/B analyses.

Arguably, such analyses are requisite for a utilitarian ethic to be credible and usable. Originating in economics, the C/B analysis is widely employed in public policy decision-making (Rhoads, 1979). Given complex social and environmental conditions in which there are a great number of low probability risks to health and life, policy-makers often must choose not to save lives. For example, they may choose to widen roads rather than to require air bags. Various methods are available to get the most risk reduction per dollar. "Discounted future earnings" computes the value of a life exclusively in economic terms, while "quality adjusted life years" adds extramonetary considerations and "willingness to pay" evaluates the benefits of a program by surveying what people are willing to pay for it.

Assessment of Costs

Beginning on the costs side, concepts and instruments are available that assess the ethical costs both to animals in the lab and to people. Given their availability, generalized assertions denying that there is much pain are inadequate. They are also implausible when we consider that psychologists have attempted to model virtually every pathological and disordered human condition. The catalogues of the extremes of vivisection produced by animal rights organizations and their supporters (Diner, 1979; Doncaster, 1982; Pratt, 1976; Singer, 1975) are as long as the lists of benefits that research defense organizations offer in response.

The assertion, unsubstantiated in any case, that a laboratory rat is better off than a rat in the dump is irrelevant. Laboratory rats are additional animals produced to meet the demands of researchers. In any utilitarian accounting, whether or not it is greater than that of other animals, their suffering is additional suffering and adds to the ethical costs (Shapiro, 1988, p. 50).

Phillips (1993) studied the attitudes toward and use of analgesics (pain-relieving drugs) in 23 biomedical laboratories. She observed no instances of analgesics being administered and found that researchers' attitudes toward its use ranged from being surprised at her raising the question to assurances that animals do not need pain-killers, even following surgical procedures. Further, the annual reports, filed with the United States Department of Agriculture (USDA) by the institutions with which these laboratories are affiliated, show that from 0–5 % of animals are used in research involving pain or distress, without administration of appropriate analgesia (1993, p. 73). This percentage is low, as even procedures that are obviously painful and distressing, such as the lethal dose 50, are reported as painless. Yet while their research involved "many instances of survival surgery," these researchers maintained that postoperative analgesia was not used and was not indicated (p. 74). This ethnographic study of animal research scientists documents their denial of pain in research conditions where the clear consensus of the scientific community is that significant pain and distress is present (p. 74). It also shows that the data often used to argue the absence of pain, USDA annual reports submitted by the scientist conducting the research, are not reliable.

In the light of this study, it is clearly not adequate for spokespersons for psychological animal research simply to assert that there is little pain involved. As scientists noted for their special ingenuity and interest in measuring even the most intangible and complex phenomena, psychologists have a clear burden to provide scientific data based on adequate measures to support such a claim.

Laboratory animals are not willing participants in our economy. As discussed, they were constructed more as tools and resources than laborers, even enslaved laborers. Any measure of their "willingness to pay" forgets this fact. However, Dawkins (1980; 1990) has developed methods which provide an estimate of the relative strength of an animal's preference or "willingness to pay" for some condition through measuring the effort expended or the amount of food given up to obtain it.

In more theoretical biological terms, Elzanowski (1991) credits nonhuman animals with the capacity to assess their own costs. In his view, birds and other higher vertebrates demonstrate adaptive behavior "...in some proportion (in terms of time, energy, speed or other parameters) to actual fitness costs and gains of incurring the present situation and to potential costs of failing to reach or to avoid an expected situation" (p. 1923). These investigators both imply that observation of animals' preferential behavior provides some handle on the costs of different painful conditions within the experimental situation.

As discussed earlier, several rating scales have been developed which measure "degree of invasiveness" and other components of "ethical cost" (de Cock Buning & Theune, 1993; Obrink, 1982; Orlans, 1987; Porter, 1993; Ross, 1981; Field & Shapiro, 1988). According to Orlans, the idea of rating scales to measure pain originated with Smyth in 1978 (Orlans, 1993). I have described one such scale which is specific to psychological animal research (Field & Shapiro, 1988). Most of the scales are scientifically reliable in that raters using different scales agree on the scoring of similar phenomena (inter-test reliability) (Shapiro & Field, 1987, p. 7) and different raters agree on scores using the same scale (inter-rater reliability) (Field, Shapiro & Carr, 1990, p. 3).

Such scales have been incorporated into the legislation and regulatory mechanisms of several countries, notably Sweden, the Netherlands, the United Kingdom, and Canada (Orlans, 1993, pp. 118–27). However, "[i]n the United States, efforts to adopt a pain scale nationally have so far

failed" (p. 119). The USDA annual reports mentioned earlier do require categorizing procedures into three pain related categories (no pain, no pain-relieving drugs; pain,
with drugs; pain, no drugs). However, the classification
scheme provides no information on level of pain, and, in
any case, provides no information on the 80% of laboratory animals that have been excluded from the Animal
Welfare Act (AWA) (pp. 125–6). The U.S. District Court
ruled in January, 1992 that the exclusion of rats, mice, and
birds from the implementing regulations of the AWA is
illegal (pp. 59–60). However, in July of 1994 the U.S. Court
of Appeals for the District of Columbia overruled the decision, asserting that the plaintiffs (the Animal Legal Defense Fund, the Humane Society of the United States, and
two individuals) have no legal standing. Also unsuccess-
fully, the Humane Society of the United States recently
petitioned the USDA to change these reporting procedures, including the adoption of a more effective pain
scale (p. 126).

As mentioned, while "... mandat[ing] that psychologists should weigh the probable costs and benefits of procedures involving animals," the APA "Guidelines" (1992)
does not even reference let alone suggest the use of the
available pain scales, scales of invasiveness or ethical
costs. Again, published articles involving animal subjects
almost never indicate the level of invasiveness of procedures nor, more generally, do they provide discussion of
"weigh[ing] the probable costs and benefits of procedures
involving animals."

Also, as indicated earlier, studies of the language utilized find a bias in published scientific reports. Lederer
(1992) and Birke and Smith (1995) find a rhetorical laundering that sanitizes and minimizes animal suffering, that
directs attention away from it to descriptions of apparati
and measures, and that obscures and minimizes description of death. Field (1993) found that introductory psychology textbooks also minimize the presentation of ani-

mal suffering, more by providing appealing and cute photographs than by emphasizing technical features. Consistent with these studies, in an informal survey of biomedical literature, Nace (1993) found that trends since 1990 are
toward more "technical descriptions to denote the death
of animals" (p. 4). However, Nace also reports that the
direct term "kill" is commonly used while the more eu-
phemistic "sacrifice" is no longer used. I have described
how the social construction of laboratory animals involves their being made part of or blended into the instrumentation and technology of the lab. Of course, these obscuring devices add to the difficulty of assessing costs,
even when scales of invasiveness are utilized.

Related to the development of scales of ethical costs is
the recent broadening of the concept of suffering in laboratory animals to include the emotional reaction to distress and anxiety, as well as to pain. Until recently, the
literature on housing and care dealt only with minimal
standards of comfort, while the experimental procedures
considered only limits on pain where possible within the
given demands of the study. Evidence from biology and
comparative psychology indicates that nonhuman animals, at least vertebrate animals, also experience the complex emotions, such as anxiety and distress, that typically
accompany pain in humans (Rose and Adams, 1989). Valenta and Rigby (1968) reported that rats can discriminate
between other stressed and unstressed rats and that they
react with stress to the former. Knott (cited in Staff, 1991)
concluded that rats were also stressed by the death of their
cagemate, as indicated by physiological differences in
stress indicators between the rat killed first and the rat
killed a few minutes later.

These extensions of the concept of suffering and its application owe some debt to the decline of behaviorism in
psychology. Due to its reluctance to talk about consciousness, in the behaviorist program pain and suffering were
reduced to physicalistic considerations. Pain was physical

in that it could be described in terms of behavior, such as avoidance of a certain stimulus, and in terms of physiology, such as injury to tissue. As Rollin described in his aptly titled work, *The Unheeded Cry* (1989), the dominance of the behaviorist ideology with its refusal to allow consciousness in a scientific enterprise delayed the inclusion of consciousness in psychology. Since the 1970s, the cognitive revolution has overturned this traditional prejudice and signalled "a dramatic comeback" for "the contents of conscious experience" (Sperry, 1993, p. 879). As mentioned, this "re-minding of psychology" has spilled over into the study of nonhuman animals known now as cognitive ethology (Shapiro, 1992). Pain itself as well as the response to it which is defined as suffering is now recognized to include subjective or conscious experience (DeGrazia & Rowan, 1991, p. 194). Clearly, the contemporary scientific answer to the philosophic query posed in the 18th century by Bentham, a founder of the utilitarian ethic—"The question is...can they suffer?"—is, unequivocally, "yes."

Beyond both pain and the experience of suffering, laboratory animals also suffer harm. For example, when we deprive an animal of the capacity to use a limb or of the capacity to fly, the animal may experience that deprivation as distressing or, in some instances, even as painful. A broadened notion of suffering includes such harms.

The caging of laboratory animals can induce another form of suffering. Chronic caging results in bored behavior, seen in stereotypical movements and postures remarkably similar for animals of different species. Wemelsfelder concludes that such repetitive behavior indicates a "process of behavioral disintegration [that] may be regarded as direct evidence of chronic suffering" (1993, p. 155). Radical loss of interest in the immediate environment and its replacement with the repetitive and nonspecific behaviors of boredom is a distinctive form of suffering (Shapiro, 1989b, pp. 187–92). As discussed in Chapter

2, to the degree that an animal experiences the loss of interest in his or her surroundings that constitutes chronic boredom as distressing, that boredom is accompanied by suffering.

As a result of these various developments —the decline of behaviorism, the rise of cognitive ethology, and the broadened sensitivity to the contexts in which suffering can occur, the earlier exclusive focus on reduction of pain and distress has been expanded, at least in some quarters and for some species, to include the positive provision of "well-being." This notion of well-being was embodied in the 1985 amendment of the Animal Welfare Act which required the development of regulations that promote the "psychological well-being of nonhuman primates" (Food Security Act of 1985).

Measurement of Benefits

As indicated, official psychology and its spokespersons take the position that the benefits of animal research have been great *and* that the benefits of any given proposed study cannot be known in advance and, particularly in basic research, are often much delayed. This is a convenient and self-serving position. It attempts to justify animal research on utilitarian grounds, while disclaiming the possibility of using utilitarian criteria to assess any given research proposal. In effect, a global judgment about the benefits of the entire body of animal research in psychology is used in place of making a judgment about a proposed study.

In addition to arguing that it cannot substitute for the obligation to assess a proposed study on its own merits, I will show: (1) that, in any case, the global judgment is unsubstantiated; and (2) that, while complex, an educated judgment about any given proposed study can and should be made using C/B analysis.

It is worth noting that the criteria that undergraduate psychology students most commonly used when asked to make ethical decisions about particular proposed studies involving animals was a C/B analysis (Galvin & Herzog, 1992b, p. 276). More specifically, "perceived benefit of a proposal was the major contributing variable to predicting approval on four of the five experimental procedures" (p. 270). Apparently, these students have not yet learned the official position that such an assessment cannot be made. Also, not incidentally for the present analysis, while some of them referred to the rights of animals, they reflect the culturally dominant emphasis on instrumentalism in employing usefulness rather than a rights principle as the primary guide in ethical decision making.

A study of Dutch scientists involved in animal research also supports this emphasis (Stafleu, Baarda, Heeger & Beynen, 1993). The scientists judge a proposed animal experiment ethically acceptable if the human benefits ("human interests") "balance" costs to the animals ("animal discomfort"). In fact, the study also found that while costs to the animals do significantly affect acceptability, these scientists utilize benefits to humans more than costs to animals in their judgments. If a rights position were operative, the opposite would be the case as animal suffering would preempt any human benefits.

Regarding the global claim of the overall benefits of animal research, the profession's presentation consists largely of sweeping assertions rather than the application of any rigorous scientific evaluation. Even so, the generalized claim of benefits provided in such catalogues is paltry when taken against the larger body of nonanimal research in psychology, with its relatively more direct application to human welfare.

Miller's article, "The Value of Behavioral Research on Animals" (1985a), is the most extensive and prominent treatment of the issue. First presented as an invited address at the APA Convention in 1983, it was subsequently reprinted in the APA's *American Psychologist*, with the highly unusual device in that staid scholarly publication of including graphic photographs (nine of them—almost all of children), purporting to illustrate how people have benefited from animal research.

Miller's primary form of argumentation is to describe a particular animal model and then its application in a human setting. It is important to understand that the connections he claims among models and their alleged applications are not themselves scientific facts. The simple presence of research on an animal model of a particular human condition obviously itself provides no scientific evidence of the benefits of that research. While hypotheses were tested in that research, they did not ask the question, "Is this animal model likely to provide benefits?" In technical terms, the animal model research itself provided no test of the null hypothesis of beneficiality. Nor did it include a scientific assessment of the amount of benefit.

At the outset of the article, Miller is at pains to distinguish the evidence he will present, which he calls "the true facts," from the "grossly false statements" of animal rights activists (p. 423). While Miller knows better, his propagandist program and style in this article could mislead readers into thinking that he is presenting scientific evidence bearing on the issue of benefits. He is not. Yet, while Miller is doing no more than describing animal models of selected pathologies, subsequent claims about the importance of animal research rest on citation of just those descriptions. Baldwin offers that "[t]he most persuasive argument for using animals in behavioral research... is the untold benefit that accrues to humans..." (1993, p. 123) and then lists Miller as the first of two references. In the context of my argument, the unintended meaning of "untold" is telling.

But it is possible to obtain scientific evidence regarding benefits. At least two of the scales of invasiveness mentioned earlier include assessment of benefits (Porter, 1992; de Cock Buning & Theune, 1992) through categories that assess aim, realistic potential of reaching it, necessity of product, scientific significance, medical significance, social significance, and the like.

Further, as I have shown, methods such as citation analysis are available that provide scientific evidence directly bearing on the influence of any given published research (Garfield, 1980a; 1980b). Through the *Science Citation Index*, one can document the degree to which articles in journals of applied psychology actually cite animal research. This gives some measure of clinical researchers' perception of the beneficiality of research allegedly bearing on their own area of expertise.

In fact, Kelly (1986) did a citation analysis of the references Miller employed to, in Miller's words, "prove beyond any reasonable doubt the value of behavioral research on animals" (1985a, p. 423). Through this analysis Kelly obtained valid scientific data which tested Miller's unsubstantiated contention that animal research is "directly linked to the development of clinical interventions for human psychological and behavioral disorders" and Miller's implication that "treatment interventions for [these disorders] could not proceed without laboratory animal studies" (Kelly, 1986, p. 840).

Kelly examined all the references in all the articles appearing in two journals publishing clinical research in those areas included in Miller's catalogue of benefits. The results are a striking refutation of Miller's claims. As reported in Chapter 4, only a very small percentage of the references in the *Journal of Consulting and Clinical Psychology* and in *Behavior Therapy* in 1984 were references to animal studies. Obviously, these researchers publishing in applied journals do not "depend critically on laboratory animal research," and "Miller's conclusions [about the value of behavioral research on animals] are inaccurate" (p. 840).

A second study also tested the hypothesis of beneficiality. Employing reference lists from course materials for the national licensure exam in psychology (the 1985 Association for Advanced Training in the Behavioral Sciences [AATBS]), Giannelli (1985) compared the references cited by Miller "documenting" the value of animal research with those references selected by experts as critical to an understanding of the field of psychology. His findings echo those of Kelly. "Of Miller's 118 specific citations (hand-picked to demonstrate the critical value of animal research to psychological knowledge), only seven (5.9%) can be found in the massed AATBS references" (p. 125).

Giannelli also reviewed in a less formal manner Miller's various claims of benefits. In most instances, he found "no compelling evidence" connecting animal research and the development of applications to human conditions, or of the "indispensability" of animal research in a given application, or of a "direct application" from animal-based research (pp. 127–137). He concludes that "Miller's reconstruction of the history of psychology placed undue emphasis on the role of animal research" (p. 125).

These two studies and the data provided in Chapter 4 on citation of animal models of eating disorders infer the degree of influence of animal-based research from the references cited in published applied research studies, presumably a literature read by clinicians. Another method to test scientifically the benefits derived from animal research involves going directly to clinicians and assessing their perception of the usefulness of the results of such research in their practices. How aware are they, for example, of the animal models Miller discussed? Is their familiarity merely with the existence of the models or do they actually know particulars? Do the particulars actually influence their clinical intervention?

In their campaigns targeting specific animal researchers, animal rights groups often utilize testimonials from clinicians who deny the benefits of animal research in particular disorders. However, to my knowledge, there are no scientific studies in which such information is acquired through random sampling of clinicians, using standardized inquiry and the like. The results of the informal survey presented in Chapter 4 suggest that such a study would not support psychology's official position regarding benefits. As mentioned earlier in another context, non-research clinicians, who are the majority of psychologists in clinical practice, and animal researchers read different journals, and, as I have just described, the applied literature only infrequently refers to the animal literature.

There are other complexities in the global assessment of benefits which reach beyond the limits of scientific assessment and require historical interpretation. Before discussing these, I will briefly describe the use of C/B analysis at the level of a particular study. As mentioned, published studies very rarely include any discussion of such an analysis or of any other ethical issues considered.

At the level of proposed studies, a primary mechanism devised to oversee animal research is the institutional animal care and use committee (IACUC). These committees were mandated by the Animal Welfare Act (as amended in 1985) and Public Health Service policy to monitor government-sponsored research using animals. While IACUCs have resulted in some reduction of pain and distress and some enhancement of well-being, they have not realized their full potential (Dresser, 1993, p. 141). They do not provide meaningful limits on research, whether through the application of C/B analysis or other ethical criteria. One of the reasons for their inadequacy is that they currently are "dominated by scientific members" who will not change the status quo (p. 136). While some scientists are genuinely open to addressing ethical issues, according to Brody, "...these committees are hand-picked by the chief executive officer of the facility" (1989, p. 427). Further, "[w]hen nine of ten committee members either receive funding or are involved in some capacity with animal research, there is tremendous conflict of interest" (p. 428).

Dresser concludes, "...committees require little more than a perfunctory claim to research value to justify extensive animal harm" (Dresser, p. 141). In her study of the current federal protective scheme, published in the Harvard Environmental Law Review, Brody agrees: "The legal regime hardly considers whether a research project's potential value can justify its cost in terms of animal suffering" (1989, p. 423). In fact, Brody supports the argument presented earlier regarding the use of global judgment in place of the obligation to evaluate each given proposed study on its own merits: "The existing federal scheme accepts, as a *sweeping premise rather than as a judgment to be made on a case-by-case basis*, that the anticipated benefits of animal research outweigh the ethical costs" (p. 425, emphasis added). Miller argues against such a case-by-case application of a C/B analysis:

> T[he] fact, that many of the most useful clinical advances have depended on basic research that had no obvious clinical relevance, shows the fallacy of requiring that any specific experiment that causes animals to suffer must be justified by a cost-benefit expectation of directly producing a sufficient reduction in human suffering (1985, p. 434).

Despite the pervasive use of utilitarian language in the relevant enabling legislation and professional guidelines, there are two sleights of hand at play here that undermine the genuine provision of a C/B analysis at the level of proposed research, beyond the less subtle use of raw political control by vested interests and a defensive posture. There is the failure to actually conduct a C/B analysis on a proposed study, while justifying that proposal under the umbrella of a global judgment about the entire animal research enterprise. As we have seen, that umbrella leaks badly as that judgment, although lined with C/B language, is unsubstantiated by any scientific evidence.

Second, there is the disingenuous use of scientific findings beyond their proper purview. The simple presence of an animal model on a particular topic itself provides no scientific evidence of the benefits of that research. Neither official pronouncements by the APA nor publications by prominent proponents of the value of animal research seem to recognize that limitation. We have shown that scientific instruments to measure the costs are available and that the hypothesis of beneficiality can be tested scientifically. The results of both belie the official position: It is not the case that the benefits and value of animal-based research are great while the costs are minimal.

Historical Considerations

There are other parameters to consider that, although still within a utilitarian framework, begin to overreach the power of scientific measurement to provide C/B analyses. Some of these require historical interpretation. While pertinent empirical data may be gathered, in the final analysis they require a reading of the history of science to judge costs and benefits.

I mention some of these, beginning with the less problematic. It is common knowledge that in psychology, as in other research fields, not all studies are completed and not all completed studies are published. As LaFollette and Shanks have noted (1995), often an investigator who fails to develop a model of particular disorder in a series of studies will not report that effort in the scientific literature. In addition, a certain percent of both studies with such negative findings and others with positive findings are rejected for publication. As noted earlier, journal rejection rates are higher in psychology than in the physical or biological sciences, and it is not known what percent of completed studies never see the light of day. Presumably, only the more "successful" studies are published. Clearly, unpublished studies have costs to the animals that are real but unknown, and add an indeterminate cost to any global judgment of the research enterprise. Further, the fact that an unknown percent of them will involve ethical costs without any possible benefits complicates the evaluation at the level of any proposed study. Some pain will be in vain and, therefore, unjustifiable from a utilitarian viewpoint.

Fraudulent research is related to rejected and other unpublished studies. The Subcommittee on Oversight and Investigation of the U.S. House of Representatives has investigated recent cases of fabrication and falsification of data and of plagiarism. Dingell (1993), committee chair, notes that while the extent of such misconduct is not known a number of indicators suggest that it is widespread. For example, 27% of scientists surveyed by the American Association for the Advancement of Science said that they had witnessed, on average, two such incidents in the previous 10 years (p. 1611).

Citation analyses show that of those studies published only half will be cited (Cole & Cole, 1972). It is possible that an investigator learns lessons from his or her uncited or even unpublished research which then enhance the benefits of his or her future research efforts. However, by and large, uncited studies are those that lead to no applications, beneficial or otherwise. I have also offered evidence that many studies, although cited, only circulate in a restricted animal research literature, and do not lead to clinical applications.

Some studies are cited in an applied literature but do not have a beneficial effect. In toxicology testing as distinguished from psychological research, this is sometimes dramatically the case. Some substances are nontoxic for certain species of nonhuman animals, while toxic to humans (thalidomide, Opren). Conversely, some are toxic when tested on nonhumans but may be of value in humans (aspirin, penicillin). There is no easy solution to this dilemma in toxicology. Employing more stringent criteria for approval may keep out the thalidomides, but it also might keep out the aspirin (LaFollette & Shanks, 1993a, p. 118). More radically, many critics of the use of animals in product and drug testing argue that extrapolation to a different species is always speculative and that the whole strategy of using one species as a kind of king's taster for another is suspect (Bross, 1987; Sharpe, 1988; Zbinden, 1981).

As described in Chapter 4, the situation in psychology is even more problematic, for a psychological disorder is rarely reducible to a toxic reaction. I have described various less than beneficial uses and some misuses of animal models of human psychological disorders. For example, some models merely provide a graphic metaphor or loose analogy without adding to understanding or effectiveness of treatment.

More generally, there are dense problems of historical evidence and interpretation in any thoughtful consideration of the benefits of animal model research in animals. We need to assess the actual role of the model in any purported benefit: Did it suggest a new understanding or treatment, or was its use limited to the refinement of an existing benefit? Or was it used to merely add the legitimating stamp of approval, "tested in laboratory-based animal research," to a discovery already made in a non-animal setting?

Consideration of the larger historical context in which animal research occurs allows an examination of reliance on such approaches as the animal model strategy. I have shown that the results of animal model research typically do not result in specific applications. But this is not to say that animal research has not had an important influence on the directions taken by modern psychology. Which of those directions are beneficial, which are delays, and which are misleads? For example, in the heyday of behaviorism, a significant proportion of a generation of research psychologists were trained in and conducted animal-based research. If they had instead directly investigated human behavior, would behavior therapy have advanced more rapidly, as Drewett and Kani (1981, p. 197) contend? Would the turn to cognitive approaches and interventions in the 1970s, such as the use of imagery, have occurred earlier?

When psychologists learn sophisticated laboratory animal experimental techniques, their careers have a certain trajectory which generally precludes learning sophisticated human-based experimental techniques. Further, having learned surgery and other invasive techniques on animals, that is what they teach to the next generation of research psychologists.

Those who invest in the strategy of developing animal models and those others who would have taken their places in the research enterprise would have produced their own research. These roads not taken, these unrealized benefits, are, in effect, additional costs. Every time we choose to fund one project, we fail to fund others that also have associated C/Bs. Clearly, the effects of any delays and misleads require a historical interpretation of the enterprise of animal research.

Science is determined by the philosophy of science and the methods it employs as well as by the objects under investigation (Suppe, 1977; Shapiro, 1986a). The construction of the lab as the site and the lab animal as the object of study, and the adoption of the animal model strategy strongly affects the kinds of questions investigators asked. In turn, these affect the kinds of answers and the kinds and power of applications derived. What are the limiting effects of framing research questions in terms of the construction of an animal model? What are the effects when that animal model strategy is joined to a behavioristic approach which deemphasizes the study of consciousness? Did this have an impact on the recognition, measurement, and ethical consideration of pain and suffering of laboratory animals used as models? On the degree of suffering allowed to be imposed? What are the effects when that strategy, shaped by a positivistic philosophy of science, valorizes findings that require and are only evident with high technology instrumentation and sophisticated statistics; when that strategy is biased toward physiological explanations and pharmacological treatments? Again, these questions require the scientist to turn to historians of science for answers.

While it cannot substitute for a C/B analysis for any given proposed research, a global judgment about the value of animal research is relevant to the present debate. However, it must be founded in rigorous historical analysis, as well as in scientific evidence developed to directly test the hypothesis of beneficiality. Of course, while the past is the best predictor of the future, even a well-founded view of the past does not promise a future consistent with it. Whatever the benefits of animal research in the past, as new sophisticated technologies are developed, any past need and efficiency of extrapolating from animal models will be superceded by forms of investigation that directly reveal those human disorders.

Conclusion

I have shown how official psychology exploits certain openings in a utilitarian philosophy to override the provision of any meaningful limitation on animal suffering in research and, more generally, to sidestep its potential for an egalitarian ethic across species. Its self-conscious identification as a rigorous empirical science notwithstanding, official psychology, through its publication of guidelines, white papers, and numerous scientific journals, oversees a research enterprise that fails to deliver any more than a lipservice to utilitarianism. In place of the application of available scientific instruments that can measure the costs and benefits of a proposed or published study, we are offered unsubstantiated claims of benefits globally attributed to the animal research enterprise as a whole.

I have also argued that any scientific data providing a C/B analysis must be supplemented by consideration of the historical contexts in which both the particular results and the general strategy of animal model research are evaluated.

To reset the context of this discussion, I have been critically analyzing the second of two ethical positions espoused by official psychology and its spokespersons. The discussion is extensive for the situation is more involved than it appears at first glance. As did "necessary suffering" in the humane ethic, the knee-jerk slogan here—"it is beneficial"— carries much conceptual and empirical freight. Our considerable attempts to unpack that freight does not imply that I favor a utilitarian ethic, even one closer to Singer's restrictive utilitarianism and one rigorously and justly applied.

On the contrary, one inference that I draw from the formidable task involved in the application of a utilitarianism ethic is that its use is limited. The limitations reflect the basic premises of the philosophy as well as the mechanics of its application to the particular ethical problem of animal suffering. There is an extensive literature in philosophy critical of utilitarianism, notably for the relative devaluation of individuals. Of course, the critique of individual-based rights philosophies is also extensive. Still, while utilitarianism is utilized as a tool in much social policy decision making, individual rights is the more basic ethical framework in our democratic system. Recall Nash's argument that both the animal rights and the environmental movements are in the historical tradition of continually recognizing the rights of, and therefore of giving moral consideration to, more and more entities, beginning with an elite of propertied, white males and now extending to animals and rivers (Nash, 1989).

Another limitation of utilitarianism as applied to the problem of animal suffering in research is that the animals are not participants in the economy in which the cost-benefits analysis is undertaken. They are produced involuntarily, confined and harmed for the sake of a system in which they are commodities and resources, not participating beneficiaries. The animals are only occasionally and only incidentally beneficiaries of animal-based research in psychology. It is really only in a metaphoric sense that I include them in a calculus of costs and benefits.

Put another way, Singer's attempt to extend moral consideration to nonhuman animals is peculiar in that, typically, the premise of a utilitarian accounting is that attendant costs and benefits can accrue to all those affected. It presumes one community composed of individuals who agree to bear costs for the overall good of the community. Each individual is more or less equally a potential beneficiary as well as bearer of costs. That is the sense in which utilitarianism is fair. We are all in this together, rain or shine. We take our chances for the good of the community as a whole, providing that there is an equal consideration of our interests, that is, we have an equal chance to share in those overall benefits. However, in the case of animal-based research, costs accrue exclusively to one group (the animal subjects), while benefits, if there are any, by and large accrue to a distinct group (human animals). The only difference between the two groups is species membership. As applied to the problem of animal suffering, even using a substantial scientific and historical accounting, utilitarianism seems to have a speciesist bias. This is why, as I discussed, Singer's own version of utilitarianism typically leans heavily on a test of species bias, in place of a C/B analysis.

One philosopher combines utilitarian and rights principles. In response to current political realities, Rollin suggests a two tier ethic in which first a utilitarian and then a rights principle are applied, in that order (1981, pp. 92–95). If the benefits of a proposed study are judged to "clearly outweigh" the costs, the rights principle is then invoked to prohibit any animal suffering beyond that intrinsic to the experimental procedure. Of course, the last qualifier is significant as it means that the experimental procedure is preemptive; the rights of the animals are safeguarded only outside the demands of the experiment. The discussion to this point suggests that, in practice, this would not be much of a gain for the animals.

However, alternatively, the two principles could be combined giving priority to rights. Elsewhere, I have suggested that any proposed research that employs an experimental procedure that is "intrinsically objectionable" be prohibited (Shapiro, 1983, p. 190). One rating scale measuring degree of invasiveness prohibits procedures that fall into the most severe category (Orlans, 1987). British regulations also embody this notion of prohibiting certain procedures (Orlans, 1993, p. 119). This concept supersedes utilitarian considerations by precluding certain procedures in principle, independent of any possible resulting benefits. In effect, this concept trumps the rights of an individual against the possible benefits to the group. Only after this rights-based criterion is met is the proposed research then judged on utilitarian grounds, along the extensive lines I have described. This mixed ethic is more true to the spirit of a deontological or rights philosophy in that it makes a certain principle preemptive. At the same time, it takes advantage of the pragmatic power of utilitarianism, the weighing of practical results— arguably, its most attractive feature. Of course, Rollin may be accurate in his judgment of the lack of political readiness for such an ethic, even his less radical suggestion. But is ethics a matter of political expediency, or of providing the most cohesive and reasonable account of what is morally permissible (Regan, 1983, p. 382)?

Epilogue

About 30 years ago, a first year graduate student in clinical psychology left his carrel to emerge momentarily from his studies of the dense writings of Freud and Jung. On his study break, he treated himself to a tour of a part of the psychology building that he had not yet explored.

As he walked past basement rooms from which emanated a peculiarly pungent and musky smell, he suddenly became aware that he was being watched. Turning, he did a double-take for it was a cat on a table that stared at him, wide-eyed and unblinking. As he looked more closely now, he saw that the animal, while conscious, was immobilized, held in place by a metal frame at his or her temples and jaw. Atop the cat's head some surgical paraphernalia obtruded and exposed what appeared to be the animal's brain.

The incident took only an instant, as the student barely broke stride, but he was filled with a sense of horror, almost terror. Upon reflection, he quickly realized that he was not somehow lost, that, indeed, this was part of the psychology building. For, as he was learning in his studies, the discipline of psychology housed both the study of personality, a child's wishes and conflicts, and of physiology, a cat's neural system.

However, the sense of horror and, dimly beneath that, of having lost his way, remained, tucked away and largely unexplicated. While he understood, at least naively, why the cat was there, he did not then have a vocabulary with which he could work through the feelings that had been aroused. While adjoining the clear intuition that something was terribly wrong, the sense of horror remained, ambiguously, as much in the region of the aesthetic as the ethical.

In retrospect, analyzing myself now for, of course, I was that graduate student, this treatise is the working through of those feelings and the clarifying of that intuition. In the decades since that traumatic beginning of my own graduate education, moral philosophy has provided several different ethical discourses which allow such experiences to be articulated in that region, as they should be.

In my view, the major ethical systems, particularly rights philosophy, taken together provide a clear and powerful indictment of the animal model strategy in psychology. One could begin and end with that analysis for it is a strong and, for many, an overriding argument. Given only the exploited condition of the nonhuman animals involved, these ethical discourses proceed largely independent of scientific practice, the institutions and subcultures in which it is embedded, and its philosophical underpinnings. In the case of rights philosophy, the analysis is independent, too, of the weighing of any resultant benefits.

However, the present study had a different point of departure and center, one which partially bracketed ethical systems by limiting consideration of them to their implications for the practice of animal research and their impact on the policies regulating it. Instead, my focus was an extensive and intensive examination of the practice of animal research, in terms both of an enterprise of science and an institution that utilizes nonhuman animals. On balance, the results of this study also indict that animal model strategy, confirming that young graduate student's as yet inarticulate intuition.

In the introduction, I mentioned that some research advocates believe that if the public only understood more about animal research they would be more accepting of it. I also cited literature indicating that there was no consistent relation between level of general scientific knowledge and attitudes toward animal research. However, in contrast with the above assertions, I believe that increased understanding of the specific enterprise of the animal model research in psychology will result in diminished acceptance of it by the public and the profession of psychology itself. More particularly, when people realize how this branch of psychological science is exploiting animals, what it is subjecting them to, and the limited relation of the results of these procedures to advances in understanding and treatment interventions, both the public and the profession will demand its radical curtailment.

Summary

To review some of the main findings, in its effort to emulate the natural sciences, particularly physiology, modern psychology borrowed from them the ideas of objectivity effected through radical detachment of the investigator and of controlled experimentation. These borrowings led to the development of the laboratory as the site of study and the lab animal as the proper object of study for this budding science. In fact, the lab and the lab animal were constructed to fit each other. I noted that at that time "lab animal" did not yet exist as a common category. The resultant lab animal is a peculiarly deindividuated, despecified and, even deanimalized entity, more a part of the highly instrumentalized laboratory itself than an autonomous, living individual.

I believe that the account in the present work linking both the ideological frame of positivism and the literal architectural frame of the lab with the construction of the lab animal is an important contribution to our understanding of the enterprise of animal-based laboratory research in psychology.

A predominant way in which psychology utilizes lab animals is as models of human disorders. Properly utilized, a model in science functions heuristically as an analogue to the actual object of study. It is a generative device that helps the investigator to think about and develop hypotheses about the actual phenomenon under study. Through this analysis of the concept of model, I reached the insight that, while important, the degree of similarity between the model and the modeled is not critical to the evaluation of the former. In the final analysis, empirically- and historically-based criteria must be applied to evaluate whether a particular model in fact fulfilled an effective generative function. It is possible that a model of low fidelity, one only vaguely analogous to the original, could nonetheless be a stimulus to a creative insight into the object of study. Conversely, a model that is quite similar to the original may yet fail to advance its understanding. Another important feature of the present work is a systematic attempt to provide such a critical analysis for a selected set of animal models.

Through a combination of historical misunderstanding and plain misrepresentation, the proper generative function of models has been lost in psychology, as well as in the biomedical sciences. Both fields attempt to oversell the benefits of animal models through the claim that they are identical rather than simply analogous to the target human disorder. The popularized notion is that the model somehow actually reproduces the human disorder in the animal as if, in effect, the animal is reducible to a host of a disorder that is transportable and invariable in different species.

In fact, psychology's use of animal models typically falls short of even the proper, more modest goal of providing a generative function. Rather than suggesting new understanding, animal models degenerate into a rhetorical or graphically demonstrative function.

If either the field's inflated claim was true or the proper function of the model as a heuristic was effectively being employed, one would expect a constructive interaction between the lab and the clinic. The present study of selected animal models of eating disorders lead to the opposite conclusion. The enterprise is impressively ingrown. An examination of the investigative process showed that, rather than arising from direct experience with the disorders in clinical settings, the models build on procedures already in the repertoire of experimental procedures. More critically, rather than continually going back to the target phenomenon for mid-course correction and eventual validation, the development of the models proceeds largely through recursive and duplicatory investigation of other already studied variables and other models. Validation is limited to this insular consistency within the lab enterprise.

The logic of experimental thought further fosters this insularity. Models typically are built on one or two features that while readily reduced to simplified, observable, and measurable procedures are only coarsely analogous to the target disorder. For example, eating disorders are grossly operationalized such that any experimental procedure that affects the amount of food consumed is a putative model of either the etiology or the treatment of the disorder. This justifies the investigator in trying out any and all available variables. More insidiously, it truncates thought. Instead of a productive interaction between the target phenomenon in its human clinical setting and the evolving model, an interaction that would likely produce a sensitivity to the nuances and the deep structure of the disorder, available variables are lined up and marched through. From my review of animal models of eating disorders, I conclude that virtually everything was tried and nothing worked.

Ironically, an enterprise governed by a regulative ideal that valorizes direct observation of the phenomenon of interest is decidedly indirect and removed from the target phenomenon. Turning away from the actual object of study and, in any case, with limited prior direct experience with it, the investigator observes a model of the original rather than the thing itself. That model is (or is "in") an individual animal of a different species, and that species has been genetically modified to fit the constraints of the lab. Further, despite this constructed adaptiveness, that individual is clearly living in a highly artificial environment and is, then, once-removed from the natural habitat he or she requires to be him or herself. That model is further removed from the original in that, again, it mimics it in only one or two gross features.

Finally, that model is not directly observed. He or she is typically first reduced to a preparation, to an isolated aspect of a physiological process. To produce that preparation requires the application of high technology apparati, such as the development of a chamber in which an animal can be held and subjected to experimental manipulation while various physiological indices are recorded. What is "observed" are the results of the experimental manipulation of that process. These results are expressed quantitatively as levels of physiological indices or frequencies of behavior. In effect, they are not observed either for they must be subjected to sophisticated statistical operations before the results can be "seen."

What begins as an effort to construct a vantage point from which the investigator can directly and without personal bias be present at the phenomenon itself, ends up as a view through a hall of mirrors.

A close examination of the several selected animal models of eating disorders examined indicated that they are shaped more by the ideology of laboratory-based experimentalism with its emphases on quantification, technology, and explanation at a micro-process level than by direct clinical knowledge of these particular disorders. A survey of clinicians specializing in the treatment of eating disorders revealed that they are largely unaware of this animal model research enterprise and that studies from it are seldom cited in the applied literature which these clinicians read. Consistent with these findings, a major study of attitudes of psychologists toward animal research indicated that clinicians do not value the contribution of animal research to their work (Plous, 1996a).

A review of studies which assess treatments of the eating disorders showed that these models have not contributed effective treatment innovations. This conclusion was also supported by the results of a citation analysis of the publications of investigators who have developed animal models of eating disorders which demonstrated that their level of citation is relatively low. In addition to its failure to produce effective interventions, the emphasis on physiology and the search for an effective drug treatment in this animal models literature is at variance with the predominant view among clinically oriented researchers, who have published a substantial literature establishing that these eating disorders are largely culturally determined.

The last two chapters document a final sense in which animal model research in psychology and animal-based research generally is a closed shop. It is insulated from certain relevant intellectual currents, most notably the spate of progressive moral philosophies developed in the last two decades. Although employing distinct and even competing discourse, in common they reach the conclusion that nonhuman animals are owed moral consideration and that, accordingly, the practice of laboratory-based invasive animal research must be significantly curtailed. Yet a survey of relevant policy statements and guidelines within the profession of psychology and federal legislation and regulations showed that these fail to incorporate these philosophies in ways that are consistent with their progressive spirit. Rights and the emerging feminist philosophies are absent from policy documents, while Singer's utilitarian ethic is given lip-service. In place of systematic analyses of costs to the animals and benefits

for us, there are on the costs side only gross categoriza-
tions of severity of pain and distress, and on the benefits
side global and unsubstantiated assertions rather than
case by case assessments. Largely developed prior to the
emergence of contemporary progressive philosophies regarding the treatment of nonhuman animals, the language of a "humane" ethic is adopted in a form that
serves as an apology for existing and customary practices.

Recommendation

We human beings study everything. There is no phenomenon, no entity, living or dead, animate or inanimate, present or past, close or far, significant or trivial, "relevant"
or extraneous that escapes our intellectual curiosity. It is
unthinkable that we would suspend study of the mind-
boggling and marvelous array of phenomena, species,
and individuals that constitute the animal world.

The present work provides a strong set of arguments
against the research enterprise of developing animal models of human psychology. Like human slavery, to which
the term was first applied, it is a "peculiar institution"—
one that, far from being inevitable or indispensable, becomes intelligible only through an account of the complex
set of cultural forces that created and maintained it. However, this present indictment does not imply that it is de-
sirable or ethical to end the study of nonhuman animals.
The results of this work are consistent with a narrower
position: that study should be limited to investigations of
animals for their own sake, to attempts primarily to understand them and only incidentally ourselves; and to
noninvasive and only minimally manipulative studies to
that end that are conducted in naturalistic or semi-naturalistic settings.

References

Adams, P. M. (1981). Using animals in research. *Testimony before the United States House of Representatives Subcommittee on Science, Research, and Technology.* Washington: The Association for the Advancement of Psychology.

Adams, P. M. (1984). *Animal research and animal welfare: Putting the issues into context.* Paper presented at the American Psychological Association Convention, Toronto, Canada.

American Medical Association (March 1988). *Use of animals in biomedical research: The challenge and response.* (Available from AMA, 515 North State St. Chicago, IL 60610).

American Psychiatric Association (1994). *Diagnostic and Statistical Manual of Mental Disorders* (4th ed.). Washington, DC: Author.

American Psychological Association (1984). *The use of animals in psychological research. Backgrounder.* Washington: Author.

American Psychological Association (1985a). *The use of animals in psychological research. Backgrounder.* Washington: Author.

American Psychological Association (1985b). *Guidelines for ethical conduct in the care and use of animals.* Washington DC: Author.

American Psychological Association (1989). *Directory of the American Psychological Association* (1989 ed., vol. 1). Washington, DC: Author.

American Psychological Association (1992). *Guidelines for ethical conduct in the care and use of animals* (revised). Washington DC: author.

Animals in research have friends and foes. (1982, January). *APA Monitor*, pp. 1, 12.

Antelman, S. M. & Szechtman, H. (1975). Tail-pinch induces eating in sated rats which appears to be dependent on nigrostriatal dopamine. *Science, 189*, 731–3.

Antelman, S. M., Szechtman, H., Chin, P., & Fisher, A. E. (1975). Tail pinch-induced eating, gnawing and licking behavior in rats: Dependence on the nigrostriatal dopamine system. *Brain Research, 99*, 319–337.

Arluke, A. (1988). Sacrificial symbolism in animal experimentation: Object or pet? *Anthrozoos, 2*, 2, 98–117.

Auerbach, S. (1985). Response of serotonin-containing neurons in nucleus raphe magnus to morphine, noxious stimuli, and periaqueductal gray stimulation in freely moving cats. *Experimental Neurology, 88,* 609–628.

Bakay, R. A. E. (1991). What we have learned from primate research. In O. Lindvall, A. Bjorklund and H. Widner (Eds.)., *Intracerebral Transplantation in Movement Disorders* (pp. 53–62). New York: Elsevier Science Publishers.

Baldwin, E. (1993). The case for animal research in psychology. *Journal of Social Issues, 49,* 121–131.

Balzar, J. (1993, December 25). Creatures great- and equal? *Los Angeles Times,* pp. 1, 30, 31.

Bannister, D. (1981). The fallacy of animal experimentation in psychology. In D. Sperlinger (Ed.), *Animals in Research.* New York: John Wiley & Sons.

Barrett, E. S. and Adams, P. M. (1972). Chronic marijuana usage and sleep-wakefulness cycles in cats. *Biological Psychiatry, 6,* 3, 1973.

Bateson, P. (1992, April). Do animals feel pain? *New Scientist,* pp. 30–33.

Beach, F. (1950). The snark was a boojum. *American Psychologist, 5,* 115–124.

Bekoff, M. (1991, September-October). [Letter to the editor]. *Hastings Center Report,* p. 45.

Benedict, J. & Stoloff, M. (1991). Animal laboratory facilities at "America's Best" undergraduate colleges. *American Psychologist, 46,* 535–536.

Benus, R. F., Koolhaas, J. M., & Van Oortmerssen, G. A. (1992). Individual strategies of aggressive and non-aggressive male mice in encounters with trained aggressive residents. *Animal Behaviour, 43,* 531–540.

Bernard, C. (1927). *An introduction to the study of experimental medicine.* New York: MacMillan.

Bernstein, E. (1987). Empathy toward animals and other sentient beings: A very personal account. *Between the Species, 6,* pp. 153–157.

von Bertalanffy, L. (1968). *General system theory.* New York: George Braziller.

Bertiere, M. C., Mame Sy, T., Baigts, F., Mandenoff, A., & Apfelbaum, M. (1984). Stress and sucrose hyperphagia: Role of endogenous opiates. *Pharmacology, Biochemistry, and Behavior, 20,* 675–679.

Birke, L. (1993). [Review of *The sexual politics of meat, Meat: A natural symbol, and Beyond beef: The rise and fall of the cattle culture*]. *Society and Animals, 1*, 2, 191–207.

Birke, L. & Smith, J. (1995). Animals in experimental reports: The rhetoric of science. *Society and Animals, 3*, 23–42.

Blass, E., Shide, D., & Weller, A. (1989). Stress-reducing effects of ingesting milk, sugars, and fats: A developmental perspective. In L. H. Schneider, S. J. Cooper, & K. A. Halmi (Eds.), *The psychobiology of human eating disorders: Preclinical and clinical perspectives*, pp. 292–307.

Boneau, C. A. (1992). Observations on psychology's past and future. *American Psychologist, 47*, 12, 1586–1596.

Booth, D. A. (1989). Mood- and nutrient-conditioned appetites: Cultural and physiological bases for eating disorders. In L. H. Schneider, S. J. Cooper, & K. A. Halmi (Eds.). *The psychobiology of human eating disorders: Preclinical and clinical perspectives* (pp. 122–135). New York: The New York Academy of Sciences.

Boring, E. G. (1963). *The physical dimensions of consciousness.* New York: Dover.

Bott, L. (1993, April). *A scale for measuring content in magazine articles on animal rights.* Paper presented at the symposium of the Eastern Communications Association, New Haven, CT.

Bowd, A. D. (1980). Ethical reservations about psychological research with animals. *The Psychological Record, 30*, 201–210.

Bowd, A. D. & Bowd, A. C. (1989). Attitudes toward the treatment of animals: A study of Christian groups in Australia. *Anthrozoos, 3*, 20–24.

Bowd, A. D. & Shapiro, K. J. (1993). The case against laboratory animal research in psychology. *Journal of Social Issues, 49*, 133–142.

Bower, G. H. (1993) The fragmentation of psychology? *American Psychologist. 48*, 8, 905–907.

Brain, P. F. (1993, November). *Pain and distress in laboratory animals: What we know and what we assume.* Paper presented at the World Congress on Alternatives and Animal Use in the Life Sciences, Baltimore, MD.

Brody, M. (1989). Animal research: A call for legislative reform requiring ethical merit review. *Harvard Environmental Law Review. 13*, 423–477.

Broida, J., Tingley, L., Kimball, R., & Miele, J. (1993). Personality differences between pro- and anti-vivisectionists. *Society and Animals, 1*, 129–144.

Bross, I. (1987). *Crimes of official science: A casebook.* Buffalo: Biomedical Metatechnology.

Brownell, K., & Rodin, J. (1994). The dieting maelstrom: Is it possible or advisable to lose weight? *American Psychologist, 49,* 9, 781–791.

Bruch, H. (1973). *Eating Disorders: Obesity, Anorexia Nervosa, and the Person Within.* New York: Basic Books.

Burghardt, G. M. (1992). Who's looking? *Contemporary Psychology, 37,* 12, 1333–1335.

Burros, M. (1994, July 17). Despite awareness of risks, more in U.S. are getting fat. *New York Times,* pp. 1, 18.

Butters, N. (1993). Editorial: Some comments on the goals and direction of *Neuropsychology. Neuropsychology, 7,* 3–4.

Cahan, E. D. and White, S. H. (1992). Proposals for a second psychology. *American Psychologist. 47,* 2, 224–235.

Cain, A. O. (1985). Pets as family members. In M. Sussman (Ed.), *Pets and the family* (pp. 5–11). New York: Hathorn.

Callicott, J. B. (1980). Animal liberation: A triangular affair. *Environmental Ethics, 2,* 311–38.

Callicott, J. B. (1989). *In Defense of the Land Ethic.* Albany, NY: State University of New York Press.

Callicott, J. B. (1992). Animal liberation and environmental ethics: Back together again. In E. Hargrove (Ed.), *The animal rights/environmental debate: The environmental perspective* (pp. 249–262). Albany: State University of New York.

Capshew, J. H. (1992). Psychologists on site: A reconnaissance of the historiography of the laboratory. *American Psychologist. 47,* 2, 132–142.

Caplan, A. (Ed.). (1978). *The sociobiology debate.* New York: Harper and Row.

Carruthers, P. (1992). *The animals issue: Moral theory in practice.* New York: Cambridge University.

Carson, R. (1969). *Interaction concepts of personality.* Chicago: Aldine.

Cartmill, M. (1993). *A view to a death in the morning: Hunting and nature through history.* Cambridge: Harvard University.

Casper, R. (1992). Integration of psychodynamic concepts into psychotherapy. In Halmi, K. (Ed.), *Psychobiology and treatment of anorexia nervosa and bulimia nervosa* (pp. 287–305). Washington DC: American Psychiatric Press.

Castelli, W. (1984). Epidemiology of coronary heart disease. *American Journal of Medicine, 94,* 7–11.

Cavalieri, P. & Singer, P. (Eds.). (1993). *The Great Ape project: Equality beyond humanity.* New York: St. Martin's.

Cheney, D. & Seyfarth, R. (1990). *How monkeys see the world.* Chicago: Chicago University.

Clark, S. R. L. (1977). *The Moral Status of Animals.* Oxford, UK: Oxford University Press.

Clifton, M. (1993, October). Count finds 5 million euthanasias a year – AHA says 12 million. *Animal People,* pp. 1, 8.

Cohen, P. S. & Block, M. (1991). Replacement of laboratory animals in an introductory-level psychology laboratory. *Humane Innovations and Alternatives, 5,* 221–225.

Coie, C. & Miller, N.E. (1984). How radical animal activists try to mislead humane people. *American Psychologist, 39,* 700–701.

Cole, J. & Cole, S. (1972). The ortega hypothesis. *Science, 178,* 368–375.

Corsini, R. (Ed.). (1979). *Current psychotherapies* (2nd ed.). Itasca, IL: F. E. Peacock.

Covino, B., Dubner, R., Gybels, J., Kosterlitz, H., Liebeskind, J., Sternbach, R., Vyklicky, L., & Zimmerman, M. (1980). Ethical standards for investigations of experimental pain in animals. *Pain, 9,* 141–143.

Corrigan, T. (1990). A woman is a horse is a dog is a rat: An interview with Ingrid Newkirk. In T. Corrigan & S. Hoppe, *And a deer's ear, eagle's song and bear's grace: Animals and women* (pp. 162–180). Pittsburgh: Cleis.

Coscina, D. V. & Dixon, L. M. (1983). Body weight regulation in anorexia nervosa: Insights from an animal model. In P. L. Darby, *Anorexia Nervosa: Recent developments in research* (pp. 207–219). New York: Alan R. Liss, Inc.

Coscina, D. V. & Garfinkel, P. E. (1991). Animal models of eating disorders: A clinical perspective. In P. Willner (Ed.), *Behavioural models in psychopharmacology: Theoretical, industrial and clinical perspectives* (pp. 237–250). Cambridge, UK: Cambridge University Press.

Crandall, C. (1988). Social contagion of binge eating. *Journal of Personality and Social Psychology, 55,* 588–598).

Dahles, H. (1993). Game killing and killing game: An anthropologist looking at hunting in a modern society. *Society and Animals, 1,* 169–184.

Davidson, T. L., McKenzie, B. R., Tujo, C. J., & Bish, C. K. (1992). Development of tolerance to endogenous opiates activated by 24-h food deprivation. *Appetite, 19,* 1–13.

Davis, H. (1981). Ethical considerations in the aversive control of behavior. *Social Science Medicine, 15,* 61–67.

Davis, H. & Balfour, D. (Eds.). (1992). *The inevitable bond: Examining scientist-animal interactions.* Cambridge, UK: Cambridge University Press.

Davis, J. D. (1989). The microstructure of ingestive behavior. In L. H. Schneider, S. J. Cooper, & K. A. Halmi (Eds.), *The psychobiology of human eating disorders: Preclinical and clinical perspectives* (pp. 106–121). New York: The New York Academy of Sciences.

Davis, J. D. & Campbell, C. S. (1973). Peripheral control of meal size in the rat: Effect of sham feeding on meal size and drinking rate. *Journal of Comparative and Physiological Psychology, 83,* 379–387.

Dawkins, M. (1980). *Animal suffering: The science of animal welfare.* London: Chapman and Hall.

Dawkins, M. (1990). From an animal's point of view: Motivation, fitness, and animal welfare. *Behavioral and Brain Sciences, 13,* 1–9.

de Chardin, T. (1959). *The phenomenon of man.* New York: Harper and Row.

de Cock Buning, T. & Theune, E. (1993). A comparison of three models for ethical evaluation of proposed animal experiments. *Animal Welfare, 3,* 107–128.

DeGrazia, D. (1992). Review of Singer: *Animal liberation* (second edition). *Between the Species, 8,* 1, 44–53.

DeGrazia, D. & Rowan, A. (1991). Pain, suffering, and anxiety in animals and humans. *Theoretical Medicine, 12,* 193–211.

Denenberg, V. H. and Rosenberg, K. M. (1967). Nongenetic transmission of information. *Nature, 216,* 549–550.

Dennett, D. (1981). *Brainstorms: Philosophical essays on mind and psychology.* Cambridge: Massachusetts Institute of Technology.

Devenport, J. A., & Devenport, L. D. (1990). The laboratory animal dilemma: A solution in our backyards. *Psychological Science, 1,* 215–216.

Devereux, G. (1967). *From anxiety to method in the behavioral sciences.* The Hague: Mouton.

Devine, L. A. (1990). The "rat lab:" A critique and review of alternative methods. *PSYeta Bulletin, 10,* 1, 12–13.

Dewsbury, D. A. (1990). Early interactions between animal psychologists and animal activists and the founding of the APA Committee on Precautions in Animal Experimentation. *American Psychologist, 45,* 3, 315–327.

Dewsbury, D. A. (1992). Comparative psychology and ethology: A reassessment. *American Psychologist, 47,* 2, 208–215.

Dewsbury, D. A. (1993, February). *A documentary history of the Committee on Research and Ethics of the American Psychological Association.* Unpublished manuscript.

Diner, J. (1979). *Physical and mental suffering of experimental animals.* Washington DC: Animal Welfare Institute.

Diner, J. (1985). *Toward an ethic of animal use in psychology research.* Chicago: The National Anti-Vivisection Society.

Dingell, J. (1993). Shattuck lecture: Misconduct in medical research. *The New England Journal of Medicine, 328,* 1610–1615.

Dollard, J. & Miller, N. (1950). *Personality and psychotherapy: An analysis in terms of learning, thinking, and culture.* New York: McGraw-Hill.

Dombrowski, D. (1988). *Hartshorne and the metaphysics of animal rights.* Albany: State University of New York.

Doncaster, A. (1982). *Experiments on animals: A review of the scientific literature.* Mississauga, Canada: Mississauga Animal Rights Society.

Donovan, J. (1985). *Feminist theory: The intellectual tradition of American Feminism.* New York: Ungar.

Donovan, J. (1990). Animal rights and feminist theory. *Signs: Journal of Women in Culture and Society, 15,* 21.

Doncaster, A. (1982). *Experiments on animals: A review of the scientific literature.* Mississauga, Ontario: Author.

Dresser, R. (1993). Animal care committees: Between the scientific community and the government. In E.K. Hicks (Ed.), *Science and the human-animal relationship* (pp. 135–143). Amsterdam: SISWO.

Drewett, R. & Kani, W. (1981). Animal experiments in the behavioural sciences. In Sperlinger, D. (Ed.), *Animals in Research* (pp. 175–201). New York: Wiley.

Driscoll, J. W. (1992). Attitudes toward animal use. *Anthrozoos, 5,* 1, 32–39.

Ehrenfeld, D. (1978). *The arrogance of humanism.* New York: Oxford University Press.

Elias, M. & Schlager, G. (1974). Discrimination learning in mice genetically selected for high and low blood pressure: Initial findings and methodological implications. *Physiology and Behavior, 13,* 261–67.

Ellis, A. (1973). *Humanistic psychotherapy.* New York: McGraw Hill.

Elzanowski, A. (1991). Motivation and subjective experience in birds. *Congressus Internationalis Ornithologici, 20,* 3, 1921–1929.

Fahy, T., Eisler,I., & Russell, G. (1993). A placebo-controlled trial of d-fenfluramine in bulimia nervosa. *British Journal of Psychiatry, 162,* 597–603.

Fairburn, C., Jones, R., Peveler, R. & Hoope, R. (1993). Psychotherapy and bulimia nervosa: Longer-term effects of interpersonal psychotherapy, behavior therapy, and cognitive behavior therapy. *Archives of General Psychiatry, 50,* 6, 419–428.

P. Fallon, M. Katzman, & S. Wooley (Eds.) (1994). *Feminist perspectives on eating disorders* (pp. 3–16). New York: Guilford Press.

Faull, J. R. and Halpern, B. P. (1972). Taste stimuli: Time course of peripheral nerve response and theoretical models. *Science, 178,* 73–75.

Feeney, D. (1987). Human rights and animal welfare. *American Psychologist, 42,* 593–99.

Field, P. (1993). Animal images in college psychology textbooks. *Between the Species, 9,* 193–203.

Field, P. (1988, August). *Surveying the behavior of researchers with a scale of invasiveness.* Paper presented at the American Psychological Association Annual Convention, Atlanta, GA.

Field, P. & Shapiro, K. (1988). A new invasiveness scale: Its role in reducing animal distress. *Humane Innovations and Alternatives in Animal Experimentation, 2,* 43–46.

Field, P. & Shapiro, K. (1990) Invasiveness of experiments conducted by leaders of psychology's animal research committee (CARE). *PSYeta Bulletin, 10,* 1.

Field, P., Shapiro, K., & Carr, J. (1990). Invasiveness of experiments conducted by leaders of psychology's animal research committee (CARE). *PSYeta Bulletin. 10,* 1, 1–10.

Five-year trends in scientific procedures. (1994, February). *FRAME News,* p. 10.

Flynn, F. W. & Grill, H. J. (1988). Intraoral intake and taste reactivity responses elicited by sucrose and sodium chloride in chronic decerebrate rats. *Behavioral Neuroscience, 102,* 93–941.

Food Security Act of 1985, 7 U.S.C. _ 2131–2156.

Forum (1991, July). *APA Monitor, 22,* 7, 4–5.

Foucault, M. (1970). *The order of things: An archaeology of the human sciences.* New York: Vintage Books.

Fouts, R. (in press). Science in Zoos: Arrogance of knowledge vs the humility of ignorance. In M. Hutchins, T. Maple, B. Norton, & E. Stevens (Eds.), *Ethics on the ark: Zoos, animal welfare, and wildlife conservation.* Washington DC: Smithsonian Institute Press.

Fox, M. (1992). *Superpigs and wondercorn.* New York: Lyons and Burford.

Franks, C. (1984). Behavior therapy: Problems and issues. In R. Corsini (Ed.), *Encyclopedia of psychology,* (vol. 1, pp. 139–141). New York: John Wiley & Sons.

Frey, R. (1980). *Interests and rights.* New York: Oxford University.

Fuchs, S. (1993). Positivism is the organizational myth of science. *Perspectives on Science, 1,* 1, 1–23.

Fulero, S. (1992, August). *A survey of student opinions on animal research.* Poster session paper presented at the American Psychological Association Annual Convention, Washington, DC.

Fullerton, D., Getto, C., Swift, W., & Carlson, I. (1985). Sugar, opioids, and binge eating. *Brain Research Bulletin, 14,* 673–680.

Furnham, A. & Pinder, A. (1990). Young people's attitudes to experimentation on animals. *The Psychologist: Bulletin of the British Psychological Association, 10,* 444–448.

Gaard, G. (Ed.). (1993). *Ecofeminism: Women, animals, nature.* Philadelphia: Temple University.

Gallistel, C. R. (1981). Bell, Magendie, and the proposal to restrict the use of animals in neurobehavioral research. *American Psychologist, 36,* 4, 357–360.

Gallup, G. (1985). Alternatives to the use of animals in psychological research. *American Psychologist, 40,* 10, 1104–1111.

Gallup, G. G. & Beckstead, J. W. (1988). Attitudes toward animal research. *American Psychologist, 43,* 6. 474–476.

Gallup, G. & Suarez, S. D. (1980a). On the use of animals in psychological research. *The Psychological Record, 30,* 211–218.

Gallup, G. & Suarez, S. D. (1980b). Reply to Bowd. *The Psychological Record, 30,* 427–428.

Gallup, G. & Suarez, S.D. (1987). Antivivisection: Questions of logic, consistency, and conceptualization. *Theoretical and Philosophical Psychology, 7,* 81–94.

Galvin, S. L. & Herzog, H. A. (1992a). Ethical ideology, animal rights activism, and attitudes toward the treatment of animals. *Ethics & Behavior, 2,* 3, 141–149.

Galvin, S. L. & Herzog, H. A. (1992b). The ethical judgment of animal research. *Ethics & Behavior, 2,* 4, 263–286.

Garfield, E. (1979). Is citation analysis a legitimate evaluation tool? *Scientometrics, 1,* 4, 359–375.

Garfield, E. (1980a). Citation analysis and the anti-vivisection controversy. In Garfield, E. (Ed.), *Essays of an information scientist, 3* (pp. 103–108). Philadelphia: ISI Press.

Garfield, E. (1980b). Citation analysis and the anti-vivisection controversy. Part II. An assessment of Lester R. Aronson's citation record. In Garfield, E., (Ed.), *Essays of an information scientist, 3* (pp. 316–323). Philadelphia: ISI Press.

Garfield, E. (1983, November 7). How to use citation analysis for faculty evaluations, and when is it relevant? Part 2. *Current Comments, 45,* 5–14.

Garfield, E. (1985, October 28). Uses and misuses of citation frequency. *Current Comments, 43,* 3–9.

Garfield, E. (1987, April 6). Citation data is subtle stuff. *The Scientist,* p. 9).

Garner, R. (1993). *Animals, politics, and morality.* Manchester: University of Manchester.

Gendin, S. (1982). The animal experiments controversy. *American Psychologist, 37,* 595–596.

Gergen, K. J. (1973). Social psychology as history. *Journal of Personality and Social Psychology, 26,* 2, 309–320.

Gergen, K.J. & Davis, K. E. (Eds.)(1990). *The social construction of the person.* New York: Springer Verlag.

Giannelli, M. (1985). Three blind mice, see how they run: A critique of behavioral research with animals. In M. W. Fox & L.D. Mickley (Eds.), *Advances in Animal Welfare Science, 1985/86* (pp. 109–164). Washington DC: Humane Society of the U.S.

Gibbs, J., Young, R. C., Smith, G. P. (1973). Cholecystokinin elicits satiety in rats with open gastric fistulas. *Nature, 245,* 323–325.

Gilligan, C. (1982). *In a different voice.* Cambridge: Harvard University.

Gitlin, T. (1980). *The whole world is watching: Mass media in the making and unmaking of the New Left.* Berkeley: University of California.

Gleick, J. (1987). *Chaos: Making of a new science.* New York: Penguin.

Gluck, J. P. & Kubacki, S. R. (1991). Animals in biomedical research: The undermining effect of the rhetoric of the besieged. *Ethics & Behavior, 1,* 3, 157–173.

Goffman, E. (1961). *Asylums: Essays on the social situation of mental patients and other inmates.* Garden City: Anchor.

Goldman, D. (1995, December 5). Making room on the couch for culture. *Washington Post,* pp. C1, C3.

Goodall, J. (1990). *My thirty years with the chimpanzees of Gombe.* Boston: Houghton-Miflin.

Goodkin, S. (1987). The evolution of animal rights. *Columbia Human Rights Law Review, 18,* 259–288.

Gould, E. & Bres, M. (1986). Regurgitation in gorillas: Possible model for human eating disorders (rumination/bulimia). *Developmental and Behavioral Pediatrics, 7,* 5, 314–319.

Greenberg, D. & Ackerman, S. (1984). Genetically obese (ob/ob) mice are predisposed to gastric stress ulcers. *Behavioral Neuroscience, 98,* 435–440.

Griffin, D. R. (1984). *Animal thinking.* Cambridge: Harvard University Press.

Griffin, D. R. (1992). *Animal minds.* Chicago: Chicago University.

Guardiola-Lemaitre, B. (1991). D-Fenfluramine and animal models of eating disorders. In Sandler, M., Coppen, A. & Harnett, S. (Eds.), *5-hydroxtryptamine in psychiatry: A spectrum of ideas,* pp. 303–308.

Guillermo, K. S. (1993). *Monkey Business.* Washington, DC: National Press Books.

Hagan, M. & Moss, D. (1991). An animal model of bulimia nervosa: Opioid sensitivity to fasting episodes. *Pharmacology, Biochemistry and Behavior, 39,* 421–422.

Hall, J. & Hanford, P. (1954). Activity as a function of a restricted feeding schedule. *Journal of Comparative Physiological Psychology, 47,* 362–363.

Hargrove, E. (Ed.). *The animal rights/environmental ethics debate: The environmental perspective.* Albany: University of New York.

Haraway, D. (1989). *Primate visions: Gender, race, and nature in the world of modern science.* New York: Routledge.

Harper-Giuffre, H. & MacKenzie, K. (Eds.), (1992). *Group psychotherapy for eating disorders.* Washington DC: American Psychiatric Press.

Harré, R. (1972). *The philosophies of science.* New York: Oxford.

Harris, B. S. & Martin, R. J. (1986). Influence of diet on the production of a "lipid-depleting" factor in obese parabiotic rats. *Journal of Nutrition, 116,* 2013–2027.

Haslam, C., Stevens, R. & Donohoe, T. P. (1987). The influence of cyproheptadine on immobilisation and oestradiol benzoate induced anorexia in ovariectomised rats. *Psychopharmacology, 93,* 201–6.

Heim, A. (1978). *The proper study of psychology.* Paper presented to the Psychology Section of the British Association for the Advancement of Science.

Hempel, C. (1966). *Philosophy of natural science.* Englewood Cliffs, NJ: Prentice-Hall.

Hendrickson, R. (1983). *More cunning than man: A social history of rats and men.* Briarcliff, NY: Stein and Day.

Herink, R. (Ed.). (1980). *The psychotherapy handbook.* New York: New American Library.

Herzog, H. A. (1988). The moral status of mice. *American Psychologist, 43,* 473–476.

Herzog, H. A. (1991). Conflicts of interest: Kittens and boa constrictors, pets and research. *American Psychologist, 46,* 3, 246–247.

Hills, A. M. (1989). The relationship between Thing-Person Orientation and the perception of animals. *Anthrozoos, 3,* 2, 100–110.

Hoebel, B. G., Hernandez, L., Schwartz, D. H. , Mark, G. P., & Hunter, G. A. (1989). In L. H. Schneider, S. J. Cooper, & K. A. Halmi (Eds.), *The psychobiology of human eating disorders: Preclinical and clinical perspectives* (pp. 171–193). New York: The New York Academy of Sciences.

Hsu, L. (1992). Critique of follow-up studies. In Halmi, K. (Ed.), *Psychobiology and treatment of anorexia nervosa and bulimia nervosa* (pp. 125–150). Washington DC: American Psychiatric Press.

Hurnik, F. & Lehman, H. (1982). Unnecessary suffering: Definition and evidence. *International Journal for the Study of Animal Problems, 3,* 131–139.

Huskey, C. A. (1990). *Attitudes toward animal research among contemporary psychologists.* Unpublished manuscript.

Huskey, C. A. (1991). Attitudes toward animal research among contemporary psychologists [extended abstract]. *Humane Innovations and Alternatives, 5,* 258–262.

Jamison, W. V., & Lunch, W. M. (1992). Rights of animals, perceptions of science, and political activism: Profile of American animal rights activists. Science, *Technology, and Human Values, 17,* 4, 438–458.

Jasper, james & Nelkin, D. (1992). *The animal rights crusade: The growth of a moral protest.* New York: Free Press.

Johnson, C & Sansone, R. (1993). Integrating the twelve-step approach with traditional psychotherapy for the eating disorders. *International Journal of Eating Disorders, 14,* 2, 121–134.

Jonas, J., & Gold, M. (1988). The use of opiate antagonists in treating bulimia: A study of low-dose versus high-dose naltrexone. *Psychiatry Research, 24,* 195–199.

Kanigel, R. (1987, January/February). Specimen no. 1913: A rat's brief life in the service of science. *The Sciences, 27,* 1, 30–37.

Kaufman, S. (1993). Scientific problems with animal models. In A.

Rowan & J. Weer (Eds.), *Proceedings of Tufts Center for Animals and Public Policy Symposium* (pp. 21–30). North Grafton, MA: Tufts Center for Animals and Public Policy.

Kaufman, S. & Hahner K. (Eds.). (1993). *Perspectives on Medical Research, 4.*

Keith-Spiegel, P., Tabachnick, B., & Allen, M. (1993). Ethics in academia: Students' views of professors' actions. *Ethics and Behavior, 3,* 2, 149–162.

Kellert, S. (1978). *Policy implications of a national study of American attitudes and behavioral relations with animals.* Washington DC: United States Government Printing Office.

Kelly, J. A. (1986). Psychological research and the rights of animals: Disagreement with Miller. *American Psychologist, 41,* 839–841.

Kimball, R. (1989). Liberal/conservative voting records compared to interest in animal protection bills. *PSYeta Bulletin, 9,* 7–9.

Kimble, G. (1984). Psychology's two cultures. *American Psychologist, 39,* 833–839.

King, F. A. (1984a, September). Animals in research: The case for experimentation. *Psychology Today,* pp. 56–58.

King, F. A. (1984b, May). Human benefits and current problems in behavioral research with animals. Paper presented at the meeting of the Association for Behavioral Analysis, Nashville.

Koch, S. (1993). "Psychology" or "the psychological studies"? *American Psychologist, 48,* 902–904.

Kotre, J. (1992). Experiments as parables. *American Psychologist, 47,* 162–163.

LaFollette, H. & Shanks, N. (1993a). Animal models in biomedical research: Some epistemological worries. *Public Affairs Quarterly, 7,* 113–130.

LaFollette, H. & Shanks, N. (1993b). The intact systems argument: Problems with the standard defense of animal experimentation. *Southern Journal of Philosophy, 31,* 323–33.

LaFollette, H. & Shanks, N. (1993c). Animal modelling in psychopharmacological contexts. *Behavioral & Brain Sciences,* commentary, (653–4).

LaFollette, H. & Shanks, N. (1995). Two models of models in biomedical research. *Philosophical Quarterly, 45,* 179, 141–160.

Lambert, K. G. (1993). The activity-stress paradigm: Possible mechanisms and applications. *The Journal of General Psychology, 120,* 21–32.

Latour, B. (1987). *Science in action.* Milton Keynes: Open University Press.

Lawson, D., Schiffman, S., & Pappas, T. (1993). Short-term oral sensory deprivation: Possible cause of binge eating in sham-feeding dogs. *Physiology and Behavior, 53,* 1231–1234.

Leahy, M. (1991) *Against liberation: Putting animals in perspective.* New York: Routledge.

Lederer, S. E. (1992). Political animals: The shaping of biomedical research literature in twentieth-century America. *ISIS, 83,* 61–79.

Leitenberg, H., Rosen, S., Wolf, J., Vara, S. et al. (1994). Comparison of cognitive-behavior therapy and desipramine in the treatment of bulimia nervosa. *Behaviour Research & Therapy, 32,* 1, 37–45.

Leopold, A. (1970). *A sand county almanac.* New York: Sierra Club/Ballantine.

Levine, A. & Billington, C. (1989). Opioids: Are they regulators of feeding? In L. H. Schneider, S. J. Cooper, & K. A. Halmi (Eds.), *The psychobiology of human eating disorders: Preclinical and clinical perspectives,* pp. 209–219.

Levinas, E. (1969). *Totality and infinity.* Pittsburgh: Duquesne University.

Li, T., Lumeng, L., McBride, W., & Murphy, J. (1987). Alcoholism: Is it a model for the study of disorders of mood and consummatory behavior? *Annals of the New York Academy of Sciences, 499,* 239–249.

Lindquist, T. (1990). *The effectiveness of the animal welfare movement in psychology: Evidence from APA publications in experimental animal behavior.* Unpublished manuscript.

Lockard, R. B. (1968). The albino rat: A defensible choice or a bad habit? *American Psychologist, 23,* 734–724.

Lockwood, R. & Hodge, G. (1986, summer). The tangled web of animal abuse: The links between cruelty to animals and human violence. *Humane Society News.*

Luke, B. (1992). Justice, caring and animal liberation. *Between the Species, 8,* 100–113.

Lutherer, L. & Simon, M. (1992). Targetted: *The anatomy of an animal rights attack.* Norman OK: Oklahoma University.

Lynch, M. E. (1988). Sacrifice and the transformation of the animal body into a scientific object: Laboratory culture and ritual practice in the neurosciences. *Social Studies of Science, 18,* 265–289.

Lytle, L. D. (1977). In R. J. Wurtman & J. J. Wurtman, (Eds.), *Nutrition and the Brain* (p. 1). New York: Raven.

Marrazzi, M. A., Mullings-Britton, J., Stack, L. Powers, R.J., Lawhorn, J. Graham, V., Eccles, T., & Gunter, S. (1990). Atypical endogenous opiod systems in mice in relation to an auto-addiction opioid model of anorexia nervosa. *Life Science, 47,* 1427–1435.

Maslow, A. (1972). *The farther reaches of human nature.* New York: Viking.

McArdle, J. (1988). AV fact finding. *The AV, 96,* 14–15.

McArdle, J. (1990). The research career of Adrian Morrison. *The AV, 98,* 6–8.

McCullough, M. L. (1979). The primacy of the experiment: Some reservations. *The British Psychological Society, 32,* 409–412.

McKeown, T. (1979). *The role of medicine.* Oxford: Blackwell.

Meiselman, H. (1992). Methodology and theory in human eating research. *Appetite, 19,* 49–55.

Mechling, E. & Mechling, J. (1991). Kind and cruel America: The rhetoric of animal rights. In M. Medhurst & T. Benson (eds.), *Rhetorical dimensions in media: A critical casebook.* Dubuque, Iowa: Kendall/Hunt.

Menzel, E. & Johnson, M. (1978). Should mentalist concepts be defended or assumed? *Behavioral and Brain Sciences, 4,* 586–7.

McLaughlin, C. L. & Baile, C. A. (1984). Increased sensitivity of Zucker obese rats to naloxone is present at weaning. *Physiology & Behavior, 32,* 929–33.

Midgley, M. (1981). Why knowledge matters. In D. Sperlinger (Ed.), *Animals in Research,* pp. 319–36. New York: John Wiley & Sons.

Midgley, M. (1983). *Animals and why they matter.* Athens, GA: University of Georgia.

Midgley, M. (1987). Are you an animal? In G. Langley (ed.), *Animal experimentation: The consensus changes,* 1–19. New York: Chapman and Hall.

Miller, N. E. (1983). Understanding the use of animals in behavioral research: Some critical issues. In J. A. Sechzer (Ed.), *The Role of Animals in Biomedical Research. Annals of the New York Academy of Sciences,* 1983, *406,* 113–118.

Miller, N. E. (1984). Value and ethics of research on animals. *Lab Primate Newsletter, 22,* 1–10.

Miller, N. E. (1985a). The value of behavioral research on animals. *American Psychologist, 40,* 423–440.

Miller, N. E. (1985b, February). Rx: Biofeedback. *Psychology Today,* pp. 54–59.

Miller, N. E. (1986). The morality and humaneness of animal research and stress and pain. *Annals of the New York Academy of Science, 467,* 402–404.

Minuchin, S. (1974). *Families and family therapy.* Cambridge: Harvard University.

Mitchell, J., & Raymond, N. (1992). Cognitive-behavioral therapy in treatment of bulimia nervosa. In Halmi, K. (Ed.), *Psychobiology and treatment of anorexia nervosa and bulimia nervosa* (pp. 307–328). Washington DC: American Psychiatric Press.

Mitchell, J., Raymond, N. & Specker, S. (1993). A review of the controlled trials of pharmacotherapy psychotherapy in the treatment of bulimia nervosa. *International Journal of Eating Disorders, 14,* 3, 229–247.

Montgomery, A. M. J. (1991). Animal models of eating disorders. In P. Willner (Ed.), *Behavioural models in psychopharmacology: Theoretical, industrial and clinical perspectives* (pp. 177–214). Cambridge, UK: Cambridge University Press.

Mook, D. G. (1989). Oral factors in appetite and satiety. In L. H. Schneider, S. J. Cooper, & K. A. Halmi (Eds.), *The psychobiology of human eating disorders: Preclinical and clinical perspectives* (pp. 63–74). New York: The New York Academy of Sciences.

Moran, T. H. & McHugh, P. R. (1982). Cholecystokinin suppresses food intake by inhibiting gastric emptying. *American Journal of Physiology, 242,* 491–497.

Morley, J.E. (1989a). General discussion: Part II. In L. H. Schneider, S. J. Cooper, & K. A. Halmi (Eds.), *The psychobiology of human eating disorders: Preclinical and clinical perspectives* (pp. 63–74). New York: The New York Academy of Sciences.

Morley, J. E. (1989b). An approach to the development of drugs for appetite disorders. *Neuropsychobiology, 21,* 22–30.

Morley, J. E. & Levine, A. S. (1980). Stress-induced eating is mediated through endogenous opiates. *Science, 209,* 1259–61.

Morley, J. E., Levine, A. S., Murray, S. S., Kneip, J., & Grace, M. (1982). Peptidergic regulation of stress-induced eating. *American Journal of Physiology, 243,* 159–163.

Morris, P. (1989). Magnetic resonance and the use of animals. In M. Kapis & S. Gad (Eds.), *Non-animal techniques in biomedical and behavioral research and testing* (pp. 237–254). Boca Raton, FL: Lewis.

Morrison, A. (1992). What's wrong with "animal rights." *The Education Digest, 57,* 57–60.

Mroczek, N. S. (1992, October). Recognizing animal suffering and pain. *Lab Animal,* pp. 27–31.

Mrosovsky, N. (1984). Animal models: Anorexia Yes, Nervosa No. In K. M. Pirke & D. Ploog (Eds.), *The Psychobiology of Anorexia Nervosa* (pp. 22–34). New York: Springer-Verlag.

Nace, P. (1993, summer). The use of euphemisms in research. *Science and Animal Care, 4,* 2, 1–4.

Nash, R. (1989). *The rights of nature: A history of environmental ethics.* Madison, WI: University of Wisconsin.

National register of health service providers in psychology. (1993). (11th ed.) Washington DC: Council for the National Register of Health Service Providers in Psychology.

Nemeroff, C. B., Osbahr III, A. J. Bissette, G., Jahnke, G., Lipton, M. A., Prange, Jr., A. J. (1978). Cholecystokinin inhibits tail pinch induced eating in rats. *Science, 200,* 793–794.

Neuman, P. A. & Halvorson, P. A. (1983). *Anorexia nervosa and bulimia: A handbook for counselors and therapists.* New York: Van Nostrand Reinhold.

Neuringer, A. (1984). Melioration and self-experimentation. *Journal of the Experimental Analysis of Behavior, 42,* 397–406.

Nibert, D.A. (1994). Animal rights and human social issues. *Society and Animals, 2,* 2, 115–125.

Nicolaidis, S. & Even, P. (1989). Metabolic rate and feeding behavior. In L. H. Schneider, S. J. Cooper, & K. A. Halmi (Eds.), *The psychobiology of human eating disorders: Preclinical and clinical perspectives* (pp. 86–105). New York: The New York Academy of Sciences.

Norgren, R., Nishijo, H., & Travers, S. P. (1989). Taste responses from the entire gustatory apparatus. In L. H. Schneider, S. J. Cooper, & K. A. Halmi (Eds.), *The psychobiology of human eating disorders: Preclinical and clinical perspectives* (pp. 246–263). New York: The New York Academy of Sciences.

Noske, B. (1989). *Humans and other animals.* London: Pluto.

Novak, M. A. (1991, July). "Psychologists care deeply" about animals. *APA Monitor,* p. 4.

Nozick, R. (1981). *Philosophical explanations.* Cambridge: Belknap.

Nuland, S. (1994) The pill of pills. *New York Review of Books, 41,* 11, 4–8.

Obrink, K. (1982). Swedish law on laboratory animals. In W. Dodds & F. Orlans (Eds.), *Scientific perspectives on animal welfare* (pp. 55–58). New York: Academic Press.

Opotow, S. (1993). Animals and the scope of justice. *Journal of Social Issues, 49,* 71–86.

Orlans, F. B. (1984, Nov.-Dec.). What institutional animal research committees can do to improve humane care. *Lab Animal,* 24–29.

Orlans, F. B. (1987). Research protocol review for animal welfare. *Investigative Radiology, 22,* 253–258.

Orlans, F. B. (1993, April). Attitudes toward animals. *Lab Animal,* pp. 42–43.

Orlans, F. B. (1993). *In the name of science: Issues in responsible animal experimentation.* New York: Oxford University Press.

Orlans, F. B. (1994). Data on animal experimentation in the United States: What they do and do not show. *Perspectives in Biology and Medicine, 37,* 2, 217–231.

Orlans, F. B. (1996). The three Rs in research and education in the USA. *ATLA, 24,* 2, 151–158.

O'Sullivan, J. (1993). *Psychologists' attitudes on the ethics of animal research.* Unpublished doctoral dissertation, University of South Dakota.

O'Sullivan, J., Quevillon, R. P., & Granaas, M. M. (in press). *Psychologists' attitudes on the ethics of animal research.*

Overmier, J. B. and Burke, P. D. (Eds.). (1992). *Animal models of human pathology: A bibliography of a quarter century of behavioral research, 1967–1992.* Washington, DC: American Psychological Association.

Overmier, J. B., Murison, R., and Ursin, H. (1986). The ulcerogenetic effect of a rest period after exposure to water-restraint stress in rats. *Behavioral and Neural Biology, 46,* 372–382.

Overmier, J. B. and Murison, R. (1989). Poststress effects of danger and safety signals on gastric ulceration in rats. *Behavioral Neuroscience, 103,* 6, 1296–1301.

Overmier, J. B. and Murison, R. (1991). Juvenile and adult footshock stress modulate later adult gastric pathophysiological reactions to restraint stresses in rats. *Behavioral Neuroscience, 105,* 2, 246–252.

Pate, J. E., Pumariega, A. J., Hester, C., Garner, D. M. (1992). Cross-cultural patterns in eating disorders: A review. *Journal of the American Academy of Child & Adolescent Psychiatry, 31*(5), 802–809.

Paul, E. (1995). Us and them: Scientists' and animal rights campaigners' views of the animal experimentation debate. *Society and Animals, 3,* 1–22.

Perhach, J. L. & Barry, H. (1970). Stress responses of rats to acute body or neck restraint. *Physiology & Behavior, 5,* 443–8.

Peyser, C. (1984). Psychotherapy techniques. In R. Corsini (Ed.), *Encyclopedia of psychology* (vol. 3, pp. 190–192). New York: John Wiley & Sons.

Phillips, M. T. (1991). *Constructing laboratory animals: An ethnographic study in the sociology of science.* Unpublished doctoral dissertation: New York University.

Phillips, M. T. (1993). Savages, drunks, and lab animals: The researcher's perception of pain. *Society and Animals, 1,* 61–83.

Phillips, M. T. (1994). Proper names and the social construction of biography: The negative case of laboratory animals. *Qualitative Sociology, 17,* 2, 119–143.

Phillips, M.T. & Sechzer, J. (1989). *Animal research and ethical conflict.* New York: Springer-Verlag.

Physicians' Desk Reference. (1994). (48th Edition). Montvale, NJ: Medical Economics Data.

Pierce, W. D. & Epling, W. F. (1991). Activity anorexia: An animal model and theory of human self-starvation. In A. Boulton, G. Baker, & M. Martin-Iverson (Eds.), *Neuromethods, Vol. 18: Animal Models in Psychiatry I* (pp. 267–311). Clifton, NJ: Humana Press.

Pifer, L, Shimuzu, K, & Pifer, R (1994). Public attitudes toward animal research: Some international comparisons. *Society and Animals, 2,* 2, 95–113.

Plous, S. (1991). An attitude survey of animal rights activists. *Psychological Science, 2* (3), 194–196.

Plous, S. (1993). Psychological mechanisms in the human use of animals. *Journal of Social Issues, 49* (1), 11–52.

Plous, S. (1996a). Attitudes toward the use of animals in psychological research and education: Results from a national survey of psychologists. *American Psychologist, 51,* 1167–1180.

Plous, S. (1996b). Attitudes toward the use of animals in psychological research and education: Results from a national survey of psychology majors. *Psychological Science, 7,* 352–358.

Polivy, J. & Herman, C. P. (1985). Dieting and binging. *American Psychologist, 40,* 193–201.

Polkinghorne, D. (1992). Research methodology in humanistic psychology. *The Humanistic Psychologist, 20,* 218–243.

Popper, K. (1968). *The logic of scientific discovery.* New York: Harper.

Porter, D. G. (1992). Ethical scores for animal experiments. *Nature, 356,* 101–102.

Povinelli, D. J. (1993). Reconstructing the evolution of mind. *American Psychologist, 48* (5), 493–509.

Pratt, D. (1976). *Painful experiments on animals.* New York: Argus Archives.

Presidents, APA Division 28, Psychopharmacology and Substance

Abuse. (1992, December). In defense of animal research [Letter to the editor]. *APA Monitor*, p. 3.

Pro-steel jaw leghold trap ôexpertsö meet behind closed doors to produce a final draft of ôhumaneö trap standards. (1993, spring). *AWI Quarterly*, p. 12.

Prozac as bulimia therapy. (1994, April 27). *Washington Post.*

Psychologists for the Ethical Treatment of Animals. (1993, March). The middle ground [Letter to the editor]. *APA Monitor*, p. 3.

Quinn, M. (1993). Corpulent cattle and milk machines: Nature, art and the ideal type. *Society and Animals, 1*, 2, 145–159.

Rajecki, D. W. (1983). Successful comparative psychology: Four case histories. In D. W. Rajecki, (Ed.), *Comparing behavior: Studying man studying animals* (pp. 67–109). Hillsdale, NJ: Lawrence Erlbaum])

Raskin, N. (1984). In R. Corsini (Ed.), *Encyclopedia of psychology*, (vol. 3, pp. 187–188). New York: John Wiley & Sons.

Regan, T. (1983). *The case for animal rights.* Berkeley: University of California.

Reines, B. (1982). *Psychology experiments on animals.* Boston: New England Anti-Vivisection Society.

Reines, B. (1991). On the locus of medical discovery. *The Journal of Medicine and Philosophy, 16*, 183–209.

Rhoads, S. (Ed.). (1979). *Valuing life.* New York: Westview.

Richards, R. and Krannich. (1991). The ideology of the animal rights movement and activists' attitudes toward wildlife. *Transcription of the 56th North American Wildlife and Natural Resources Conference*, 363–371.

Riger, S. (1992). Epistemological debates, feminist voices: Science, social values, and the study of women. *American Psychologist, 47*(6), 730–740.

Robbins, T. W., Phillips, A. G. & Sahakian, B. J. (1977). Effects of chlordiazepoxide on tail pinch-induced eating in rats. *Pharmacology, Biochemistry, & Behavior, 6*, 297–302.

Robbins, T. W. & Fray, P. J. (1980). Stress-induced eating: Fact, fiction or misunderstanding? *Appetite, 1*, 103–33.

Robinson, D. N. (1990). Comment on animal research labs. *American Psychologist, 45*, 1269.

Rollin, B. E. (1981). *Animal rights and human morality.* Buffalo, NY: Prometheus.

Rollin, B.E. (1989). *The unheeded cry: Animal consciousness, animal pain, and science.* New York: Oxford University Press.

Rorty, M., Yager, J., & Rossotto, E. (1993). Why and how do women recover from bulimia nervosa? *International Journal of Eating Disorders, 14,* 249–260.

Rose, M. & Adams, D. (1989). Evidence for pain and suffering in other animals. In G. Langley (Ed.), *Animal experimentation: The consensus changes* (pp.42–72). New York: Chapman and Hall.

Rosenblum, L. A. and Smiley, J. (1984). Therapeutic effects of an imposed foraging task in disturbed monkeys. *25, 3,* 485–497.

Rosenzweig, M. (1992). Psychological science around the world. *American Psychologist, 47, 6,* 718–722.

Ross, M. (1981). The ethics of experiments on higher animals. *Social Science in Medicine, 13,* 51–60.

Roszack, T., Gomes, M., & Kanner, A. (Eds.). (1995). *Ecopsychology: Restoring, the earth, healing the mind.* San Francisco, Sierra Club Books.

Rotton, J., Levitt, M., & Foos, P. (1993). Citation impact, rejection rates, and journal value. *American Psychologist, 48,* 911–912.

Rowan, A. (1982). The Silver Spring 17. *International Journal for the Study of Animal Problems, 3,* 219–227.

Rowan, A. (1984a). *Of mice, models, and men.* Albany: State University of New York.

Rowan, A. (1984b). Appropriate care for deafferented primates. *Journal of Medical Primatology, 13,* 175–181.

Rowan, A. (1993). Analysis of the arguments against animal research. In A. Rowan & J. Weer (Eds.), *Summary and Proceedings: The Value and Utility of Animals in Research* (pp. 3–20). North Grafton, MA: Tufts Center for Animals and Public Policy.

Rowan, A. (1993, December). Laboratory animal numbers. *The Animal Policy Report, 7,* 4, p. 1.

Rowan, A. (1994). Laboratory animal numbers: Trends and problems. *The Animal Policy Report, 8,* 1–3.

Rowland, N. E. & Antelman, S. M. (1976). Stress-induced hyperphagia and obesity in rats: A possible model for understanding human obesity. *Science, 191,* 310–312.

Ruesch, H. (1978). *Slaughter of the innocent.* New York: Bantam.

Russell, G., Dare, C., Eisler, I., & LeGrange, P. (1992). Controlled trials of family treatments in anorexia nervosa. In Halmi, K. (Ed.), *Psychobiology and treatment of anorexia nervosa and bulimia nervosa* (pp. 237–262). Washington DC: American Psychiatric Press.

Russell, W. & Burch, R. (1992). *The principles of humane experimental technique.* (Original work published 1959). South Mimms, UK: Universities Federation for Animal Welfare.

Russell, G. F. M. (1979). Bulimia nervosa: an ominous variant of anorexia nervosa. *Psychological Medicine, 9,* 429–448.

Ryder, R. (1975). *Victims of science: the use of animals in research.* London: Davis-Poytner.

Sackett, E. (1988). Animal rights, human rights, scientific rights: Who's right? [Review of the book *Maternal deprivation studies in psychology: A critique]. Contemporary Psychology, 33,* 1.

Sahakian, B. J. & Robbins, T. W. (1977). Isolation-rearing enhances tail pinch-induced oral behaviour in the rat. *Physiology & Behavior, 18,* 53–8.

Sarason, S. (1984). If it can be studied or developed, should it be? *American Psychologist, 39*(5), 477–485.

Scalafani, A. (1984). Animal models of obesity: Classification and characterization. *International Journal of Obesity, 8,* 491–508.

Scalafani, A. (1989). Dietary induced overeating. In L. H. Schneider, S. J. Cooper, & K. A. Halmi (Eds.), *The psychobiology of human eating disorders: Preclinical and clinical perspectives* (pp. 281–291). New York: The New York Academy of Sciences.

Schmorrow, D. D. (1993). *The use of nonhuman subjects in behavior analysis: A review of JEAB studies.* Unpublished doctoral dissertation, Western Michigan University, Kalamazoo.

Schneider, L. H. (1989). Orosensory self-stimulation by sucrose involves brain dopaminergic mechanisms. In L. H. Schneider, S. J. Cooper, & K. A. Halmi (Eds.), *The psychobiology of human eating disorders: Preclinical and clinical perspectives* (pp. 307–320). New York: The New York Academy of Sciences.

Schneider, S. (1990). Psychology at a crossroads. *American Psychologist, 45*(4), 521–529.

Scholtmeijer, M. (1993). *Animal victims in modern fiction: From sanctity to sacrifice.* Toronto: University of Toronto Press.

Scientific procedures on living animals in Great Britain in 1991. (1992, October). *FRAME News,* pp. 8–9.

Sechzer, J. (1981). Historical issues concerning animal experimentation in the United States. *Social Science & Medicine, 15F,* 13–17.

Sechzer, J. (1983). The ethical dilemma of some classical animal experiments. In J. A. Sechzer (Ed.), *The Role of Animals in Biomedical Research,* (pp. 5–11). New York: New York Academy of Sciences.

Seed, J. Macy, J., Fleming, P., & Naess, A. (1988). *Thinking like a mountain.* Philadelphia: New Society.

Segal, E. F. (Ed.). (1989). *Housing, care and psychological well-being of captive and laboratory primates.* Park Ridge, NJ: Noyes Publications.

Seid, R. (1994). Too "close to the bone": The historical context for women's obsession with slenderness. In P. Fallon, M. Katzman, & S. Wooley (Eds.), *Feminist perspectives on eating disorders* (pp. 3–16). New York: Guilford Press.

Seligman, M. (1975). *Helplessness: On depression, development and death.* San Francisco: W. H. Freeman.

Serpell, J. (1986). *In the company of animals.* New York: Blackwell.

Shapiro, K. J. (1983). Psychology and its animal subjects. *International Journal for the Study of Animal Problems, 3,* 188–191.

Shapiro, K. J. (1986a). Verification: Validation or understanding. *Journal of Phenomenological Psychology, 17,* 2, 167–181.

Shapiro, K. J. (1986b). Foreword. In M. L. Stephens, *Maternal deprivation experiments in psychology: A critique of animal models.* Jenkintown, PA: The American Anti-Vivisection Society.

Shapiro, K. J. (1988). Galloping sophistry: A rat in the lab is worth two in the dump. *Theoretical and Philosophical Psychology, 8,* 2, 47–53.

Shapiro, K. J. (1989a). The Silver Spring monkeys and APA. *PSYeta Bulletin, 9,* 1–6.

Shapiro, K. J. (1989b). The death of an animal: Ontological vulnerability and harm. *Between the Species, 5,* 4, 183–195.

Shapiro, K. J. (1990a). Animal rights v. humanism: The charge of speciesism. *Journal of Humanistic Psychology, 30,* 2, 9–37.

Shapiro, K. J. (1990b). Learning and unlearning empathy. *Phenomenology and Pedagogy, 8,* 43–49.

Shapiro, K. J. (1992). Reminding animals: Developments in the scientific study of nonhuman animals. [Review of *Interpretation and explanation in the study of animal behavior*, volume 1]. *Between the Species, 8,* 2, 74–80.

Shapiro, K. J. (1993). Scientist-animal bond: Better late than never. [Review of *The inevitable bond: Examining scientist-animal interactions*]. *Psychology, 4,* 38.

Shapiro, K. J. & Field, P. (1987). A new scale of invasiveness in animal experimentation. *PSYeta Bulletin, 7,* 5–8.

Sharpe, R. (1985). *Psychological and behavioral research.* London: Mobilisation for Laboratory Animals Against the Government's Proposals.

Sharpe, R. (1988). *The cruel deception: The use of animals in medical research.* Wellingborough, U.K.: Thorsons.

Sharpe, R. (1993). The polio files. *The AV Magazine, 101,* 8–13.

Shisslak, C. & Crago, M., (1994). Toward a new model for the prevention of eating disorders. In P. Fallon, M. Katzman, & S. Wooley (Eds.), *Feminist perspectives on eating disorders* (pp. 419–437). New York: Guilford Press.

Shyan, M. R. & Sanders, L. (1991). The laboratory animal dilemma: A reply to Devenport and Devenport. *Psychological Science, 2*(2), 127.

Silcock , S. (1992, April). Is your experiment really necessary? *New Scientist,* pp. 32–34.

Silverman, P. (1994). It's the "m" word. [Review of *Animal models in psychiatry, I* and *II*]. *Contemporary Psychology, 39,* 659–660.

Singer, P. (1975). *Animal liberation: A new ethic for our treatment of animals.* New York: Avon.

Skinner, B. F. (1953). *Science and human behavior.* New York: Free Press.

Smith, G. P. (1989). Animal models of human eating disorders. In L. H. Schneider, S. J. Cooper, & K. A. Halmi (Eds.), *The psychobiology of human eating disorders: Preclinical and clinical perspectives* (pp. 63–74). New York: The New York Academy of Sciences.

Smith, G. P., Bourbanais, K. A., Jerome, C., & Simansky, K. J. (1987). Sham feeding of sucrose increases the ratio of 3/4-dihydroxy-phenylacetic acid to dopamine in the hypothalamus. *Pharmacology of Biochemical Behavior, 26,* 585–591.

Smith, G. P. & Gibbs, J. (1988). The satiating effect of cholecystokinin. In M. Winick (Ed.), *Control of appetite: Current concepts in nutrition* (Vol. 16, pp. 35–40). New York: John Wiley & Sons.

Smith, J. & Boyd, K. (Eds.). (1991). *Lives in the balance: The ethics of using animals in biomedical research.* New York: Oxford.

Smith, L. D. (1992). On prediction and control: B. F. Skinner and the technological ideal of science. *American Psychologist, 47*(2), 216–223.

Spence, J. T. (1987). Centrifugal versus centripetal tendencies in psychology: Will the center hold? *American Psychologist, 42*(12), 1052–1054.

Sperry, R. W. (1993). The impact and promise of the cognitive revolution. *American Psychologist, 48,* 8, 878–885.

Spitzer, R. L., Skodol, A. E., Gibbon, M., & Williams. J. B. W. (Eds.). (1981). *Diagnostic and Statistical Manual of Mental Disorders (3rd ed.): Case book.* (1st ed.). Washington, DC: American Psychiatric Association.

Stafleu, F., Baarda, B., Heeger, F., & Beynen, A. (1993). The influence of animal discomfort, human interest and scientific quality on the ethical acceptability of a projected animal experiment as assessed with questionnaires. *ATLA, 21*, 121–137.

Staff. (1991, spring). Rat communication. *ACCART News, 4*, 3, 4–5.

Steinmetz, P & Tillery, S. (1994). Animal models: Some empirical worries. *Public Affairs Quarterly, 8*, 287–298).

Stephens, M. L. (1986). *Maternal deprivation experiments in psychology: A critique of animal models.* Jenkintown, PA: The American Anti-Vivisection Society.

Stephens, M. L. (1988). Animal rights, human rights, scientific rights: Who's right? *Contemporary Psychology, 33*, 23–25.

Stephens, M. L. (1989). Replacing animal experiments. In G. Langley (Ed.), *Animal experimentation: The consensus changes* (pp. 144–168). New York: Chapman and Hall.

Stillings, N., Feinstein, M., Garfield, J., Rissland, E., Rosenbaum, D., Weisler, S., & Baker-Ward, L. (1989). *Cognitive Science: An introduction.* Cambridge: MIT Press.

Stone, C. (1974). *Should trees have standing? Toward legal rights for natural objects.* Los Angeles: William Kaufmann.

Strupp, H. (1986). Psychotherapy: Research, practice, and public policy. *American Psychologist, 41*, 2, 120–131.

Strupp, H. Hadley, S., & Gomes-Schwartz, B. (1977). *Psychotherapy for better or worse: The problem of negative effects.* New York: Jacob Aronson.

Styles, W., Shapiro, D., & Elliott, R. (1986). Are all psychotherapies equivalent? *American Psychologist, 41*, 2, 165–181.

Sugarman, C. (1994, May 3). A greater variety of eating disorders. *Washington Post Health,* p. 16.

Suomi, S. J. & Harlow, H. F. (1972). Depressive behavior in young monkeys subjected to vertical chamber confinement. *Journal of Comparative Physiological Psychology. 80*, 11–18.

Suppe, F. (Ed.) (1977). *Structure of scientific theories.* Urbana: University of Illinois.

Szasz, T. (1961). *The myth of mental illness.* New York: Delta.

Takooshian, H. & Blacher, A. (1988). Opinions on animal research: Scientists versus the public? *PSYeta Bulletin, 7*, 2, 5–9.

Takooshian, H. (1993, April). Lab animal controversy: Scientists versus the public? Paper presented at the meeting of the Eastern Communication Association, New Haven.

Tannenbaum, J. (1989). *Veterinary ethics.* Baltimore: Williams and Wilkins.

Tannenbaum, J. & Rowan, A. (1985). Rethinking the morality of animal research. *Hastings Center Report, 15,* 5, 32–43.

Tennov, D. (1973). Pain-infliction in animal research. Paper presented at the meeting of the Eastern Psychological Association, Washington DC.

Tester, K. (1991). *Animal and society: The humanity of animal rights.* New York: Routledge.

Thackwray, D., Smith, M., Bodfish, J. & Meyers, A. (1993). A comparison of behavioral and cognitive-behavioral interventions for bulimia nervosa. *Journal of Consulting & Clinical Psychology, 61,* 4, 639–645.

Thomas, G. V. & Blackman, D. (1991). Are animal experiments on the way out? *The Psychologist, 4,* 5, 208–212.

Thomas, G. V. & Blackman, D. (1992). The future of animal studies in psychology. *American Psychologist, 47,* 1679.

Thomas, K. (1983). *Man and the natural world.* New York: Pantheon.

Tuan, Y. (1984). *Dominance and affection: The making of pets.* New Haven: Yale University Press.

Ulrich, R. E. (1992). Animal research: A reflective analysis. *Psychological Science, 3*(6), 384–386.

U.S. Congress, Office of Technology Assessment (1986). *Alternatives to animal use in research, testing, and education* (OTA-BA-273, February). Washington DC: U.S. Government Printing Office.

Valenta, J. G & Rigby, M.K. (1968). Discrimination of the odor of stressed rats. *Science, 161,* 599–601, 1968.

Van Vort, W. B. (1988). Is sham feeding an animal model of bulimia? *International Journal of Eating Disorders, 7,* 797–806.

Van Vort, W. B., & Smith, G. P. (1981). Pregastric stimuli are sufficient for the hedonic value of a meal in the rat (Abstract No. 215.8). *Society for Neuroscience, 7,* 654.

Vandereycken W. & Hoek, H. W. (1992). Are eating disorders culture-bound syndromes? In K. A. Halmi (Ed.), *Psychobiology and treatment of anorexia nervosa and bulimia nervosa* (pp. 19–36). Washington, DC: American Psychiatric Press.

Vaswani, K., Tejwani, G. A., & Mousa, S. (1983). Stress induced differential intake of various diets and water by rat: The role of the opiate system. *Life Sciences, 32,* 1983–1996.

Viney, W., King, D. W., & Berndt. (1990). Animal research in psychology: Declining or thriving? *Journal of Comparative Psychology, 104,* 4, 322–325.

de Waal, F. (1989). *Peacemaking among primates. Cambridge:* Harvard University Press.

Walsh, B. T. (1992). Pharmacological treatment. In K. A. Halmi (Ed.), *Psychobiology and treatment of anorexia nervosa and bulimia nervosa* (pp. 329–340). Washington, DC: American Psychiatric Press.

Watanabe, K., Hara, C., & Ogawa, N. (1992). Feeding conditions and estrous cycle of female rats under the activity-stress procedure from aspects of anorexia nervosa. *Physiology & Behavior, 51,* 827–832.

Webster, J. (1994). *Animal welfare: A cool eye toward Eden.* Oxford: Blackwell Science.

Weisstein, N. (1971). *Psychology constructs the female: Or, the fantasy life of the male psychologist.* Boston: New England Free Press.

Wemelsfelder, F. (1984). Animal boredom: Is a scientific study of the subjective experiences of animals possible? In M. W. Fox & L. D. Mickley (Eds.), *Advances in Animal Welfare Science* 1984–1985 (pp. 115–154). The Hague: Martinus Nijhoff.

Wemelsfelder, F. (1993). *Animal boredom: Toward an empirical approach of animal subjectivity.* Utrecht: Elinkwijk.

Wertz, F. (1986a). The rat in psychological science. *The Humanistic Psychologist, 14,* 3, 143–168.

Wertz, F. (1986b). The question of the reliability of psychological research. *Journal of Phenomenological Psychology, 17,* 2, 181–207.

Weston, A. (1994). *Back to earth: Tomorrow's environmentalism.* Philadelphia: Temple University Press.

Willner, P. (1991). Animal models as simulations of depression. *Trends in Pharmacological Sciences, 12,* 131–136.

Wilson, S. & Fairburn, C. (1993). Cognitive treatments for eating disorders. *Journal of Consulting & Clinical Psychology, 61,* 2, 261–269.

Wolff, H. (1943). *Human gastric functioning: An experimental study of man and his stomach.* New York: Oxford.

Wyers, E. (1994). Comments on behavioral research in naturalistic settings. In E. Gibbons, E. Wyers, E. Waters, & E. Menzel (Eds.), *Naturalistic environments in captivity for animal behavior research* (pp. 19–36). Albany: State University of New York Press.

Wolf, E., & Fairburn, C. (1992). An evaluation of behavioral and cognitive-behavioral group interventions for the treatment of bulimia nervosa in women. *International Journal of Eating Disorders, 11,* 1, 3–15.

Yates, A. (1989). Current perspectives on the eating disorders: I. History, psychological and biological aspects. *Journal of the American Academy of Child and Adolescent Psychiatry, 28,* 6, 813–828.

Yates, A. (1990). Current perspectives on the eating disorders: II. Treatment, outcome, and research directions. *Journal of the American Academy of Child and Adolescent Psychiatry, 29,* 1, 1–9.

Zbinden, G. & Flury-Roversi, M. (1981). Significance of the LD50 test for toxicological evaluation of chemical substances. *Archives Toxicology, 47,* 77–99.

Index

treatment 113, 117, 140, 144, 167,
170, 172, 179, 187, 188, 189,
191, 192, 193, 202, 207, 208,
210, 214, 226, 245
– of eating disorders 10
– innovations 10
– interventions 12
trend 22, 24, 26, 40
two psychologies 58
typical conditions 28, 29
typical harm 32

U
undergraduate(s) 18, 19, 47
United States Department of
Agriculture (USDA) 24, 264,
266
unlikeness 87, 102
unnecessary 257
unnecessary suffering 251, 252
utilitarian 226, 229, 231, 243,
244, 260, 264, 283
– ethic 204

– philosophy 231
utilitarianism 241, 244, 283

V
validation 101
validity 89
victimization 83
vivisection 46
vomiting 114, 122, 124, 125

W
weak analogy 88, 219
weigh 266
weight 114, 122, 123, 124, 134,
141, 154, 157, 180, 181
welfare 52
welfarists 217
Wemelsfelder, F. 76
Wertz, F. 65

Y
Yates, A. 179, 183, 184, 185